ITALIAN LITERATURE AND THOUGHT SERIES

The Italian Literature and Thought Series makes available in English some of the representative works of Italian culture. Although it focuses on the modern and contemporary periods, it does not neglect the humanistic roots of Italian thought. The series will include new scholarly monographs, anthologies, and critically updated republications of canonical works, as well as works of general interest.

PIERO GOBETTI

ON LIBERAL
REVOLUTION

Edited and with an introduction by
Nadia Urbinati

Translated by
William McCuaig

Foreword by Norberto Bobbio

Yale University Press   New Haven & London

To my friends at the Istituto Gramsci of Bologna

Published with the funding assistance of Centro Studi Piero Gobetti of Turin and the City Council of Turin.

Designed by James J. Johnson and set in Aster Roman types by Tseng Information Systems, Durham, North Carolina. Printed in the United States of America by Vail-Ballou Press, Binghamton, New York.

Library of Congress Cataloging-in-Publication Data

Gobetti, Piero, 1901–1926.
[Rivoluzione liberale. English]
On liberal revolution / Piero Gobetti ; edited and with an introduction by Nadia Urbinati ; translated by William McCuaig.
p.   cm. — (Italian literature and thought series)
Includes bibliographical references and index.
ISBN 0-300-08117-0 (cloth : alk. paper) —
ISBN 0-300-08118-9 (paper : alk. paper)

1. Italy—Politics and government—1914–1945.   2. Liberalism—Italy—History—20th century—Sources.   3. Anti-fascist movements—Italy—History—20th century—Sources.   I. Urbinati, Nadia, 1955–   II. McCuaig, William, 1949–   III. Title.
IV. Series.
JN5450 .G6313 2000
945.091—dc21   00-025022

A catalogue record for this book is available from the British Library.

The paper in this book meets the guidelines for permanence and durability of the Committee on Production Guidelines for Book Longevity of the Council on Library Resources.

10   9   8   7   6   5   4   3   2   1

CONTENTS

3. Socialism and Communism

4. Fascism and the Missed Liberal Revolution

FOREWORD

I am old enough that I would have been able to know Piero Gobetti if he had not died so young. Between us there was a difference of only eight years: he was born in 1901, I in 1909. When he died in Paris on 15 February 1926, he was only twenty-five, and I was still in high school. As I have written on previous occasions, I heard his name for the first time from the teacher of Italian in our school, Umberto Cosmo, a noted antifascist who was forced to give up his teaching position the same year. Upon entering the classroom on that day in February 1926, he read the news of the death of Gobetti from *La Stampa* and added a few words of his own, with deep emotion.

When I was at university, enrolled in the same faculty that Gobetti had chosen—jurisprudence—his life was over, but he was survived by one of the three journals that he had founded, *Il Baretti*, which had not immediately been shut down when the exceptional laws on curbing press freedom were put into effect in 1926, because it was a journal of literature, not politics. One of our high-school teachers, Augusto Monti, had become the covert editor (covert because he too was the object of fascist hostility), and he got us to subscribe. Not long ago, while sorting through some old drawers, I discovered that I still had a few copies, which I had jealously guarded like precious relics.

The publishing house that Gobetti founded, which in the space of a few years published more than a hundred books on philosophy, literature, history, and politics, had also been shut down. Many of these editions wound up in the stalls of second-hand book dealers. I bought a few, which now form part of my library, and I recall with particular gratitude a work by one of my university professors, Francesco Ruffini, with whom Gobetti had also studied a few years earlier. This work, which later had a notable success when fascism collapsed, was entitled *Diritti di libertà* [*The Rights of Freedom*], and was one of the last affirmations of free thought prior to the onset of the dictatorship.

When fascism became a regime and suppressed the basic freedoms, a blanket of silence fell on Gobetti and all the other adversaries who had opposed it. Only with the end of the war and liberation from fascism did some of his writings begin to be republished and his journals reprinted, thanks to the Centro Studi Piero Gobetti, founded in 1961 by Ada Prospero, his widow, with the collaboration of old friends. Three volumes of collected writings have already been published by Einaudi: *Scritti politici, Scritti letterari, storici e filosofici,* and *Scritti di critica teatrale* [*Political Writings; Literary, Historical, and Philosophical Writings; Theater Criticism*]. The fourth volume, in preparation, will comprise his rich correspondence. *Guida bibliografica degli scritti su Piero Gobetti (1918–1975)* [*Bibliography of Writings on Piero Gobetti, 1918–1975*], edited by Giancarlo Bergami and consisting of approximately three thousand entries, came out in 1981, and a second edition, updated and augmented, is being published.

Gobetti died at the age of only twenty-five, but his achievements as a writer and as a promoter of cultural initiatives are astonishing, even though they were accomplished in the space of a mere seven years, between the age of seventeen, when, barely out of high school, he founded his first journal, *Energie Nuove,* in November 1918 (World War I had just ended), and his death. In the Manifesto of that journal the formula "liberal revolution" encapsulates a historical judgment, a political ideology, and a program of action. From the historical standpoint, the journal announces a series of articles dedicated to a "reconsideration of Italy's political formation in the Risorgimento"; as for political ideology, it promises to focus "on a scrutiny of the political strengths of the parties and of their development"; as regards action, it heralds the constitution of local groups committed to democratic agitation.

Meanwhile, Gobetti studied Russian with his fiancée in order to be able to read for himself the texts of the revolution that had burst upon Russia in 1917. He translated a few works by an author and playwright of note, Andreiev, who had gained wide renown for his writings against the folly and horror of the First World War. It was in this period that Gobetti composed his essays on the Russian Revolution and wrote theater criticism for Gramsci's journal, *Ordine Nuovo*, which had become a daily. He did his conscripted military service and passed all his exams in jurisprudence, taking his degree in 1922 with a dissertation on the political thought of Vittorio Alfieri, under the supervision of Professor Gioele Solari, with whom I myself took my degree nine years later, in 1931.

The first issue of *La Rivoluzione Liberale* came out on 12 February 1922. In April 1921 the second national election since the war, based on universal male suffrage, had taken place, and the National Bloc, headed by Giovanni Giolitti, had won. But the first fascist deputies, a little over thirty of them, had also won seats in parliament. The communists too had stood for election for the first time, following their secession from the socialists at Livorno in January 1921, and had won sixteen seats in the Chamber of Deputies. The Giolitti ministry was followed by the ministries of Bonomi and then Facta—the last ministry preceding the march on Rome that ended on 28 October 1922, when the king gave Mussolini the mandate to form a new government. This was the beginning of the fascist era, which would last for more than twenty years.

La Rivoluzione Liberale was conceived for the purpose of combating fascism when it was advancing toward the conquest of power. Three days before the march on Rome, in response to an accommodationist article by Giuseppe Prezzolini proposing the foundation of a club for those who were not prepared to "swallow it" [i.e., those who refused to get involved in the tumult of politics], Gobetti wrote: "Faced with a fascism that, by abolishing the freedom to vote and freedom of the press, would stifle our action at its source, we would be forming, not the congregation of those who refuse to swallow it, but a companionship of death." In the first article written after the march on Rome, when many of the old liberals were paralyzed, or were actually conniving, and waiting to see how things turned out in hopes of a rapid reconfiguration of the traditional powers of the state and the return of constitutional freedoms, he wrote: "We will stay at our post . . . whether that means witnessing a democratic farce or suffering the persecution that awaits us." And on 23 November, a month after Mussolini had become the head of the government, Gobetti delivered his sarcastic "praise of the guillotine," writing, "We want blows so as to wake a few people up, we want the hangman so as to make it clear how things stand."

When he wrote these courageous, burning words, he was twenty-one. The persecution and the blows duly followed. He was arrested for the first time on 16 February 1923 and again on 29 May. On 9 June 1924 his home was searched. On 5 September he was assaulted and beaten by a group of fascists as he left his house.

Throughout 1925, when, following the murder of Matteotti in June 1924 and Mussolini's speech of 3 January, fascism was being transformed into a regime, the journal was continually confiscated. And the life of Piero Gobetti became ever more difficult and dangerous.

In June 1925 he began seriously to contemplate going into exile; and when the journal, in the wake of repeated confiscations, was forced to cease publication in November, he decided to leave for Paris. He departed on 3 February 1926. These are the last words he wrote as he left Turin:

> My last sight of Turin: through the glass of the lurching carriage as it moves through the snow, the driver's voluminous cloak looms. . . . A Nordic farewell to my Nordic heart. But am I Nor-

dic? And do these words make any sense? These doctrinal contrasts are useful in debate, along with opposite tastes, habits, and
ideals. I will feel myself more akin to an intelligent Frenchman
than I will to a boorish Italian—but only when my mind turns to
intellectual experiences, when I regard others in terms of my acquired culture. In Saffron Hill I felt how much I am still attached
to humble things, to the life of my folk. I feel that my ancestors
had this suffering, this humility, for their destiny; that they were
chained to this soil, and though they cursed it, it was their ultimate tenderness and weakness. One cannot be countryless.

He ends by outlining, in a few bare words, his own moral portrait: "The outcome doesn't concern me because I accept it as the
measure of my action. . . . The goal: to be everywhere oneself."

On 11 February, within a few days of his arrival in Paris, he
fell ill. On the 13th he was brought to a clinic. On the 15th, toward
midnight, he died. He was buried in the cemetery of Père La-
chaise, not far from the Mur des Fédérés.

His last letter from Paris was addressed to a friend in order
not to alarm his wife. He wrote: "I am in bed with a fever. . . .
Naturally I ask you not to write anything about my indisposition
to Ada in Turin." The last letter from Ada, which he would never
read, bears the date 14 February: "They tell me you are fatigued:
don't worry if you cannot write at length, but make sure not to
get overtired, and to take care of yourself. I beseech you, on behalf of Pussin as well" (Pussin was their nickname for their son,
Paolo, born in December).

What did Gobetti mean by "liberal revolution"? He meant
principally a movement from below, aimed at radically transforming Italian society, which had never been shaken by a revolutionary upheaval. The Risorgimento, which was referred to as
the Italian revolution, had in reality been a war, in part of liberation and in part of conquest, undertaken by the Kingdom of Piedmont. Italy had been governed for centuries by small princely
courts, even by foreign powers, and, after national unity, by narrow cliques, the last of which, for Gobetti (a follower of Salve-

mini), was the Giolittian liberals. A liberal revolution would be a revolution bringing liberation from the traditional ills of Italian society, in the name of a liberalism understood philosophically as an antagonistic conception of history, economically as the theory of the free market, and politically as a state ruled by law, a state that guarantees the exercise of the fundamental civil liberties and, as such, stands in opposition to any form of autocratic state (of which fascism was to be the brutal incarnation).

These memorable words are his: "Fascism is the autobiography of the nation."

NORBERTO BOBBIO

PREFACE

This book is a collection of representative writings of a radical liberal, Piero Gobetti, who lived in Italy immediately before the establishment of the fascist regime. This edition fills a gap on the shelves of Anglo-American scholars, who already have books by the main intellectual companions of Gobetti: Antonio Gramsci, Benedetto Croce, and Carlo Rosselli. Nevertheless, the reason that I came to collect and edit some of Gobetti's writings is not historiographic. Rather, it is my belief that *On Liberal Revolution* can enrich multifaceted liberalism, for it brings to the foreground two political categories of relevance today: conflict and political autonomy. Gobetti goes to the sources of liberalism; he reads liberalism as a theory and politics of liberation, a theory and politics that is culturally revolutionary because the individual is posited as its moral principle. His democratic conception of liberalism leads him to stress the roles of political agency and social movements in the expansion of the public sphere, which he sees as intermediary between the economic sphere of needs and the coercive sphere of the state. Only within this perspective, he thinks, can politics retain an ethical character and have a critical meaning.

This book has been made possible by the generous help of Paolo Bagnoli of the Bocconi University in Milan; John A. Davis of the University of Connecticut; and Charles Maier of Harvard University, who recommended its publication to Yale University Press; and the Centro Studi Piero Gobetti of Turin and the City Council of Turin, which provided financial support for its translation. I wish to express my most sincere gratitude to the staff of the Centro Studi Piero Gobetti, and Carla Gobetti in particular, whose friendly help was determinant in the fulfillment of this project. William McCuaig was able to render Gobetti's complex and tense style into elegant English and to assist me in the critical annotations with competence and patience. I own a very special debt to Norberto Bobbio, the most original interpreter of Gobetti's liberalism and my most beloved teacher, whose challenging reading of my introduction and whose unforgettable conversations with me have been of invaluable help.

William McCuaig wishes to thank Franco Andreucci of the University of Pisa and other members of the Internet list H-Italy; Robert E. Johnson of the University of Toronto; the Centro Studi Piero Gobetti of Turin, which generously supplied books and other materials, including a draft translation of Norberto Bobbio's preface by Carolyn Hardy; Marco Scavino, for his valuable scholarly help; and Mary Pasti and everyone else at Yale University Press who contributed their efforts to the making of this book.

INTRODUCTION:

LIBERALISM AS A

THEORY OF CONFLICT

The rise of liberalism has reflected and inspired the economic and political transformation of Western societies. The ideas of Locke and Jefferson, of Mill and Dewey, testify to the historical evolution of liberalism from the age of liberal revolutions, to the age of constitutionalism, and finally to the age of the democratic transformation of the liberal state. Seen from the vantage point of the present day, the story of liberalism is decidedly one of success.[1] With few exceptions, both the authors and the principles embodying what we call liberalism today belong to those few countries in which liberalism completed both its intermediary stages and its overall project. The contemporary theory of liberalism is deeply marked by a consciousness of its success; it is smugly gratified by its sense of irresistible destiny.

What I am proposing to offer here is an account of the liberal experience viewed as a project in crisis, not at its culmination. Piero Gobetti's essays are witness to a liberalism conscious of its imminent and perhaps long-lasting twilight. My aim is not to reconstruct the historical reasons for that defeat (the advent of fascism) but to disclose the characteristics peculiar to a liberalism that acquired an awareness of its own value out of a perception of being marginalized and ultimately thwarted. How does liberalism explain its own failure? Which principles does it stress most in order to prove its value and validity? Which theoreti-

---

1. I use the word "success" in a descriptive sense. By it I mean the opposite of "fall," "defeat," capitulation."

cal strategies and ideal resources does it deploy to counter the threat of a defeat and to gain stability within both the society and the state? These are the questions that Italian scholars and intellectuals have posed in each generation since the rise of fascism (1922) and that are threaded through Gobetti's essays. Taken together, his essays constitute the first Italian document of a militant liberalism.

GOBETTI'S LIBERALISM

Gobetti's writings, with their scourging, merciless criticism of Italian political culture, are challenging in many ways. They show a clear understanding of the link between liberal institutions and moral culture; they point out the antiliberal role played by Catholicism and its encouragement of a dreadful indifference toward the rule of law; and they denounce the threat to political liberty posed by communitarian corporatism and the misguided longing for a utopia of social unity. Antithetical to both Catholicism and fascism, Gobetti's liberalism refers not only to an institutional and political system but, more importantly, to a philosophy of life inspired by the principles of individual freedom and moral and political autonomy.

Gobetti's conception of liberalism has three constituent elements. First, it professes to be a secular philosophy that recognizes no forms of transcendence in the domains of knowledge, history, or morals. In this sense, his liberalism is "synonymous with immanentism and historicity" and views the human condition as one of possibility, not necessity.[2] Gobetti's liberalism is conscious of its social and cultural sources. It does not look for metahistorical foundations, nor for justifications that transcend the will and praxis of individuals. Nor does it aim at doctrinal

2. On Gobetti's liberalism, see Norberto Bobbio, *Italia fedele. Il mondo di Gobetti* (Florence: Passigli, 1986), 54–55.

purity; it is willing to maintain links with other political traditions, such as republicanism and socialism.

The second element pertains to Gobetti's economic ideas, which were firmly anchored in a full recognition and acceptance of the market. The principles of private enterprise are deeply constitutive of what he called modernity, while strongly embodying the philosophy of individual responsibility and risk ("Henry Ford").[3] Gobetti, however, did not maintain a deterministic identification of liberalism with capitalism. He recognized that liberalism emerged as economic relations were defeudalized and was unable to establish itself in societies in which the economic structure was still communitarian and noncompetitive. Indeed, Gobetti may even be considered a libertarian, at least insofar as he rejected state protection and contested the ethical theory of the state coming out of the Hegelian tradition. He saw in tariff policy a perverted class tactic, oligarchic in its outcome, by which "a few lucky insiders" aimed at protecting their privileges against "the whole nation" and at shielding themselves from future risk ("Toward a New Politics"). But, unlike other libertarians, he did not limit the benefits of competition to trade; rather, he thought of social conflict between the owners of capital and the owners of labor as not only unavoidable but even positive, because it helped to protect and to advance the realization of individual autonomy while forcing economic management to pursue restless innovation. Consequently, to Gobetti, liberalism was the most radical alternative to both socioeconomic corporatism (fascism) and protective state socialism (etatism).

Third, Gobetti endorsed the principle of toleration and defended the theory and politics of instituting and maintaining a wall between the church and the state. However, he grasped the complex implications of tolerance and perceived the ambiguity of its classical liberal interpretation, its apparent tendency to

3. Like Weber, he detected a sort of asceticism in the creative vocation of the founders of industry.

merge with indifference and to support a rationalist detachment from politics. By contrast, Gobetti showed the ambiguity of the boundaries between toleration and intolerance, both in relation to the exercise of political liberty and in relation to the very existence of pluralism.

Now, if one looks at pluralism from the point of view of the individual, one may say that it implies the existence of principles and values that people are not ready to give up or to compromise on easily. The persistence of those values depends on personal engagement; they demand a certain degree of belief and loyalty, whose formation and endurance presume some kind of isolation from, and resistance to, other beliefs and loyalties.[4] According to Gobetti, political life cannot and should not avoid "intransigence" (or integrity) unless it is reduced to being simply a bargain among organized interests or to being a rationalistic form of deliberation from which disagreement is supposed to disappear as truth advances. As we shall see in the penultimate section of this introduction, Gobetti thought that politics retained an "ethical" thickness of its own and could be reduced neither to a market kind of behavior nor to a Platonic exercise of dialectical skill. His conclusion was less simplistic: to view the public space as an aseptic exercise of reason is unrealistic and misleading, precisely because people do not elaborate objective opinions out of neutral information. Rather, people share beliefs that lead them to interpret the information they receive in one way or another; that is, politics does not exclude the irrational altogether. "If you are in politics, you are a combatant. Either you pay court to the new bosses, or you are in opposi-

4. On the tension between passion and reason (or convictions and obligations) in politics, see the two options offered by Walzer and Shklar. Michael Walzer, "The Obligation to Disobey," in *Obligations: Essays on Disobedience, War and Citizenship* (Cambridge: Harvard University Press, 1970), 3–23; and Judith N. Shklar, "Obligation, Loyalty, Exile" (1993), in *Political Thought and Political Thinkers*, ed. Stanley Hoffman (Chicago: University of Chicago Press, 1998), 38–55.

tion. Those in the middle are neither independent nor disinterested" ("Against the Apolitical Ones"). Even in "civilized nations," in which liberal toleration has succeeded in fostering a moral education of respect and understanding, politics does not cease to be an open field of struggle among differing, and often antagonistic, convictions.

From the point of view of society, pluralism presumes and entails the absence of any external authority from which members of society may derive neutral and objective criteria to sort and judge values. Gobetti was aware that the political sphere could hardly avoid the threat of being captured by winning majorities. However, just as for Gaetano Mosca, the important question for Gobetti was not so much how to prevent political seizure as how to prevent the blockage of competition. The "rules of the game," that is, the constitutional limits of political competition, were the reasonable guarantees able to protect pluralism from the manipulations of the winner: "the true contrast is not that between dictatorship and freedom, but between freedom and unanimity."[5]

Gobetti's statement recalls similar ideas put forth by other critical observers of modernity, such as Mill and Tocqueville. All convey the awareness of a growing hostility in modern society toward individuality and differences of opinion on what the society chooses as its shared values. What Gobetti was denouncing, however, was not unanimity per se but the homogeneity induced by a coercive state power. He was equally suspicious of the nostalgia for a premodern order and of the aristocratic disdain for democracy. Nonetheless, his modernism did not prevent him from perceiving the corporatist vocation of industrial society or, as we will see, the inner link between the post-Enlightenment myth of an organizational rationality and the fascist project of eradicating all forms of conflict and "irrationality." Awareness of that link convinced him that liberalism and the persistence of

5. *La rivoluzione liberale* (ed. Perona), 25.

conflict were crucial for the defense of individual liberty, both moral and political.

Thus, freedom and conflict are symbiotically attached, the former being thwarted when the latter is in jeopardy. "The method of liberalism," wrote Gobetti, "both in economic and political life, rests on the recognition of the necessity of political struggle in modern society. . . . Our liberalism, which we call revolutionary in order to avoid any equivocation, is inspired by an inexorable libertarian passion, and sees reality as a contrast of forces able to produce always new aristocracies provided that new popular classes enliven the struggle with their desperate will of emancipation."[6] Civic education, he contended, grows out of action, which is the most concrete "experimental training" for the development of moral character and personal dignity. It was within this theoretical framework that Gobetti appealed to the ethics of "intransigence" and set limits to toleration. To him, toleration was the art of handling conflict, not that of preventing it.

Over and above the three constitutive elements—immanentism, the market, and toleration—Gobetti's conception of liberalism is based on a clear and indisputable acceptance of individual rights and the limits to state interference in the lives and affairs of individuals. Gobetti did not derive rights from either natural law or from a metahistorical conception of human nature. Rather, he interpreted them as historical achievements by which Western societies coped with their cultural and political transformations. As moral and legal instruments created for the protection of individual life and personal integrity, civil rights are endowed with a legitimizing authority; they are normative criteria for distinguishing autocratic from consensual uses of state authority. Gobetti viewed rights as consistent with the character of the modern individual and with the decline of transcendental philosophy. He saw them as the immanent outcome of a worldly

6. Piero Gobetti, "Revisione liberale" (1923), in *Scritti politici*, 515.

morality and politics, both entirely grounded on activity and the relation between personal initiative and material results. Rights are the transcription of individual autonomy from an external and superior authority and, consequently, the recognition of a basic equality of consideration due to all.

Gobetti's originality rests on the two principles that mark his conception of liberalism and that distinguish it from those of other liberal thinkers: first, the distinction between politics and the state and, second, as a consequence, an interpretation of liberalism as also a theory of political conflict and political autonomy. To this vision he gave the name "liberal revolution" to stress the difference between the conception of liberalism as a process of liberation and liberalization and the conception of liberalism as either a system of judicial guarantees or as a form of state organization and management. Whereas the conception of liberalism as a system of judicial guarantees promotes a restriction of politics, and its conception as a state organization confines politics to the sphere of government, Gobetti's conception of liberalism accords a salient value to political action and to social movements because self-government and emancipation from subjection are perceived as the "revolutionary" implications of liberal ideals. In his mind, liberalism was born revolutionary because it articulated that the individual's autonomy of judgment and the individual's equal value in relation to others are the underpinning values of modernity. To complete the picture of his immanentistic liberalism, one must remark that it is not, in fact, groundless. Indeed, the priority Gobetti accorded the individual shielded his strongly agonistic conception of politics from the risk of being transformed into an unlimited relativism and a nihilistic exaltation of the political struggle for power.

Politics, which Gobetti was very careful to keep distinct from policy, is necessarily characterized by conflict. Its endurance depends on the survival of liberty and the persistence of antagonism among social and political actors. Politics, freedom, and conflict are interdependent; they settle on a relation of reciprocity and circularity. This assumption involves two conceptions of liberalism. On the one hand, it qualifies the very conditions of liberty and political action. But this liberalism is not to be confused with a political movement: this is the "constitutional" dimension of the rules of the game. On the other hand, it is one ideology among others; it upholds some specific values and thus can neither claim neutrality nor avoid partisanship. Indeed, because of its principled defense of the two main tenets of modernity—economic competition and individualism—liberalism will hardly go unchallenged. A market economy invariably generates, or at least is not able to impede the growth of, social inequality. As a consequence, the justice, equality, and liberty called for by liberalism will become the legitimate opponents of the effects of a market economy, as will the principles nurturing the growth of common interests and alternative visions of the just society. Liberal ideology cannot expect, nor should it want, to go unchallenged.

Besides being inescapable, conflict between ideas and interests is positive. Its value rests on the stipulation that in the midst of dissent, people may have the chance to develop a sense of self-reliance. The practical experience of antagonism may bring them to change their minds, switch their loyalties, or stick with their beliefs. Whatever the practical outcomes might be, politics is invariably characterized by a process of public and free dialectics among citizens and groups holding different convictions and having different interests. One might say that the value of democracy lies more in the process itself than in its empirical outcomes.

The limits of conflict coincide with the very possibility that conflict will endure. The difference between liberal and antiliberal movements rests on the fact that the latter regard political competition as a means for achieving a political order that may very possibly suppress competition. The stability of liberal society rests on antiliberal movements being in the minority. As long as this remains the case, there is no need to impede their development or to repress them. Gobetti's apparently paradoxical conclusion was that in a constitutional state—that is, one in which the rules of political competition are respected and upheld—political movements that are not themselves liberal can in fact contribute to making the society more free and liberal. This point recalls the ideas of Madison and Mill on what makes for a liberal society: pluralism itself, the certainty that no competitor will enjoy a monopoly or be in a position to put an end to political competition. Thus, it is pluralism, along with basic liberal guarantees, that constitutes the fundamental condition for freedom and for politics itself. As we shall see in a following section, it is on these premises that Gobetti grounded his anti-etatism and his positive evaluation of the role played by the communist movement led by Antonio Gramsci.

For Gobetti, liberalism was more than a mere formalistic theory of judicial guarantees, then; it was also a belief and a praxis. He ascribed to it an ethical character and viewed it as a mode of interaction among actors (groups as well as individuals) who give one another an equal chance to speak and be heard and who learn to listen to and respect one another.[7] Liberalism bestows dignity on politics by making it an open arena among contenders who recognize each other as equally legitimate participants by expressing their dissent; as Gobetti put it, liberalism makes politics human. In short, I would say that the main ideas shaping Gobetti's thoughts are, first, that politics, freedom, and conflict are inseparable and, second, that liberalism denotes both the practice of politics and its normative value.

---

7. Paolo Bagnoli, *Piero Gobetti: Cultura e politica in un liberale del Novecento* (Florence: Passigli, 1984), 177–237.

A PUBLIC CRITIC

Piero Gobetti was born in Turin on 19 June 1901. He died in Paris, in political exile, on 15 February 1926, at the age of twenty-five. The seven years of his intellectual activity coincided with several dramatic events: the etatist transformation of the liberal state; the Bolshevik revolution; and the democratization of Italy, a process that fascism would violently interrupt. As for Gramsci, Gobetti's intellectual laboratory was Turin, the city in which national unification and Italian industrialization had begun. Between the end of World War I and the establishment of fascist despotism (1918–25) Turin also became the laboratory for the political and intellectual ideas that would shape post-fascist Italy: democracy, liberalism, and Marxism.

Gobetti's life was short not because he longed for heroism, but because he claimed the basic right to live freely. Mussolini's police arrested him twice, put his journals under severe censorship, and exposed him to periodic harassment and violence. He chose exile in order to remain free to express his ideas and died fifteen days after he arrived in Paris. He was the victim of a regime that had suspended the basic liberal guarantees of life and liberty and turned a constitutional state into a despotism.

The only child of a recently urbanized petty bourgeois family, Gobetti was as precocious in his intellectual life as he was in his death. More than a professional theorist, he was a theorist who tested his ideas through political action and cultural activity. To use a contemporary expression, his world was that of the public sphere of journals and newspapers; his work was that of a public critic.

Gobetti founded a publishing house (which printed, among many other books, *Cuttlefish Bones* by the Nobel laureate in poetry Eugenio Montale) and three important journals: *New Energies* (*Energie Nuove*), started when he was seventeen and still a high school student; *Liberal Revolution* (*La Rivoluzione Liberale*), started when he was twenty-one and a law student at the University of Turin; and *Il Baretti* (a literary journal named after an eighteenth-century intellectual who revived the tradition of Machiavelli in Piedmont), started when he was twenty-three. His mentors and interlocutors were Benedetto Croce, Giovanni Gentile, Gaetano Mosca, Vilfredo Pareto, Luigi Einaudi, Gaetano Salvemini, Antonio Gramsci, and Georges Sorel, who all helped to define some of the theoretical coordinates of contemporary political language, including theories of the separation of life-spheres, the formation and circulation of elites, hegemony, and the role of the irrational in politics.

Gobetti belonged to the generation of Antonio Gramsci and Carlo Rosselli, with whom he shared the same tragic destiny. Rosselli published his first article on liberal socialism in Gobetti's *Rivoluzione Liberale*. Gramsci got Gobetti involved in his own journal, *Ordine Nuovo,* and regarded him as a living example of his conception of the "new intellectual." They all represent the most radical and original expression of twentieth-century Italian political culture. Each of them engaged in a critical revision of the ideal tradition to which he adhered. Gramsci (1891-1937) revised the deterministic reading of Marx that the socialists had inherited from the Second International and from Karl Kautsky's positivism. Rosselli (1899–1937) revised socialist ideology by separating it from Marxism and linking it to the liberal tradition.[8] Gobetti revised liberalism by ridding it of its parliamentarianism and its etatist vocation. He did with the "old" liberalism what Gramsci and Rosselli did with the "old" socialism. But, unlike Gramsci and more like Rosselli, he saw the solution to the Italian political crisis in the permanence of conflict, not in the overcoming of conflict. "Where a majority holds power with complete security, you have a veiled oligarchy and nothing else" ("In Defense of Proportional Representation"). That is why he defined his liberalism as "revolutionary."

8. Carlo Rosselli, *Liberal Socialism*, ed. Nadia Urbinati, trans. William McCuaig (Princeton: Princeton University Press, 1994).

LIBERALISM AND MORAL CULTURE

The term "liberal revolution" refers to a political vision.[9] In order to explain Gobetti's conception of a liberal revolution, it is important to note that Gobetti was convinced that the fragility of a liberal regime was more than a mere political fact; it was a cultural fact as well, and its sources had to be sought in the moral and intellectual character of the national culture. If Italy was not able to preserve its liberal institutions, he reasoned, this was because it had not developed a moral culture and a social structure consistent with, and supportive of, those institutions.

By grounding his conception of liberalism on history and culture, Gobetti was in effect distancing himself from the "abstractions" of both "the demagogues" of the Enlightenment and the constitutionalists of the nineteenth century ("A Manifesto"). The fragility of liberal principles within popular culture, he cautioned, had sanctioned the reduction of liberalism to the practice of parliamentary bargaining and had made liberalism the name of a conservative ideology and the descriptor of a corrupt regime. According to Gobetti, when liberalism does not have cultural roots in society and consists simply of a constitutional apparatus, it can become the main agent of its own decline into an oligarchic state.

This conception contains the answer to the first question I posed, namely, "How does liberalism explain its own failure?" A liberalism, like Gobetti's, that has not renounced its political character is able to see its own paradoxical situation: when it is not able to inspire a moral culture sufficiently widespread and popular and to count on an open market economy, it may very well end up becoming a modern form of authoritarianism, led by and functional for the interests of a moneyed oligarchy. Capi-

9. It was also the title of both a journal (1922–25) that, coinciding with the establishment of the fascist dictatorship, attempted to inspire a political movement, and a book (1924) on the ideological sources of fascism.

talism can push a liberal government toward a foreign policy of imperialism and colonialism while demanding a protectionist policy at home. In this sense, it is not always identifiable with liberalism, whose values are instead anchored in an ethic of competition, responsibility, and equal opportunity. Now, according to Gobetti, the revolutionary character of liberalism, that is, its liberating import, must be preserved in order to counter attempts to turn it into the instrument of an oligarchic minority. As a ceaseless practice of personal engagement and enterprise, liberalism entails that everyone be in the condition of acting "freely and in this way carry[ing] out the necessary work of participation, review, and opposition" ("A Manifesto"). Accordingly, there are circumstances in which liberalism collides with capitalism and may find support in other social subjects that, precisely because of their condition of subordination, may understand its emancipatory meaning more consistently. Thus, Gobetti's conception of liberalism recognizes the value of free and fair competition more than the practice of capitalism does.

Gobetti benefited from reading Marx, but his conclusion was not Marxist. Instead of welcoming the final collapse of the liberal-capitalist regime, he though it necessary and possible to invert that trajectory by giving liberalism the chance of expressing its revolutionary potential. He thus extended the liberal notion of competition to include the phenomenon of class struggle, which he saw as a modern expression of the quest for individual self-reliance, moral as well as political.[10] The culmination of Gobetti's vision is contained in the answer to the last two questions I asked above: The principle that liberalism needs to stress in order to regain its identity and recover its credibility is politi-

10. This was not, after all, such an unorthodox move, for the notion of class conflict can be found both in Adam Smith and in James Madison. See Adam Smith, *An Inquiry into the Nature and Causes of the Wealth of Nations* (Oxford: Oxford University Press, 1976), book I, chap. 8; and James Madison, *The Federalist*, no. 10, in A. Hamilton, J. Madison, and J. Jay, *The Federalist Papers*, ed. Clinton Rossiter (New York: New American Library, 1961).

cal autonomy, that is, the value of equal citizenship. To fulfill this goal, liberalism should not hesitate to call on and use resources that belong to other political traditions but which liberalism shared in its revolutionary age: the resources of conflict and of a politics of conviction and principles.

Given these premises, one may understand Gobetti's belief that a politics of emancipation starts with the intellectual work of historical interpretation, and we may thus finally capture the significance of his book *La rivoluzione liberale*, to which the chapters composing Parts 3 and 4 of this collection belong. The search for a reason to explain the cultural weakness of Italian liberalism brought Gobetti to confront the moral legacy of Catholicism. Like Croce and Gramsci, he held Catholicism to be responsible for Italy's ineptitude in constructing a territorial state and fulfilling the project of modernity. To him, fulfilling the project of modernity meant anchoring political action and social relations in trust, individual responsibility, and moral autonomy. Catholicism meant two things: the Church of Rome as an institutional entity and the moral hegemony of its religious teachings. Italy not only has a Catholic culture; it also hosts the Vatican—the throne of Catholicism.

The theory of an incompatibility between Catholicism and politics inspired many generations of Italian thinkers, not all of them liberal. Largely accepted among intellectuals, this view has always met with great obstacles both in popular culture and in the political establishment. Niccolò Machiavelli was its first and most lucid supporter. The theory was revived during the Risorgimento by Carlo Cattaneo, a federalist and anti-Mazzinian republican. Gobetti referred explicitly to both.

Machiavelli articulated his argument in relation to both Catholicism and Christianity. On the one hand, he deemed the Church of Rome responsible for obstructing the formation of the Italian state; on the other hand, he thought that the antinational function of the church was encouraged by Christian morality. The formation of European territorial states convinced Machiavelli that emancipation from foreign domination was the basic condition for acquiring political liberty as such. Italy's dependency upon mercenary forces was a direct consequence of the papacy, which "favored the [division of the] cities in order to build up its temporal authority."[11] But it was also the effect of a system of values that praised passivity and humility instead of *virtù* and political action. The divisive policy of the popes could endure and succeed thanks to a cultural milieu that was deeply Christian and thus antipolitical.

Machiavelli developed the early nucleus of what Gramsci would later call hegemony, that is, the idea that for political action to succeed it must be able to count upon a moral culture consistent with it among both the leaders and the people. Without this link, any courageous political enterprise would fail. Indeed, *fortuna* without *virtù* would allow for achievements that were fragile because they could not profit from conscious support and direct effort on the part of their actors. In Gramsci's language, one might say that *fortuna* without *virtù* can at best generate a coercive authority, but not an authority grounded upon consensus.[12]

Gobetti's interpretation of the reasons for the failure of Italian liberalism drew on Machiavelli's insights. He theorized the distinction, and opposition, between *two* Italys, one of which was minoritarian and conscious of the "secular" virtues of political freedom, the other of which was dominant and had absorbed the habit of "discipline, order, and hierarchy."[13] The periodic acts

11. Niccolò Machiavelli, *The Prince*, in Machiavelli, *Selected Political Writings*, ed. and trans. David Wootton (Indianapolis: Hackett, 1994), 7–14.

12. I have developed this topic in "From the Periphery of Modernity: Antonio Gramsci's Theory of Subordination and Hegemony," *Political Theory* 26, no. 3 (1998), 370–91.

13. *La rivoluzione liberale* (ed. Perona), 10. In Italy the polemical debate between secular liberal intellectuals and Catholic intellectuals takes on this oppositional character quite regularly: to the former, who speak of "two Italys" in order to assert their autonomy from the Catholic tradition and their marginalization from the national cultural mainstream, the latter object that

of political rebellion among the populace, as quick in their explosion as in their sedation, seemed to him, as to Gramsci, evidence that the Italian problem originated not in a lack of authority but in a lack of autonomy. The construction of the liberal state did not change things. In fact, the new state profited from that lack of autonomy in order to impose itself on and against a people

---

Italy owns its moral and cultural identity thanks to the Church of Rome. The liberals see the Vatican (which they do not identify with Catholicism) as the main cause of Italy's lack of political unity at the beginning of modernity and of the state's subsequent political evolution; the Catholics see the church as the only repository of the spiritual identity of Italy during the many centuries of its political division.

Since the Risorgimento, attempts to seek a reconciliation between Catholicism and liberalism have been made, in particular beginning with the end of the six decades of Catholic isolationism (1870–1929) that followed from the Vatican refusal to acknowledge the Italian state and to allow the Catholics to exercise their political rights. The politics of a Catholic reconciliation with liberalism has been named *neoguelfismo,* after the medieval faction that supported the pope against the "secular" Ghibellines, who, instead, supported the emperor, who had given the free cities more autonomy in domestic affairs.

The Catholic reconciliation with liberalism is sometimes pursued through a politics of discredit and polemics against the secular liberal tradition, which includes the views of the moderate Croce as well as the radical Gobetti. Since 1989, with the decline of Marxism and Leftist ideology and with the "discovery" of liberalism, the polemic between the two factions has started again. In an attempt to oppose a "true liberalism" against the secular one, some Catholic-liberal intellectuals are pursuing a strong attack against the Italian tradition of liberalism—their main targets are Norberto Bobbio and Gobetti, but they also take aim at Carlo Rosselli and the intellectuals who, after World War II, attempted to link liberalism to non-Catholic ideas, such as socialism and republicanism. From the political point of view, their aim is to question the principle of having a wall between the church and the state and the politics of individual rights. To capture a sense of this dispute, see, for instance, issues of the following journals over the past few years: *Il Mulino, La nuova rivista di storia contemporanea, Micromega, Liberal, Critica liberale,* and *Il Corriere della Sera* and *La Stampa.* On the Catholic critique of the secular liberal tradition see Ernesto Galli della Loggia, "La democrazia immaginaria. L'azionismo e l'ideologia italiana," *Il Mulino* 42 (March–April 1993), 255–70. I have reconstructed this debate in "The Two Italies," *Correspondence: An International Review of Culture and Society,* no. 4 (Spring/Summer 1999), 7–8.

that lingered between passivity and hostility. From this perspective, the failure of Italian liberalism had to be traced back to the way political unification and the construction of the liberal state had been accomplished.

The Risorgimento is to the Italians what Americanism is to the Americans: the object of a permanent disagreement that political events repeatedly fuel and rekindle. To Gobetti, it meant a process of state construction that lacked the strength to transform the habits of its citizens and perpetuated the indifference toward a sense of the public good that Catholic morality had inculcated. "Liberalism became a word inseparable from Catholicism. Theocracy won through the very army of liberals," who endorsed the ethics of compromise and made of casuistry a practice of justification that taught people and politicians to evade personal responsibility and the rule of law. One might say that in Italy liberalism was born with a saliently illiberal vocation.[14]

Hence, to Gobetti, fascism was not an extemporaneous accident, as it was to Croce; it was the "autobiography" of a nation that had identified stability with corporatism and the avoidance or repression of conflict.[15] "Italian individualism has no confidence in itself; it lacks the courage for extreme statements. It seems that the mind of everyone here is haunted by dread of a tradition of sedition and factious unruliness, so they think that public order might be in peril every single day" ("Democracy").

Whereas Machiavelli, who did not have the chance to see the growth of Protestantism, identified Catholicism with Christianity, Gobetti stressed their distinction and contrasted the ethic of Protestantism with that of Catholicism. There is no evidence that he had read or even knew of *The Protestant Ethic and the Spirit of Capitalism,* yet his perspective on the ethic of Protestantism closely echoes that of Max Weber. For Gobetti, Protes-

14. *La rivoluzione liberale* (ed. Perona), 18.
15. Thus, Gobetti claimed that Machiavelli's project of developing a theory of politics grounded on a civil religion remained totally unintelligible to a courtly Italian bourgeoisie. Ibid., 12.

tantism meant both a spiritual experience of self-restraint and a comprehensive vision of life that fosters individual enterprise and independence. The Protestant Reformation was able to inspire the growth of liberal institutions insofar as it rooted the sense of legal duty in individual responsibility without resorting to the sanctions of an authority acting from above. It was the egalitarian character of Reformation churches that prepared the terrain for the growth of liberal hegemony.

Complaints of Italy's lack of Protestantism have been a topos in Italian secular culture, not only liberal culture. Both the detractors and the admirers of Protestantism have acknowledged that it represented the first radical expression of disobedience to an external authority and the beginning of a process of moral emancipation that would lead to the achievement of civil and political rights. The link that Gobetti articulated between it and liberalism is historically accurate and theoretically compelling. But it poses a challenging question: Can only Protestant countries become and be liberal?

To Gobetti, the French case seemed to prove that liberalism and Protestantism do not necessarily need to go together. In France, "the experiment of Reformation succeeded perfectly without Calvinism." There, republicanism was able to make up for the absence of a religious revolution by inspiring in the citizens a strong sense of political dignity. The "populace of Paris can suffer the infernal life of the factory . . . only because when they take a walk in the Champs Elysées on Sunday . . . they know they are not going to meet Marie Antoinette."[16] In France, it was "the citizen" that emancipated "the man." The revolution of 1789 could thus be seen as a "political Protestantism" (a political liberal revolution). Italy missed that revolution, too.

Significantly, Gobetti did not adopt France as a model, even though he acknowledged that it had "accomplished its liberal

16. Piero Gobetti, "La Francia republicana" (1924), in *Scritti politici*, 685–92.

revolution."[17] His ideal model was the Anglo-American world, because he regarded Protestantism as a process of emancipation that began within the individual and furthered the values of free enterprise and self-reliance. Along with "the urge for freedom on the part of the masses" against church hierarchy, Protestantism generated an "individualistic revolution of consciences trained in personal responsibility" and accustomed the individual to view himself as a dignified member of the community, indispensable and fully responsible ("Our Protestantism"). Conversely, Gobetti criticized the dogmatic attitude of the French Enlightenment in general and its "abstract language of democracy" in particular, because it tried to impose its principles by force on countries not yet prepared to receive them. In the case of Italy, the unfortunate failure of the several revolutionary upheavals that had followed the French Revolution provoked a counterreaction that was fatal for the growth of liberalism ("Manifesto").[18]

The French model and the Anglo-Saxon model represent two different strategies, one directly revolutionary and the other devoted to the work of cultural hegemony. Like Gramsci, Gobetti viewed both models as vital. In the chaotic and tragic years during which fascism arose, the former strategy was seen as more necessary, especially in the years between Mussolini's first government (1922) and the establishment of dictatorship (1925). Following the abolition of political liberties, the latter strategy became immensely important. After 1925, Gobetti stopped the publication of his militant journal *Liberal Revolution* and

17. He did not, moreover, see fascism as compatible with French culture, partly because France had a solid and independent bureaucracy, partly because of its "first-rate" political class, and partly because of its "popular republicanism." Ibid.

18. Such criticism of the Enlightenment is echoed by other Italian scholars and intellectuals, conservative and radical alike: Croce as well as Gramsci. Both also agreed that a "cultural" or "moral" revolution had to precede any radical political transformation.

founded a literary journal, *Il Baretti*. The shift was strategic; it was meant to imply that liberalism had to prepare itself for a long, and no longer open, war of resistance and had to devote itself to cultivating and spreading the values of moral resistance and personal and political integrity.

It would, however, be misleading to think that of the two models only the former is revolutionary. Both are characterized by a politics of principle and a practice of coherence, or, in Gobetti's favored expression, by an ethic of "intransigence." Gobetti's liberalism was Jacobin in the same way Protestantism was.[19]

Nonetheless, the "exception" of France was important, if only because France opened a liberal path without passing through a religious reformation and for this reason could offer useful suggestions to non-Protestant countries. Thus, even if Gobetti remained faithful to the ideals springing from the Anglo-Saxon experience, the French case nonetheless offered him the chance to reflect upon the hard problem of how to promote liberalism in a country that did not have a religious reformation.

That question had tormented the intellectuals belonging to Gobetti's generation. It haunts Gramsci's *Prison Notebooks*, which begins with the assertion of the failure in Italy of the liberal project and contrasts liberal hegemonic countries and coercive liberal governments. It shapes Guido De Ruggiero's *History of European Liberalism*, which begins with the description of the English Christian communities of the seventeenth century and their opposition to hierarchical authority and ends with a description of the growth of the socialist movement and its opposition to a new kind of hierarchy. De Ruggiero envisages socialism as a movement capable of infusing new blood into the anemic body of constitutional liberalism and of playing the same inno-

19. On the Jacobinism of the Puritans who led the Glorious Revolution see Michael Walzer, *The Revolution of the Saints* (Cambridge: Harvard University Press, 1965).

vative role as the religious congregations of the seventeenth century did.[20]

The theme of a modern or political kind of Protestantism is one of those that unites Gobetti's writings. He understood that modernity had transformed social relations and moral values. "What are the differentiating characteristics of the modern world? Its economy is based on the free market and its politics on liberalism; its philosophical outlook is immanentist and critical, its morality is activist and realistic, its logic is dialectical" ("The Bourgeoisie"). Consequently, in modern times a liberal emancipation would take a secular path, not a religious one. The modern condition itself would facilitate the liberal process, partly because the transformation of social practices would gradually promote the growth of liberal values and partly because the substitution of a religious strategy by the practices of public-opinion formation, economic transformation, and political movements would extend the range of liberalism well beyond the countries in which it had been born.[21]

La rivoluzione liberale was an early attempt to contest a codified vulgata of Italian national identity and to oppose an alternative reading against the established one. Through a radical reinterpretation of the sources and values that nationalism had constructed since the nineteenth century, Gobetti rewrote the intellectual history of the Risorgimento. In going back to forgotten and marginalized authors and ideas, he aimed at recovering and dignifying the Italian secular equivalent of a religious reformation. His *Risorgimento Without Heroes* was a national reading that pivoted around such authors as Machiavelli, Vittorio Alfieri, and Carlo Cattaneo. In the end, Protestantism came to acquire a nonreligious meaning, corresponding to a set of

20. Guido De Ruggiero, *The History of European Liberalism*, trans. Robin George Collingwood (1927; reprint, Boston: Beacon Press, 1959).
21. The portrait of Henry Ford and the essay "The Bourgeoisie" help to clarify this idea.

values representing individual liberty and cultural resistance to moral as well as political homogeneity.

Gobetti's message was that no country is a univocal community of meanings and traditions and that no country needs to copy foreign experience to develop liberal values. Within each culture one can find values and ideas critical of the dominant ones, divergent ideas from which one may start a process of democratic emancipation. "It would be absurd to generalize the Anglo-Saxon experience. What we need to do instead is to collect our own instinctive endowments, which actually will bring us more naturally toward a political than toward a moral reformation (revolution)."[22]

The conclusion of Gobetti's inquiry is that liberalism neither follows a unitary path nor profits always and everywhere from the same actors. For instance, not since the time of the early modern republics has the agent of modernity in Italy been religion. The beginning of Italy's transformation into a modern, secular state occurred in the spheres of economics and politics. Protestantism revived and rescued religion, redirected the path to modernity toward the inner self and moral principles, and marked the character of liberalism. The irony of modern society was that even though liberalism propagated itself through religious conflicts, its strength nonetheless coincided with a gradual process of secularization. Thus, economic competition and political conflict—which had marked the emergence of Italian early modernity—would become central once again. The public sphere of political competition and criticism and the social sphere of economic life and interests would become, Gobetti believed, the loci from which liberal emancipation would take place in contemporary societies. The values of trust, individual independence, and freedom could thus be revived, he argued, by keeping both domains open to competition and conflict. By

22. *La rivoluzione liberale* (ed. Perona), 13. See below, "A Teacher of Liberalism."

becoming free and responsible citizens and conscientious producers, Italians could make their own secular (or political) reformation. "Protestantism in Italy has to battle a parasitic economy and petit bourgeois unanimity and seek the cadres of heresy
and democratic revolution among workers acculturated to free
struggle and the morality of work" ("Our Protestantism"). Gobetti's interpretation explains the reason he opposed not only
Catholicism and fascism but also the "old" reformist socialism
and nonliberal versions of democracy.

ANTILIBERAL THREATS

Not unlike Marx, Gobetti was a modernist and thought that
labor contributed to promoting individual independence—
moral independence no less than material independence. Unlike
both the socialists and Marx himself, however, Gobetti did not
see collectivism and the overcoming of social conflicts as ideals
to be longed for (thus he maintained a distinction between "the
political" Marx—the theorist of the class struggle—and Marx
"the economist" and social scientist). Moreover, like Gramsci,
Gobetti was very critical of the traditional socialist ideology that
preached the messianic advent of a harmonious society and all
the while bargaining with the state. Reformist socialist leaders
used demagoguery with the masses while compromising with
the government. They renounced the "educating principle" of
political conflict and yielded to "utilitarianism." In this sense,
they were "immoral" because they taught people to relinquish
their political autonomy in exchange for assistance: "the best
weapon of the Church has always been generalized poverty.
Impoverished plebeians were Catholic because of the lure of
charity; and thus dogmatism held sway over their humbled and
submissive minds" ("Our Protestantism"). Socialist reformers of
late nineteenth century revived the Catholic practice of duplicity
and the subordination to needs as a way of securing docility. Not

only were they "immoral," they were also politically misguided, because they debilitated the political energies of their movement at the very moment it could have, and needed, to play a crucial role in the defense of political liberty.

To be sure, Gobetti did not undervalue the role of justice in policymaking. What he criticized was the barter of political liberty for social assistance. The sketch of Giacomo Matteotti, the only social reformist leader he admired, clarifies this point effectively. In a Sorelian way, Matteotti had focused on the process of emancipation pursued by the workers themselves in their everyday lives. Thus, while articulating the myth of collectivism and final revolution (in which he did believe), he focused entirely on "bringing the revolution about as the worker learned how to manage public institutions" and govern "communes, schools, cooperatives, leagues." It was political autonomy at which he aimed first, and for this reason he did not pursue a policy of state assistance ("Giacomo Matteotti").

Criticism of socialist reformism is at the core of Gobetti's work on the origins of fascism, and it parallels his critiques of "humanitarian democratism" and Catholicism. The socialist strategy of bartering social legislation for political order and the avoidance of conflict opened a new season in European and Italian politics. On the one hand, it supported a crescendo in state planning, and, on the other, it abdicated the leadership of reformism in favor of the government, which used the support of the socialists to tame its strong electoral forces. The advent of a war economy accelerated the nationalist transformation of the liberal state. The socialists were wholly unprepared to face the growth of social anxiety and conflict, and the ideological debilitation of their movement made room for the growth of fascism, which found a predictable ally in the liberal state, traditionally authoritarian and prone to compromise. Fascism was the expression of a society that demanded more organization and harmony, a society that used the state as an instrument for rationalization and protection, repression and mobilization.

According to Gobetti, fascism's proximate ancestor was the Saint-Simonian mythical vision of the replacement of politics with organization. Accordingly, social and political conflicts were a pathology to be cured through a policy of state corporatism. Gobetti detected in fascist corporatism the convergence of both the conciliatory ethics of Catholicism and the nineteenth-century myth of social harmony. "Fascism won a victory over democracy without fighting against it," because both systems valued social and cultural and political unanimity.[23] In the end, the only true alternative to fascism was liberalism, precisely because of its conflictual vocation.

Gobetti's depiction of nonliberal democracy shares some common traits with that of Carl Schmitt, whose book *The Crisis of Parliamentary Democracy* came out at the same time as Gobetti was setting forth his ideas. For Schmitt, too, democracy meant perfect equality and homogeneous unity. For him, too, democracy was, in principle, more antithetical to liberalism than it was to fascism, which indeed was "certainly anti-liberal but not necessarily antidemocratic."[24] If Gobetti was suspicious of democracy, it was because he had, as it were, a Schmittian vision of it. Or, more accurately, he was suspicious of the Schmittian conception of democracy. However, he tried to make a distinction between that conception and a liberal one. On the one hand, he held democracy to be synonymous with the myth of social harmony and arithmetical equality. It was thus not by chance that he defended proportional representation, which he regarded as a strategy to further fragment the social and political arena and to make the parliament a true agora in which opposition could not easily be silenced and in which minorities would

23. *La rivoluzione liberale*, 91. Gobetti was rearticulating one of the main themes of Mill's *On Liberty*, in which mass democracy is explicitly related to the illiberal doctrine of Auguste Comte. In 1925, Gobetti's publishing house reprinted Mill's *On Liberty*.
24. Carl Schmitt, *The Crisis of Parliamentary Democracy* (1923), trans. Ellen Kennedy (Cambridge: MIT Press, 1994), 16.

not be represented disproportionately. On the other hand, he perceived that democracy was in fact something different from its "aberrations." It meant the primacy of the individual and the acknowledgment of the priority of the political process over practical outcomes. Democracy, Gobetti thought, renders activity cardinal, and for this reason it cannot but encourage individual autonomy. Whereas nineteenth-century liberal thinkers, like Mill and Tocqueville, stressed the identification of democracy not with liberty but with equality, Gobetti offered a more subtle understanding of democracy's two distinct moments: one loyal to the utopian myth of unity and homogeneity, and the another radically oriented toward liberty.

From these premises, Gobetti derived two conclusions that puzzled Italian liberals and made them either doubt his liberalism or view it as an oxymoron.[25] The first conclusion pertained to his assessment of the Russian Revolution of 1917 as a liberal revolution; the second pertained to his assessment of the Turinese communists led by Gramsci as the modern subjects of a liberal revolution. As I will argue, in both cases Gobetti evinced a consistent conception of liberalism as a politics of emancipation from moral as well as political autocracy.

Gobetti's first opinion of the Soviet revolution was negative. In 1918, however, he started studying Russian, and within a few years he became an authority on Russian culture and literature. The outcome of his work was a book entitled *Paradox of the Russian Spirit* and numerous articles on Russian novelists and intellectuals.[26] His reading of the Soviet revolution as a liberal revolution was inspired partly by Trotsky and partly by his re-

25. See, for instance, Marco Revelli, "Gobetti 'liberal-comunista'?" in *I dilemmi del liberalsocialismo*, ed. Michelangelo Bovero, Virgilio Mura, and Franco Sbarberi (Florence: La Nuova Italia, 1994), 63–84.

26. See *Scritti storici*. His mentor was Leone Ginzburg and his wife, Natalia. Ginzburg, a Russian-born immigrant and the first Italian professor of Russian literature, was as old as Gobetti and was one of contributors to his journals; he died under torture in 1944. While in jail he edited and translated into Italian Trotsky's *History of the Russian Revolution*.

flections on the Italian case. Just as France was the background of Tocqueville's *Democracy in America*, Italy was the implicit reference point for Gobetti's *Paradox of the Russian Spirit*.

Gobetti's thesis can be synthesized as follows: To become democratic, Russia needed to develop a secular state; because the Revolution of 1917 aimed at creating a secular state, the Bolsheviks were in actuality, if not in principle, accomplishing a liberal revolution. This reading may be paradoxical, but it was inspired by an interpretation that was liberal and historicist in character. It was consistently liberal because it pivoted around secularism and a belief that the construction of a *Rechtstaat* was the first step toward political liberty. According to Gobetti, Russia did not experience the Middle Ages, which in western Europe had meant the beginning of both the conflict between the papacy and the empire and the struggle by local jurisdictions against a centralized power. Since inception, European liberalism encompassed state secularization and pluralism.

Gobetti put tsarist Russia in the category of "Asian despotism" and gave its political backwardness a cultural explanation. He thought that if in Russia the state apparatus had never been seriously challenged by popular resistance, it was mainly because the Orthodox Church embodied a form of Christianity incapable of becoming a source of political education. "No reforms or heresies arose out of concrete debate about ideas; only sects, out of otiose Byzantine questions about rites or even about orthography" ("Paradox of the Russian Spirit"). The break between the people on one side and the state and the church on the other accounted for the powerlessness of the language of the Enlightenment and the radicalism and anarchical-liberalism of the pre-Bolshevik intelligentsia; it made the principles of Locke and Rousseau politically irrelevant and abstract while justifying the need for a popular revolution. In Russia, Gobetti maintained, the Soviets represented the first modern expression of democratic spontaneity and undertook the first attempt made by a self-organizing people to give birth to a new power structure.

Gobetti wrote his essays on Russia between 1919 and 1924. He did not live long enough to see that the "Russian paradox" would repeat itself and produce a new kind of despotism. The Soviet state enfranchised politics from the old theocracy just in order to make it subservient to a new theocracy. This confirmed Gobetti's belief that a secular state and the concomitant values of individuality and autonomy are the basic conditions for democracy to grow and endure.

THE ETHICAL DIMENSION OF POLITICS

Italy was the reference point for Gobetti's *Paradox of the Russian Spirit,* but can one speak of a similarity between the two countries? After all, the church played an antiliberal role in Italy, too, while the secular state proved to be weak. The similarity cannot be taken further, however, because, as we have seen, Italy had in its tradition those elements that could bring it to accomplish a liberal revolution without exceptional means. The practices of political conflict and economic freedom were not foreign to Italian tradition, even if the conditions were not ripe for the culture of rights to become widely accepted. In Italy as in Russia, a contractarian liberalism grounded on the philosophy of reason and natural rights was unsuitable and powerless. Gobetti had no doubt that liberalism is grounded on individual rights and civil liberty. What he rejected was the contractarian justification of rights, which he deemed abstract and anti-historical and in any event unsuited to non-Protestant countries. In Italy, the "imitation" of the Anglo-Saxon model would, he considered, be anachronistic and thus powerless.

As we have seen, Gobetti regarded rights as a political construction consistent with the condition of modernity, that is, with its secular and individualist character. To secure their institutionalization, judicial recognition, and protection he trusted social and political movements even more than legal institutions. In any event, he did not see the constitution as either a final agreement or as a sufficient reason for security, especially when its implementation could not profit from a widespread liberal culture. Indeed, before the fascist assault, the Italian liberal constitution remained a silent and toothless document; the only constitutional politics would have had to come from the people had the people not been violently repressed.

In sum, one may say that Gobetti indicated two possible strategies for justifying the establishment of individual rights: a moral-religious one, which is normative and abstract, and a political-historical one, which is contextual and embedded in social and political relations. The latter has a greater potential for extending its influence, according to Gobetti, because it does not presume a specific common religious experience. It is more "universalistic" in its reach precisely because it is historicist in its foundation.

Gobetti argued that since the inception of modernity, the path of emancipation had been located in the external dimension of political action, not in the inner self. "Within the teaching of Machiavelli there is the finesse of a citizen expert in historical contingencies, not the vociferous program of a peasant who proclaims the right to free examination and feels the need of carrying on his spiritual formation in public," that is, in religious congregations. Thus, he wrote, the conditions were such that Italian liberal energies could come from the political rather than the private realm, while rights could be claimed in the name of historical transformation instead of a religious kind of universality.[27] Luther and Calvin, not Machiavelli and Alfieri, were the founding fathers of modern liberalism. And yet the trajectory of modernity toward secularism would allow Italy to profit from its own diversity; political conflict would be the channel through which citizens could develop their moral liberal values. Whereas the Luther-Calvin path changed the person in order to form the

27. *La rivoluzione liberale* (ed. Perona), 13.

producer and the citizen, the secular political path would take an opposite direction and change the morality of the citizen and the producer first.

The distinction between private and public morality is very important to understanding both Gobetti's idea that politics has an "ethical" dimension and his strategy of linking liberalism to the republican tradition.

Now, if one goes back to Machiavelli, one may see that he addressed the question of how to stay in power, not simply of how to gain power. The achievement of political stability, in particular that of a free political order, was his main concern. For Machiavelli, it was conflict itself that ensured the persistence of political liberty in a noncorrupt republic. But to him the practice of conflict presumed an ethical attitude toward politics that was wholly antagonistic to Christianity. Thus, his attempt to make politics independent of morality was in fact an attempt to make politics independent of *Christian* morality in order to endow it with its *own* morality. Gobetti built on Machiavelli's idea when he tried to define an autonomous dimension of political morality and to credit politics with an autonomous value. If the Italians could not ground their moral emancipation from authority on the intimate dimension of religion, and if they had to walk a political path, what they needed first was to endow that path with its own worth or ethics. Political action itself, Gobetti thought, would create citizens capable of obeying the law instead of someone's will, of experiencing pride in their equal rights, of defending their dignity against the power of the state, of demanding accountability from politicians, of claiming the right to articulate and advocate their opinions freely.

This is Gobetti's vision of liberal transformation in a society in which "the man" and "the citizen" are separate at birth and are, moreover, rivals. It is important to understand this premise to explain why Gobetti based his theory of liberalism on the defense of a principle that canonical liberalism does not generally stress: the principle of political autonomy. Unlike moral

autonomy, political autonomy pertains to actions, to an actuat-
ing will, and not to the will as such. In the political realm, liberty does not imply noninterference, as it does in the sphere of
morals; rather, it implies nonconstraint.[28] To be politically free—
or, as Gobetti would say, to be autonomous—means not to be
subjected to an unchecked power. Political freedom goes hand
in hand with self-restraint, that is, with laws that have received
popular consent; it goes hand in hand with self-government. One
may speak of a climate of political freedom when obedience to
the laws follows from the consent of those who have to obey
them. It is consent that gives politics autonomy, which ought to
be interpreted as an "ascending power opposite to a descending
power," that is, as a power coming from below against autocratic
imposition from above.[29]

To make his call for political autonomy consistently viable,
Gobetti had to recover the emancipating function of political
action and, more generally, the "ethical" function of politics. He
had to recover a conception of politics as character formation,
a conception that was peculiar not to liberalism but to republicanism.

Gobetti's main criticism of fascism was that it had incorpo-
rated society into the state and had stripped politics of its ethical dimension by collapsing it into the category of the "useful."
Gobetti's criticism of the fascist manipulation of politics recalls
Croce's criticism of contractarianism and Marxism: both view
politics as superstructural and as identical with state coercion
and governmental policy. In different ways and for different reasons, both of them depoliticized human relations and rendered
politics instrumental to the social realm.

However, Gobetti's view should not be seen as an idealistic
hypostatization of politics. He did not disclaim the relation between the social and the political. What he opposed was a deter-

28. Norberto Bobbio, *Politica e cultura* (Turin: Einaudi, 1955), 176.
29. Bobbio, *Italia fedele*, 55.

ministic derivation of the latter from the former. "Politics deals
with actions aimed at utility, and utility is not morality. But it is
not simply egoism either, so there is a need to defend the spiritual, and fundamentally valuable, nature of political engagement against all those who dismiss it as completely immoral, the
preserve of crooks" ("Benedetto Croce"). To Gobetti as to Croce,
the task of liberalism was thus that of recovering the dignity of
politics in the face of both Christian mistrust and "utilitarian"
manipulation. To be sure, for Gobetti, too, politics sprang from
interests. But it did not end there, because it had the capacity to
enfranchise itself from the material realm of the "useful" and to
create new kinds of needs and relations, becoming thereby an
"instrument for moral life" ("Benedetto Croce").

It needs to be stressed that Gobetti insisted on maintaining a
distinction between politics and state administration. This gave
his criticism of fascism an original and radical turn insofar as it
allowed him to grasp the main contradiction of fascism, namely,
that it represents simultaneously the apotheosis of the state (a
centralized and bureaucratic state) and the suffocation of political life. He saw fascism as a regressive phenomenon because it
reinstated a simple dualism of state and civil society by giving the
former a monopoly over politics and the public realm while forcing the latter to withdraw into the narrow dimension of private
and material interests. By debilitating politics, fascism inter-
rupted the growth of the public sphere that had begun in the age
of liberal revolutions.[30]

The term "politics" has three referents in Gobetti's writings:
that which pertains to politicians and political leaders; that
which pertains to public intellectuals; and that which pertains

30. Some of Gobetti's ideas are to be found in the contemporary, and
more sophisticated, debate over the distinction between public and private.
For a helpful reconstruction of this debate, see Jeff Weintraub, "The Theory
and Politics of the Public/Private Distinction," in *Public and Private in
Thought and Practice: Perspectives on a Grand Dichotomy*, ed. Weintraub and
Frishan Kumar (Chicago: University of Chicago Press, 1997), 1–42.

to political parties and movements. He was always very critical of the first, and he ascribed an ethical value to the latter two. With respect to the third, he referred more favorably to political movements than to political parties. His annoyance with uniformity led him to favor small groups over large ones; in general, he was distrustful of large parties.[31]

Within this perspective, he listed three political movements as the subjects of his conception of a liberal revolution: the Turinese communists led by Gramsci, the "agricultural organizations in the south," and the regionalist movement demanding the autonomy of Sardinia. In all these cases, the leading motive was political autonomy. Gramsci's followers did not ask for material and corporate benefits but for political control of the factory; southern peasant movements demanded the eradication of large landed estates and the institution of the private ownership of the land; and the Sardinian movement for autonomy demanded local self-government to replace state centralization. All three could be considered collective subjects of the liberal revolution because their claims were grounded on a belief in political equality and responsibility. They bequeathed to politics a dignity of its own by reviving its genuine function of emancipation. "In Italy now there are millions of peasants who are just starting to feel like human beings and citizens, and who will no longer stand by while their individual rights are trampled. The life of the nation depends on them, provided they organize themselves" ("Toward a New Politics"). Because the defense of those who did not yet enjoy the status of free citizens meant an expansion of liberty for the whole community, these minoritarian political movements were the natural subjects of the liberal revolution.

Gobetti ascribed to politics an ethical role when politics meant "practical activity" in regard to questions pertaining to "many individuals aiming at different results" while united by public interaction ("Our Faith"). The political actors to which he

31. Bobbio, *Italia fedele*, 131.

referred were movements belonging to the intermediary realm
between the world of economic needs and the institutionalized
sphere of the state. Politics occupies, or, more accurately, defines, the area of public life in the modern sense of the word. It
means not only *force* but *consent*, and for this reason, it requires
liberty. It is not in conflict with the individualistic character of
modern society, because it stems from individual engagement.
It is not disruptive of social cohesion; to the contrary, it links
individuals to one another by linking them to political movements, to their adversaries, and to the life of their country. Gobetti saw conflict as the modern vehicle for the achievement of
social unity. "The sense of social solidarity can come only from
the exercise of individual rights, which are naturally bounded by
the similar rights of everyone else. Those who preach abstract
solidarity are ripe to become servants at court" ("Democracy").

The language of political movements had to be principled
and symbolic, because it had to speak to issues of political emancipation while countering popular apathy. Gobetti was highly influenced by Sorel's radical criticism of reformist socialism and
his acknowledgment of the role of myth in political action. In
this sense, even if Gobetti was radically anticollectivist and did
not believe in communist propaganda, he credited Gramsci for
being able to give the Turinese workers an effective motivation
for action (without sparing Gramsci's party the criticism of becoming bureaucratic and "politically protectionist") ("The Communists"). Actually, Gobetti was convinced that through the
communist myth and in spite of its content, the workers were
fulfilling the goal that the Italian bourgeoisie had failed to
achieve, namely, that of becoming "producers" and asking for
recognition of the very principles of responsible enterprise and
self-mastery that would make them, paradoxically, the new elite
of modern bourgeois democracy. "This will be the irony of history for those who declaimed against the bourgeoisie and announced they were ready to bury it" ("The Bourgeoisie").

In short, Gobetti, who was neither socialist nor communist,

regarded the movement of factory councils as a training ground for democracy and as an instrument for renewal of political leadership. He praised the practices of that grass-roots movement much more than he did the actual goals those councils were intended to pursue, because he believed in the formative function of democratic participation. Workers' refusal to limit their strategy to unionism and salary policy led them to "spiritualize" politics by emancipating it from the dictates of material needs: when Gramsci's followers asked for factory self-government and responsibility in the workplace, they were acting as political subjects. They were wholly modern insofar as their spheres of practice—economic and politics—were secular and consistent with liberal society. In spite of their propaganda, they were not constructing socialism but reeducating themselves as citizens. They were becoming individuals conscious of their rights and of their basic political equality. "In fact we fully recognize, without waiting for the outcome, or even anticipating it, that they are *accomplishing* liberal work *even now* simply because they are pursuing a process of autonomy and liberation and translating their initiatives into political discipline. That is the substance of our liberalism, and it is diametrically opposed to any conservative practice" ("Liberalism and the Workers").

GOBETTI AND CONTEMPORARY LIBERALISM

Gobetti's writings suggest a vision of liberalism that is not conventional and that can enrich the multifaceted identity of contemporary liberalism. As I argued above, Gobetti was not a professional scholar but an intellectual confronting problems of political instability and transition. This made him attentive to the dimension of political action and the impact of liberal ideals in the everyday lives of men and women. It brought him to appreciate and stress the emancipating potential of liberalism.

Gobetti's conception of liberalism bears the mark of being

a historical conquest consistent with the modern transformation of society, in particular the growth of a market economy
and the recognition of the value of the individual. The search
for neutrality and normative detachment has brought contemporary liberal theorists to interpret liberalism as a set of principles that transcends social context and historical specificity.[32]
This trend has recently been revised by John Rawls, who argues
that a political constructivist conception of the basic principles
and procedures of a just and free society ought to be seen as the
highest form of abstraction of a historical process that can be
traced back to the age of religious wars.

Contemporary constitutional democracy reflects a political
conception of justice that ought to be understood as a translation into a general and theoretical form of certain "basic intu-
itive ideas" that are latent in the public political culture of a
democratic society or in common sense.[33] To paraphrase Hegel,
philosophy makes its appearance at the end of the day, as a reflection of a course of action that was determined in the first
place by political conflicts and the historical development of social and political structures. As Gobetti would say, constitutional
democracy is the ripened fruit of modernity, the political expression of the emancipation of the individual from both comprehensive philosophies and asymmetrical relations of power.

Both contemporary liberals and Gobetti speak of "political
liberalism," although they may place the accent on different elements and define it in different terms. As in Madison's writings,
one perceives in Gobetti's work a clear consciousness of the social affiliation of liberalism and the permanent tensions that this
affiliation brings into political debate. To stress the dimension
of politics is, for Gobetti, a reason to bring liberalism closer to

32. See, for instance, Charles Larmore, *The Morals of Modernity* (Cambridge: Cambridge University Press, 1996), 121–27.
33. John Rawls, "Justice as Fairness: Political Not Metaphysical" (1985),
in Rawls, *Collected Papers*, ed. Samuel Freeman (Cambridge: Harvard University Press, 1999), 390.

social needs and experiences. By contrast, political liberalism in the contemporary debate seems to refer mainly to the legalistic and judicial structure of the state. It is my belief that the appeal of Gobetti's approach, which distinguishes political and governmental dimensions, rests on the desirability, which he stresses, of preserving a distinction between judicial and political competence. To employ contemporary language, he gives the public sphere a broad compass, one that takes into consideration the configuration and expression of dissent and the search for new levels of consent. Thus, he holds a conception of politics that is highly relevant to us today.

Contemporary liberal theorists tend to ascribe to liberalism a *super partes* status and to expel from public discourse reasons for contest and disagreement. They seek to ascribe to the liberal structure of society a neutral character and status in order to protect it from the partisan claims that arise from "thick" conceptions of the good and from comprehensive visions of life, which may kindle intolerance and jeopardize social stability. While this approach is reasonable in relation to *certain* conceptions of the good, it does not easily fit all conceptions, nor can it be extended equally and indifferently to all institutions and citizens. One may reasonably ask whether the notion of neutrality applies equally to religious and cultural perfectionism and to issues pertaining to the concrete opportunities that individuals have to pursue their life plans. Theories of neutrality overshadow the fact that liberalism likewise has a substantive and perfectionist core—indeed, its evaluative criterion favors the individual and, above all, the individual's dignity and equal consideration as a person and a citizen. In relation to the social or cultural station in which a person finds herself or himself, this claim can easily bring a liberal to partisanship. The paradox of neutrality is that it cannot ignore factual conditions of discrimination and injustice without becoming nugatory; yet to recognize those factual conditions necessarily requires a suspension of neutrality or, more accurately, its circumscription.

Laws should neither tell us to worship nor specify how to worship, nor prescribe whether, how, or whom to love. But consensus on what the state should not do becomes more precarious and vulnerable to contestation once we come to the basic (material and cultural) conditions of individual well-being. Hence, for instance, liberalism may bring us to think that the state should not be neutral in matters concerning the choice of parents not to send their children to school, or in matters concerning the length of the working day.

Finally, no less controversial is the decision over *where* neutrality should be claimed, endorsed, and protected. Is the quest for impartiality just as appropriate in the case of a politician and representative as in the case of a judge and public official? What is the place of neutrality in legislative decisionmaking, where parties, interests, and ideas are in charge? Moreover, should the individual citizen be expected to behave like a judge and public official and give neutral justification for his or her public choices?[34]

Although Gobetti endorses the liberal principle of the separation of politics from religion, he does not subscribe to the claim of an unbounded, pervasive neutrality. The discourse of neutrality presumes a feeling of security in the government and the law (the existence of a solid democratic society and constitution)—a condition that was absent in his time and country. For him, neutrality implied an apolitical perspective, and, in this sense, it was decidedly negative. I would say, however, that living at a given time and in a given place is not solely what made him skeptical about neutrality. It was his deep sense of the value and significance of the moral premise of liberalism, his belief in the individual as an autonomous moral subject, that brought him to declare his partisanship. Like Mill, Gobetti saw self-reliance

34. For a rigorous discussion of the principle and politics of neutrality see George Sher, *Beyond Neutrality: Perfectionism and Politics* (Cambridge: Cambridge University Press, 1997), 20–44.

and self-government as the main goals of liberalism, which, in
this sense, was perfectionist. Thus, he did not feel distraught at
the emergence of political movements denouncing the promises
that liberalism did not or was not willing to fulfill, even when
those movements defended their claims on the basis of nonliberal ideals (although he understood very well that those movements must remain representative of a minority). On several
occasions, he thought of "myths" as necessary to shake off popular apathy, which he regarded as a severe threat to liberal democracy.

Gobetti was aware, in a way that recalls Isaiah Berlin, that
by endorsing pluralism he could hardly avoid the paradox of a
liberal society inhabited by loyalties that are not in themselves
liberal.[35] The solution Gobetti offers is the institutionalization
of conflict, because he regards political antagonism as a vehicle
for interaction and for learning the art of toleration.[36] Conflict
is necessary both to competitors and to the overall society: to
the former because antagonism can be a means for reciprocal
recognition and interdependence, which brings "enemies" to relate and try to reach a common ground for dialogue; to the latter
because the opposite of conflict may very well be a society that
yearns for homogeneity and is malevolent toward difference—
two attitudes that are equally detrimental to liberty.

Pluralism exposes the public realm to a degree of "intransigence," or integrity, with which liberalism has to cope. Gobetti
anticipated a problem that contemporary theorists of deliberative democracy are posing to themselves when they inquire
about the depth and extension of consensus, even if they are sus-

35. Isaiah Berlin, "Two Concepts of Liberty" (1958), in *Four Essays on
Liberty* (Oxford: Oxford University Press, 1992), 122–31; and John Rawls,
Political Liberalism (New York: Columbia University Press, 1993), 303–4.

36. Rawls himself recognizes that "the stage" on which abstract conceptions are set in motion is filled by "profound and long-lasting controversies."
"In political philosophy the work of abstraction is set in motion by deep
political conflicts." Rawls, *Political Liberalism*, 44.

picious of the presence of passions and beliefs in the collective deliberative process. Opposite forces may reach a compromise that allows for governability and policy implementation. But do they give up their convictions? Is it not the case that maintenance of the democratic process requires that consent does not exhaust the possibility of dissent?[37] Gobetti's dialectics of tolerance and intransigence might be seen as a valuable challenge to the contemporary theory of deliberative democracy.[38]

As I argued above, to Gobetti liberalism is synonymous with immanentism and historicity. Historicity implies the recognition of liberalism's "corruption" by other political traditions. Gobetti has no trouble acknowledging that the genealogy of liberalism traces back to republicanism, nor is he reticent in maintaining that, in his time, liberalism might adopt ideas from nonliberal traditions, such as socialism and Marxism. His conception of immanentism and historicity has a twofold sense. First, it suggests that liberalism has undergone, and presumably will undergo in the future, changes in its character. In a constitutional and parliamentary democracy, liberalism tends to play a

37. Some interesting thoughts on the limits of reasonable explanation and the role of beliefs in conviction formation are to be found in Gerald F. Gaus, "Reason, Justification, and Consensus: Why Democracy Can't Have It All," in *Deliberative Democracy: Essays on Reason and Politics*, ed. James Bohman and William Rehg (Cambridge: MIT Press, 1997), 214–15, 221–24, 231–36.

38. See, for instance, Amy Gutmann and Dennis Thompson, *Democracy and Disagreement* (Cambridge: Harvard University Press, Belknap Press, 1996), 134–36. Gutmann and Thompson argue, convincingly, that "deliberation cannot occur unless an issue reaches the political agenda. Nondeliberative means may be necessary to achieve deliberative ends" (135). Significantly, however, they regard rhetoric as just such a nondeliberative means, suggesting that deliberation is a rationalistic enterprise, devoid of attempts at nonrational persuasion. But if deliberation is not simply the final act of voting but is above all a public forum for reaching agreement through discussion, then rhetoric is one of its constitutive components. Gobetti recognized this when he acknowledged the rhetorical function of the "myth" in grass-roots movements.

conservative role, that is, a role of preserving the existing political institutions and guarantees. Although this represents an important achievement and a sign of liberalism's stability, playing this role can impoverish the critical function of liberalism. Gobetti distinguishes his emancipating liberalism from that of "domesticated" liberals. For this reason, he cautions that we must maintain a distinction between two different levels: the level of institutional policy, where decisions occur, and that of politics, where matters of institutional deliberation are shaped and developed. As a quest for equality and for inclusion and extension of guarantees, democratic principles stimulate political action and the growth of political movements; hence they press the extension of deliberation outside the sphere of the state and beyond the moment of voting. Even if Gobetti did not use the word "democracy," his notion of a liberal state and culture is exquisitely democratic, and more familiar to us than to his contemporaries.

The second sense of Gobetti's immanentism and historicity suggests that liberalism is not in need of developing its identity in opposition to other political traditions. The notion of conflict, which he derives from the Marxist idea of class struggle and from Machiavelli, inspired several liberals of his generation, from Mosca and Pareto to Schumpeter. The same can be said of the "ethical dimension of politics," which has a republican lineage and yet was endorsed by several liberals of his generation, for instance, Croce and Hobhouse. To speak of an ethical dimension of politics implies a recognition that politics is not simply the sphere in which interests operate and bargains take place, even if interests do lend weight to this side or that and even if agreements must be reached. Politics also expresses a vision of freedom from subjection. As has recently been argued, the dualism between republicanism and liberalism is a function of post–French Revolution liberalism that does not help us to fully appreciate the richness of the notion of freedom as self-reliance, a notion that both republican and liberal theorists have endorsed.[39] This was precisely Gobetti's ideal at the beginning of the twentieth century. In his time, his conception of liberalism was perceived as the idealistic project of a young and dissatisfied radical. Today we can see his sour radicalism as an astute anticipation of ideas that democrats would acknowledge and appreciate several decades later.

39. Mogens Herman Hansen, *The Athenian Democracy in the Age of Demosthenes* (Oxford: Blackwell, 1993), 73–85; Philip Pettit, *Republicanism: A Theory of Freedom and Government* (Oxford: Oxford University Press, Clarendon Press, 1997), 17–50.

ABBREVIATIONS:
WORKS BY PIERO GOBETTI

Scritti politici	*Opere complete di Piero Gobetti.* Vol. I, *Scritti politici.* Ed. Paolo Spriano. 1960. Reprint, Turin: Einaudi, 1997.
Scritti storici	*Opere complete di Piero Gobetti.* Vol. II, *Scritti storici, letterari e filosofici.* Ed. Paolo Spriano, with notes by Franco Venturi and Vittorio Strada. Turin: Einaudi, 1969.
La rivoluzione liberale (ed. Perona)	*La rivoluzione liberale: Saggio sulla lotta politica in Italia.* 2d ed. Ed. Ersilia Alessandrone Perona, with an essay by Paolo Spriano. Turin: Einaudi, 1983. (A new edition with an essay by Paolo Flores d'Arcais was published by Einaudi in 1995.)

ON LIBERAL REVOLUTION

1 MEN, WOMEN, AND IDEAS

LEV TROTSKY

IN the *Rivista di Milano* [*Journal of Milan*] for 20 February 1921, I showed that the Russian Revolution—by promoting the creation of an agrarian democracy, overthrowing autocracy and the *mir* [village commune], and creating a state in which the people believe because they feel they have made it themselves—is essentially, in its inner dialectic, an affirmation of liberalism.[1] Further research on the intellectual crisis in Russia in the previous century and the study of a magisterial work by Lev Trotsky (*Terrorism and Communism: A Reply to Kautsky*), which has not yet been translated into Italian and with which I am acquainted at first hand, have persuaded me to restate my thesis in philosophical terms.

Trotsky counters the abstractions of the Slavic intelligentsia, from Radishchev to Tolstoy, by proclaiming a liberal vision of history for the first time in Russia. He arrived at this conception of history as the result of free human activity by way of Marxist culture, which conceives the possibility of overcoming, in a fruitful manner, the abstract intellectualism that vitiates the stance of the Slavic thinkers as they vainly anguish over the artificial contrast between Slavophiles and westernizers. Slavophiles and westernizers share the same point of departure—the Hegelian

<hr>

1. Original title: "Trotzki"; from *Il Resto del Carlino* (Bologna), 5 April 1921. Translated from *Scritti politici*, pp. 206–210.

outlook, but with Hegel given a mystical slant, something we
have seen in Italy with the Hegelianism of Vera.[2] Two different
factors combined, each in its own way, to make these Russians
lose touch with reality, ignore the conditions in which the people
were living, and attribute a political function to an intellectual
class that was impregnated with mystical values, bemused by
the myth of pure rationality, and miserably incapable of action:
one was the redemptive mission claimed for the Russian *spirit*
from Khomiakov to Dostoevsky; the other was the importation
into Slavic obscurantism (hailed as a revelation by Belinskii and
Herzen) of the ideas of the European Enlightenment. The anarchic sentimentalism of the intelligentsia had not achieved a
reflective consciousness, nor a complete individualism capable
of reconciling itself with, and making use of, autonomous rationality. Whether these intellectuals were atheists or simply opponents of the institutionalized church, they did not succeed in for-
mulating a critique of the old theocracy, and their religiosity did
not lead to anything concrete but dissipated into messianic expectations of moral renewal. They did not understand morality
as practical social action that counts for something socially to
the extent that it is concrete and, to be frank, political; for them
it remained a pure abstract form, an object of contemplation
—a morality that finds redemption outside itself (for example,
Tolstoy's *Resurrection*) and is thus false (inadequate and sterile)
at its core.

A sound familiarity with economic ideas, however determin-
istically and materialistically they were understood at first, laid
the initial basis for a denial of a theocracy that had developed in
isolation from the real conditions of Russian life and had crys-
tallized into a centralizing force with the power to crush all activity and to hold the citizens in a state of slavery. Trotsky's entire project as a thinker is to portray the religious problem as a

2. Augusto Vera (1813–1885) was an influential but not original Neapolitan philosopher whose main merit was importing Hegel's philosophy to Italy.

purely political question, by which means he hopes to dissolve the mystical logic of churchly indifference and force it to yield a concrete self-justification; and that ought to be practically lethal to it. "Materialistic socialism," says Trotsky in a polemic against Masaryk, "is really for the workers the first stage of subjective life, of life lived for themselves." The criticism aimed at Russian theocracy by the intellectuals wandered off into a mystical vision that denied values, and reality. Russia is the birthplace of every sort of mysticism; there *thought* has to turn to *abstraction*, there idealistic values have to turn hazy and evanescent. Even Kant becomes a proponent of mysticism if he is transplanted into the Slavic environment (for example, Masaryk). Trotsky understands that to root out mysticism one has to destroy philosophy (pseudophilosophy) and affirm a materialistic conception of life.

History is made by individuals. So the individual must not become lost in a dream of fantastic transcendence or quietist contemplation; the task is to become aware of one's own responsibility.

"What does our Russian peasant suffer from? From the lack of individual consciousness, which is precisely what our populist reactionaries have celebrated, what Tolstoy glorified in the person of Plato Karataieff: the peasant who melts into his community, who obeys the soil. Socialism clearly will not be created out of Plato Karataieff, but out of workers who think, who are endowed with initiative and awareness of their own responsibilities. Whatever the cost, we have to nourish initiative in the workers. Individualism in the working class is not in contradiction with solidarity and fraternal collaboration" (*Terrorism and Communism*). Solid thinking like this, conscious of its own historical importance, is clearly a contradiction of Tolstoyan abstraction.

Trotsky's vision has taken a markedly voluntaristic turn, leaving behind the materialistic and fatalistic element that contaminates Marx's conception of history. Thus he puts the problem of the revolution in concrete terms, knowing that amid the empty anarchic hopes of Russian antitsarism the only possibility of introducing a principle of life and realization would be the creation of a class of leaders with a sense of the state, able to impose discipline and make this into a state of citizens. Against the reformism of Kerensky, who behaved in the Russian context as though he were an English democrat, Trotsky theorized the dictatorship of the proletariat, a government arising not out of the indistinct mass of the people but out of the portion of it that feels public responsibility; in this view factory councils became essential organs because they would be the road to political experience for workers and peasants, proportioned by degrees to their increasing maturity.

In countries like those of the Slavic world, where theocracy has existed side by side for centuries with a sentiment of purely anarchic libertarianism quite unable to harden into a solid awareness of individual values, Trotsky's whole critique of the natural-law metaphysics of the democrats is perfectly legitimate and profoundly liberal. To preach abstract philosophical equality is simply inane, given that in history equality has had real impact only as a political force in empirically determined and utterly transient circumstances. The democratic myth was a contingent offshoot of the French Revolution and a forceful weapon against feudalism, but it will hardly be able to create consensus in a people that is barely taking shape as such and still does not give universal credence to the value of the *individual*.

Trotsky longs for a state in which liberty is not proclaimed by law but is achieved by the citizens to the extent to which each is able to assume the responsibility. Over against abstract egalitarianism (which in Russia more properly deserves to be called by the frank term "reactionary") this is the potent inception of a liberalism that sees history as the living outcome—always unforeseeable and always outstripping the will of any individual—of what individuals themselves bring about, of what each is able to bring to the common task of humanity. And the de facto contribution of each cannot be weighted a priori, through a process of abstraction; it counts only pragmatically, in what is realized.

On these principles Trotsky defends his conception of liberalism, seeing a concrete example in the voluntary labor contributed by the workers on "communist Saturdays and Sundays." On these principles he affirms, with a resolve that leaves no room for doubt, that intellectuals have a function as the living force of civilization. And he proposes that industry be organized on the basis of a unified command, in opposition to the socialist system of collegial control and responsibility.

Only from tactical necessity and under the pressure of history in a country like Russia, the homeland of the *mir*, the country where every sort of *community* receives adoration, does this fertile movement for liberalism have to assume the name and sometimes the appearance of a movement for socialism. You cannot accomplish the education of an entire nation in the space of a few years: the masses will often reject the substance if doing so means that things retain familiar names. It falls to the historian to speak the truth, on a plane higher than political contingency.

LUIGI STURZO

THE personality of Luigi Sturzo[3] constitutes a challenge to both theorists and historians because within the man himself are contained all the insoluble difficulties and subtle equivocations that make it hard to grasp the praxis of the Popular Party —a party that, whatever its adversaries claim, is working out political positions and feelings that are quite impossible to mis-

3. Luigi Sturzo (1871–1959) was the founder of the Italian Popular Party (1919). Elected to parliament in 1919, he refused to support Mussolini's government and left for exile, first in London and then in New York. Returning to Italy in 1946, he was among the founders of the Christian Democratic Party.

take for old-style clericalism.[4] For some years the Honorable Meda[5] has found himself in a state of profound unease, and the great authority he enjoyed as quasi head of the government and unchallenged leader of the Catholics has suddenly plummeted. This is not just personal bad luck, nor does it signify the substitution of one figurehead for another. Rather, these developments signify the appearance of new ideals, a shift in concepts and methods. Today nobody views Meda as the leader of the Popular Party; he represents the old liberal reformist clericalism within the Popular Party, and since the latter encompasses the former, Meda is simply one element in the complex political game of Sturzo. Historically he figures as a precursor who hasn't yet understood, and therefore finds himself bewildered and at times bowled over by, a rationale antithetical to his own.

Within the government Meda is a man of ability, not an idea; Meda's experience will serve Sturzo as he constructs his own system of thought and pursues his own strategy. Meda reconciled Catholicism and liberalism without even seeing reconciliation as problematic. History, on the other hand, usually unfolds with a greater degree of thought and profundity: the experience of Murri[6] could not be skipped over so easily. But the imperative of Murri, resolved in such a way as not to exclude Meda, indeed in such a way as to justify him, raised much more complex problems of culture and action: new elements forced their way into

4. Original title: "Don Sturzo"; from *La Rivoluzione Liberale* 1, nos. 20–21 (July 1922), p. 76. Translated from *Scritti politici*, pp. 383–387.

5. The title "Honorable" designates a parliamentary deputy. Filippo Meda (1869–1939) was among the first prominent Catholics to enter political life. After the unification of Italy and as a sign of opposition to it, the Vatican forbade believers to take part in the political life of the country. The Vatican acknowledged the Italian state in 1929, when it signed an agreement with Mussolini's regime.

6. Romolo Murri (1870–1944) was a priest and the first prominent Catholic intellectual to enter political life against the ban of the Vatican. Because of his disobedience and his "modernist" ideas, Murri was excommunicated. As a politician, he tried to implement the social ideas of Leo XIII's *Rerum Novarum* and to promote a Christian social politics.

the hermetic circle of clerical uncertainty, which was still long-ing mystically for an idyll. Clericalism had amounted to nostal-gic literature, and its importance to society was to supply a tech-nique for diplomats: the Popular Party was supposed to become a force in the political contest.

To make Miglioli coexist with Crispolti,[7] to receive the legacy of Murri and Pius X, to praise the pseudo-economic elucubra-tions of Toniolo[8] and profit from the concreteness of Tangorra, to welcome even heresy with free and lofty superiority, to go so far as to exploit with regal sapience the elegant, combative dilettantism of Luigi Ambrosini (and compromise him instead of being compromised)—this is the majestic dialectic that the Popular Party has imposed on the disorganized life of the Ital-ians, this is the truth behind its equivocation. Taken in isolation, it is easy to explain Speranzini and Anile, Gemelli and Crispolti, Miglioli and De Rossi. But when it comes to Sturzo, the problem is to resolve all these antitheses at once, to locate the unifying factor among all these individuals. We can follow the actions of the Popular Party; we can explain its nature and form without engaging in too many dialectical acrobatics. But the past and the future of his party are immanent in Sturzo himself, and we cannot understand his personality if we do not enter a realm of logic that lies above the empirical struggle. Thus he remains an enigma to the technicians of politics. To Giolitti[9] he must have seemed a deus ex machina that suddenly materialized to cause a disturbance; philosophers themselves are disconcerted. In fact,

7. Guido Miglioli and Filippo Crispolti were among the founders of the Italian Popular Party.

8. Of the several names that Gobetti mentions here, Giuseppe Toniolo (1845–1918) and Agostino Gemelli (1878–1959) are the more noteworthy. The former, an economist, was among the protagonists of the Italian *Methoden-streit*, the reaction against the doctrine of the free market that began in Ger-many early in the 1870s. The latter, the founder of the Catholic University in Milan, was among the scholars who contributed to the revitalization of Thomist philosophy in Italy.

9. See, e.g., the essays in Chapter 3.

Luigi Sturzo could be defined as the *messianic figure of reformism,* and even that definition, complex and ungraspable as it is, does not exhaust all aspects of the man.

If we are to discuss the thought of Luigi Sturzo, the concept of *reformism* requires a double clarification. Even in abstract terms it is impossible not to distinguish between reformism and reforms. Reform is part of the art of government. But in the concept of reformism we discern elements that lead us to judge it dismissively in the specific Italian situation of today.

Luigi Sturzo takes his place in the dialectic of Italian history by taking his place in the dialectic of reformism and creating a laic logic.

From 1848 to 1914, as we have argued elsewhere,[10] the government of Italy was a form of state socialism. The Piedmontese Center-Left, the *trasformismo* of Depretis[11] and Giolitti, the socialist monarchy, all reveal the separation between government and people and the tragic absence of a laic discipline and laic values in our national life. Government has to resort to illicit pressure, dealmaking, and corruption in order to find an equilibrium at which it can function without being toppled; reforms as correlatives of the art of government are not enough, because

10. Giovanni Giolitti (1841–1928) is one of the targets of Gobetti's criticism against the old liberalism. Giolitti was several times prime minister before the advent of fascism and the main protagonist of *parlamentarismo* (translated here as "parliamentarianism"), or the degeneration of political life into lobbyism and bargaining. During the first decade of the twentieth century, *giolittismo* (translated here as "Giolittism"), or *trasformismo* (an untranslatable term explained in the following note), was able to guarantee political stability by gaining support from the strong Socialist Party in exchange for some legislative concessions. That tactic proved to be wholly inadequate to cope with the growth of social conflict as a consequence of postwar distress. Moreover, this unprincipled politics bears the responsibility for legitimizing fascism through the attempt to bargain with Mussolini's party.

11. The initiator of *trasformismo* was Agostino Depretis (1813–1887), prime minister in the 1870s; he developed the strategy of compromising policy to involve the opposition in the government's decisions and overcome the majority-minority divide.

the unstable premise is constantly having to be re-created, and that task falls to reformism, which makes liberals, too, lose touch with their principles.

In the reformist illusion, the people submit to utilitarianism, and this condition distances them yet again from the unity that has already failed twice. What we have to deal with is a new, formal degeneration. What we have to do is halt the catastrophe of disintegration that the socialists neither see nor know how to avoid. In this light, Sturzo is the *messianic figure of reformism*, taking Cavour's prescription entirely at face value and striving to make the people believe in politics through a moral a priori. He thinks of *democratic vitality*, but he does not see, enclosed within the bounds of the problem he has to resolve, the relation between politics and the state. The popular movement is viewed by Sturzo in relation to the *forces of regeneration in the future of all peoples*, and in this way he resolves the two essential problems of the life of his party and of Italian life. He can make the effort to proselytize, at which the democrats failed, because he waves the banner of messianic reformism and uses the religious illusion to bring the masses to participate in laicization. He has no fear of praxis because by accepting lame old reformist liberalism he makes it harder for the *pantheistic state* and Marxism to challenge him.

But Luigi Sturzo is having an effect not only on the history of Italy but also on the history of the Church, which makes him a more complex figure, harder to grasp. With the same approach and to exactly the same degree, he makes himself the *reformer of messianism*. Politics and religion each use their own strength to realize the other. The unique power of politics creates a religious position—and vice versa.

The European war has shown that the Church cannot fight against all of Europe on the theory that it alone stands against heresy; instead it has to present this antithesis in more cautious, dialectical terms. Sturzo, who is not enamored of revolutions, makes this too an occasion for peaceful regeneration and coun-

ters noisy demonstrations with an agile transaction. Just as he
opposed historical materialism and the liberal state on the political terrain, he opposes religious reform on this terrain. The
Risorgimento is a result that has to be accepted: this is the tactical premise that keeps Sturzo from achieving an integral solution. Religious reform is always a movement that erupts outside the Church; it is life pressing against the closed unity of
dogma and demanding that its interests be satisfied. To take the
impetus out of religious reform, what is needed is diplomatic
agility, a versatility of consensus and sympathy—not genuine internal reform. And in this respect, Sturzo exemplifies the traditional finesse and ductility of Catholicism, except that he plays
the game with fewer moral inhibitions: he steers Christianity
into politics; he goes to the people through the gospel. Some
people take a malicious and skeptical view of his religiosity, but
although a practical man and adverse to mysticism, he is in fact
one of the great religious souls of our time because of the way
he drives beyond appearances, because of the way he measures
results and nothing else, because of the certainty with which he
navigates through contradictions and adaptations. This is not
the religiosity of Giuliotti;[12] it is the faith of a Christian, optimistic and serene, acting here on earth in the knowledge that
the Divinity is always with him because it is universal. Sturzo
feels the problems of the spirit in the most immediate way without feeling the terror that they inspire in ascetics. His religiosity
is not the tormented kind but rather, if I can put it this way,
Goethean serenity practically applied.

It is hard to find in Sturzo any formal profession of Christianity, and if there were one, it would be inadequate, because
he is not intolerant, and his need to proselytize induces him to
soften his tone. But transcendence is part of his thought whether
it is expressed or not; his philosophy of history is Catholic, so

12. Domenico Giuliotti (1877–1956) was a Catholic polemicist who
scourged modernity and liberalism.

he never loses faith in the way things are going. As a realist, he has only a generic understanding of myth. As a practical man, he leaves dogma aside in order to concentrate on the problem of action as an external phenomenon.

There is a psychological premise that is necessary along the road that leads to transcendence, and Sturzo's spirit and intentions are focused on bringing this premise into action. An integrist declaration of dogma and faith in the context of the modern world might cause a scandal, but the word of faith and love spoken by the Church springs up on its own in the solitude of the individual conscience. The regenerative elements on which Sturzo counts lead indirectly to Catholicism and offer themselves to the unsatisfied hopes of weak human beings at just the right moment. So he has to create the messianic expectation that allows these impulses to come into play. Sturzo does not back down; he confronts the modern world and waits for the moment of weakness in which surrender to the universal Church may once again become a reality. For the moment, note the effort he makes to perceive moral value in every political fact; note the way he derives the moral justification of every action not from historical reality, or the objective autonomy of what comes about (as do Marx and Hegel), but from the supreme dignity of the moral individual. The Church can prevail still by relying on the fear of individuals faced with a crisis of conscience.

Sturzo's calculation is deep, but it turns into a dangerous game. The hidden strategy in this satanic plan is the abandonment of confessionalism, in an attempt to turn the weapons of liberals back on themselves. The healthy struggle for autonomy against the bureaucratic state becomes a struggle against the state and against socialism. It is easier in praxis to overcome the spirit of individuals than to overcome states, because states are not subject to the hard vigils of conscience and fear of heresy. The same tactic that was used to erode the Roman empire from within at a time when it was impossible for the Church to dominate it from without is being employed once again, two millennia later.

But will it really be possible to awaken people's consciences without also arousing their sense of responsibility? Will the self-determining wills of people today incline once more to ask for sanction? Sturzo plans his moves without remembering the inversion of praxis. He binds himself in his own game. You cannot serve God and Satan at the same time. In awakening individual consciences and arousing autonomous impulses he operates like a liberal, and he no longer knows where to stop. Will the messianic figure of practical reformism serve the Church or the state? Will the reformer of messianism remain Catholic, or will he follow out the logic of free inquiry?

Judging by the consequences of his actions, Sturzo looks as though he is not all that far from being excommunicated; and even if he should desist, the consequences won't fail to play out.[13] But the current state of affairs is much more interesting because Sturzo will not desist, and in this paradox lies the function and the importance of the Popular Party.

WOODROW WILSON

Woodrow Wilson died today at a quarter past eleven.[14] The ex-president died at home, in the arms of his wife and daughter, in his favorite room on the third floor at the back of the house, where the noise from the street can barely be heard. The windows give onto the garden, and in the distance can be seen the dome of the Capitol building and the river that flows down to Mount Vernon, where stands the historic home of George Washington. Despite the privacy of this room, vehicular traffic has

13. In fact, the Vatican did not excommunicate Sturzo.
14. Original title: "Uomini e idee [VII]: Lo stile di Wilson"; from *La Rivoluzione Liberale* 3, no. 7 (12 February 1924), pp. 25–26, signed "p.g." Translated from *Scritti politici*, pp. 591–593.

been suspended on all the streets around the house since last
Saturday by order of the authorities, so as not to disturb the
peace surrounding the dying man. But all night long a crowd
of people filed silently before Wilson's residence to read the bul-
letins on his health. And this morning around a hundred men
and women gathered on the sidewalk in front of the house and
prayed for a long time on their knees. (*From Monday's papers.*)

THIS humble newspaper story may stand as the most worthy
eulogy of Wilson. His silent, composed passing shows a style
that elevates him above all the writers who have taken the opportunity to insult him under pretext of commemoration.

The commentaries on Wilson's death are no more than a
shabby example of everyday journalism. None of the writers has
succeeded in evoking the atmosphere of history. The anger of
Italians who were either disappointed or self-interested spoke
instead, as though Wilson were merely the theorist of the Fourteen Points, or the man of Versailles. But to take the measure
of his greatness, one has to regard him as an American, in the
context of American history. His election to the presidency is a
fact of solemn importance in itself: in 1914 he had already shown
himself to be a great statesman. After the mediocrity of presi-
dents like Taft and Roosevelt, one felt in Wilson the temper of a
Lincoln.

We ought not to forget that American politics and American traditions were stamped with the name of Monroe. Wilson,
whom the obituarists of today would like to portray as a weak-
ling and a talker, had the strength to fight against and conquer
this long political tradition of closed nationalism and protectionism; he defeated the plots of America's swindling financiers;
he was the first to craft a role for his country in the world. The di-
rections he set for tariff and monetary policy, the solution to the
Panama Canal question, the decision to intervene in the war in
Europe, give such outstanding proof of his realism and his open
and intelligent spirit that they rehabilitate him even from the

debacle of Versailles. Remember that we are judging an American, not a European, and in American history the guidance he gave will outlive him: his name is on the complex of policies that will be carried into the future. The blame he bears for the failure in Europe he shares with the Europeans who left him on his own. In this solitude lies the greatness of his tragedy: at home he stood alone against American particularism while in Europe he stood alone against the particularism of the nations. Six years of power in these unusual conditions destroyed him. Few politicians had ever withstood a trial like that, and it made him one of the first modern statesmen who was truly a world statesman. Because the task he faced was unique, realism and idealism (in the sense of originality and creative political virtue) bordered one another so closely, each virtually a function of the other, that a single error, a refusal to bend, was enough to topple the whole edifice. If Wilson had been flanked at Versailles not by a stubborn nationalist like Sonnino, or a rhetorician like Orlando, but instead by a farsighted nationalist like Nitti, his rigidity would have produced results.[15] But in any case it is ridiculous for us to put our own regrets into the balance in our historical judgment of this complex, international political figure.

His death has a flavor of intimacy and solemnity of feeling that, in our view, confirms his greatness by showing us a cordial, human aspect of the man. No Americanism, no posturing. Wilson is not a dynamic hero; yet I reflect on the death of a real hero, dynamic and modern. There ought to be a room at the *Excelsior* and a poetess of vers libre to pronounce a dirge herself, or to prompt the actress of the moment, summoned expressly in memory of past favors, to do so. The dynamic hero is not sup-

15. Sidney Sonnino (1847–1922) and Vittorio Emanuele Orlando (1860–1952) represented Italy at the Conference of Versailles, which they abandoned after President Wilson refused to acknowledge the claim of Italy over Fiume. Francesco Saverio Nitti (1868–1953) was a valued social scientist and the head of the government in the difficult years 1919 and 1920 (known as the "red biennium").

posed to die quietly, but in despair for his thirst, for his aridity concealed in vain from the humdrum melodrama.

Wilson, the statesman with a vision of world politics, has *his home, his favorite room on the third floor at the back of the house, where the noise from the street can barely be heard, and the windows give onto the garden* . . .

Wilson's style leaves room for silence; and reading of his death, one comprehends how he must have found himself out of place in Paris among the exasperated veterans of the war in their new suits.

FILIPPO TOMMASO MARINETTI

"THE eldest among us are thirty, so we still have at least a decade left in which to complete our work.[16] When we are forty, other men, younger and stronger than we, can go ahead and toss us into the wastebasket, like useless drafts. That is how we want it!" That was Marinetti in 1909. And in 1919, faithful to his own promise, he found himself with a vocation and political experience: the politics of forty-year-old war veterans, fascism, which was simply the social extension of the movement he had begun in the world of art ten years before. The Nitti[17] government had a lucid intuition that although the labels had changed, the spirit and style were the same, so it concluded that the gentle correctional standards of 1910 would still do the trick, and with these fine methods it managed to generate a little publicity for these unrepentant publicity seekers. Marinetti relates what happened:

> On 20 November the fascists took part in the elections for the first time, with a list made up as follows: *Mussolini* the founder of

16. Original title: "Marinetti, il precursore"; from *Il Lavoro* (Genoa), 31 January 1924. Translated from *Scritti politici*, pp. 579–582.

17. See note 15.

fascism; *Marinetti* the founder of futurism; *Podrecca* the initiator of Italian anticlericalism; the illustrious conductor *Toscanini;* the futurist *Bolzon;* the futurist aviator *Macchi;* a few republicans and syndicalists who had favored taking part in the war; and a few anarchists. This audacious advance guard was beaten by the socialists and Nitti's faction, who succeeded in having Mussolini, Marinetti, Vecchi, and fifteen Arditi [shock troops] arrested and held in prison for twenty-one days at San Vittore, accused of jeopardizing state security and organizing an insurrection. On 29 May 1920, Marinetti and several other futurist leaders resigned from the Fasci di Combattimento,[18] after their failure to bring the fascist majority round to their antimonarchical and anticlerical point of view.

The spirit of this account is poisonously tendentious. The fact of the matter is that today Marinetti can assert his rights as maestro and superfascist against his tame jail companions. He can always extol the antimonarchical and anticlerical tendency that was betrayed.

Who can tell what would have become of Italian fascism without the split of 29 May? What would Marinetti have done if he instead of Gentile[19] had become minister of education?

Rather than let himself be bridled, Marinetti has gone back to art, to the battle for the theater. But in truth the fascist revolution has changed things for him too, if one considers the box-office

18. Fasci di Combattimento (literally, "Combat Squads") was the name of the first political movement founded by Mussolini in 1919. In the national convention of 1921 the movement changed its name to National Fascist Party.

19. Giovanni Gentile (1875–1944) was the most prominent Italian philosopher of the period; he became Mussolini's minister of education and the ideologue of the regime and was killed by the partisans. His political theory was an extreme version of the Hegelian doctrine of the ethical state. The state, as pure and true freedom (and *legibus solutus*), was the highest form of rational life, into which individuals must be absorbed. The ethical state was neither neutral nor agnostic; it was a subject with the mission of implementing the true values of the spirit.

receipts in the theaters where he has recently made his *rentrée*. Who ever heard of paying for a ticket to get in to a futurist show? At the Teatro Chiarella the other evening Marinetti demanded payment and with this candid maneuver alone was able to fill the theater. Melancholy memories of the Nitti years, when Marinetti spoke in the empty squalor of the Scribe, or the Romano! But then he was a millionaire, arriving from Tokyo one day and leaving for Madrid the next, and you could still get in to his shows for free. Today, on the other hand, even Marinetti has to *make money*. Fortune rewards the bold and comes to the aid of those who want to profit.

The melancholy Marinetti of four years ago was too pedantic and sententious. Speeches, sermons, Socratic dialogues. He declaimed the *The Alcove of Steel* [*Alcova d'acciaio*]. He improvised his shows with the faith of an apostle, never worrying about details, confident that he would move mountains with the candor of his American-style self-advertisement. It appears, however, that after forty-six years have passed for Filippo Tommaso Marinetti, he is no longer capable of moving anything, so on theater posters the new sensation and top money earner has become the beautiful Paduan operetta soubrette Mak Gill.

The march on Rome has ruined everything, even the ascetic disinterestedness of Filippo Tommaso Marinetti!

Marinetti remains the representative figure of our epoch. In him our irony will discover all the characteristics that another man has unfairly usurped. Marinetti is the genuine maestro of the Italians. Only in a provincial, philistine, carefree world like ours could such a patriotic fanatic of "internationalism" appear. Only in a country of improvisers could such a vulgar imposture, such a giddy mystification, take shape. We need not be too severe with futurism; the good bourgeois philo-fascists *ought* not to be. Marinetti is right to claim that it was futurism that got contemporary Italian art talked about abroad. We should raise a glorious pedestal for these patriotic heroes: they are true

Italians—Marinetti first and foremost, who was born in Alexandria (Italian Africa!) through pure irony and who wrote his first dozen books in French.

And, assuming that Marinetti did actually study in Paris, the best part of the story is this: the wildest French avant-gardists, the most obstreperous poets of Paris, would never have compromised their finesse as dilettantes by taking a fight too seriously. None of those gentlemen transported the elegant battles of the theater onto the plane of reality. But Marinetti set up a commercial business in Milan, a placement office, an agency for boring, insolent political hacks, an organization for publicity, advertising, drumbeating. It is no accident that the Egyptian and the Romagnol[20] had to come to Milan to get a reputation and win a place in the sun.

Milan, the only place with a sense of realism, is where romanticism comes to terms with commercial initiatives. The movement of Corso Venezia was immediately the quintessence of modern commercialism: everyone stole, got a job, had a piece of the missionary action. A new generation of futurist parasites was born every day. Marinetti paid for everyone. Long before all the Blackshirts, he announced the cult of progress and speed, sport, physical strength, rash courage, heroism and risk, as opposed to the obsession with culture, etc. With Russolo as noisemaker, the Milanese sports fans and students made the first fascist revolution.

This was the psychology of the first duce: an African fantasy of turbid and salacious images beneath the most unflinching impudence; a Romagnol need to aggrandize beneath a severe and lofty frown; the precursor of postwar man. The mask and the frown were needed to hide the emptiness of these squalid hero types, who had no capacity for private sharing, no capacity for intimacy; who preached external violence from fear of solitude,

20. Mussolini was born in Romagna (hence the qualification "Romagnol"), a region located south of Venice.

from fear of having to reckon with themselves. Everyone recalls the more grave and fearsome incarnations of these classic figures of Italian fascism, but you always have to go back to Marinetti to discover where they came from. There is only one other man in Italy who has the same compromising habit Marinetti has of doing his thinking in public.[21] And in these cases, thinking in public excludes thinking in private.

ANTONIO GRAMSCI

ANTONIO Gramsci is going to the new fascist Chamber of Deputies as the representative of the workers of the Veneto.[22] What this really means is that the defeated revolution is going to parliament to predict disaster for the victors. He is the first revolutionary to enter the Palazzo di Montecitorio! A far cry from smashing the ballot boxes and causing clamor and outrage! Bombacci and Misiano were photographic images of Enrico Ferri;[23] it was a delightful revolution for the newspapers of the good bourgeoisie. Both the ideological project and the style of these agitators strangely resembled those of Mussolini.

If Gramsci takes the floor at Montecitorio, we will likely see the fascist deputies listening to his slender, reedy voice in composed silence, and in their effort to pay attention they may imag-

21. Meaning Mussolini.

22. Original title: "Uomini e idee [X]. Gramsci"; from *La Rivoluzione Liberale* 3, no. 17 (22 April 1924), p. 66, signed "p.g." Translated from *Scritti politici*, pp. 644–647.

23. Nicola Bombacci (1879–1945) was a socialist leader who became a fascist and was killed by the partisans. Enrico Ferri (1856–1929) was a sociologist and a theorist of criminal law; along with Cesare Lombroso he was the most prominent leader of Italian positivism and the target of Gramsci's and Gobetti's harsh criticism. Gobetti also mentions Francesco Misiano, a socialist elected to parliament, and Giambattista Tuveri, editor of the newspaper *Il Corriere di Sardegna* and a politician who was active in the Kingdom of Piedmont in the years before the unification of the country.

ine they feel a new sensation—thought.[24] Instead of raising a
protest against frauds and ruses, Gramsci's dialectic, from the
pure heights of the Hegelian idea, scrupulously notes how utterly indispensable they are to a bourgeois government. His
speeches will be metaphysical condemnations; his invectives
will flash with glimpses of palingenesis.

To understand his hatred of society, you have to bear in mind
his whole spiritual formation during his university years in
Turin. Gramsci's hatred is one of the most convincing examples
I know of proud nobility and wounded dignity. His socialism is
above all a response to the hurts inflicted by society on an immigrant from Sardinia living in solitude. His ascetic sociology and
the philosophical absolutism of his Jacobin stance flow from a
personal suffering that has made him, in the marrow of his very
being, an aristocrat capable of deriding all the compassion of
bourgeois morality, of documenting the brazen cruelty of philanthropy. It is not easy to find another equally characteristic example of pure Marxism, of plebeian consciousness so firm and
proud and true to itself.

But even before that, his instinct led him to scorn all this
semi-bourgeois stuff, and that instinct matured in the Sardinian
countryside, where political opinions lead quite logically to
cattle thieving and the practice of assassination for vendetta.

A hundred years ago Tuveri demonstrated to the republicans
of the mainland that, all hypocrisy aside, as monarchomachs
they had logic on their side. Gramsci, too, follows his premises
to their conclusions, with no half measures. It is as though he left
the fields to forget his traditions, to replace the diseased inheri-
tance of Sardinian anachronism with a chill, inexorable drive
toward the modernity of the citizen. The very body of the man
bears the mark of this denial of rural life and of the near violence with which he put in its place a project constructed and

24. Gobetti's predictions came true. Gramsci delivered his speech on
18 May 1925.

animated by the force of desperation and the spiritual urgency of one who has rejected and disavowed his native innocence. Antonio Gramsci has the head of a revolutionary; his features seem the product of his own will, harshly and fatally etched to meet a necessity that he had to accept without discussion: his brain has overpowered his body. The head that dominates the ailing limbs looks as though it were made in accordance with the logical dictates of some great redemptive utopia, and the effort has imprinted on it a rough-hewn, impenetrable seriousness. Only his eyes, mobile and innocent, but curbed and veiled by bitterness, occasionally inject a pessimistic kindness into the stern rigor of his rationality. His cutting voice matches the disintegrative power of his criticism; his irony is tinged with the poison of sarcasm; the dogma by whose logical tyranny he lives robs him of the consolation of humor. His open sincerity is burdened by hidden anger; out of his condemnation to solitude and disdain for confidences there arises a dolorous acceptance of responsibilities that are stronger than life itself, as hard as historical destiny. Conversely, there is sometimes resentment and sometimes the deeper rancor of the islander who simply cannot open up except through action, who is unable to obtain release from the ancestral bond of slavery except by bringing a touch of the tyrannical to his energetic, commanding role as apostle. Instincts and affections are both concealed beneath the acknowledged necessity of giving his own life a cadence of austerity in both form and logical consequentiality. Where serene and harmonious unity simply cannot be, constraint will take their place, and ideas will dominate feelings and manifestations of resentment.

His love of categorical and dogmatic clarity, typical of the ideologue and the dreamer, forbid him sympathy and communication, so that beneath the fervor of discovery and the experience of direct inquiry, beneath the ethical preoccupations of his program, there lies an arid rigor, a cosmic tragedy, that does not permit even a moment of relaxation. The student freed himself from the innate rhetoricism of his race by denying his own instinct for literature and his own lively enjoyment of the rigors of research into comparative linguistics. The utopian now dictates his categorical imperative to the *instruments* of modern industry, regulates with infallible logic the rotating machinery in the factories, reckons like an imperturbable administrator, *counts* his battle-ready troop formations like a general. He does not try to work out how victory will arrive, nor does he make forecasts about when, because victory will be the sign of God, the mathematical result of the inversion of praxis. Here tolerance and silent self-confidence produce the ethical sense: after all, the bourgeoisie is there, working hard to bring the victory of the proletariat.

More than a tactician or a combatant, Gramsci is a prophet, unheeded except by fate, in the way that a prophet must be today. His eloquence will not cause any government to fall. His catastrophic polemic and desperate satire are not looking for easy satisfaction. All of humanity, the entire present state of things, he regards with suspicion; he demands justice from the future—in the form of a ferocious vindication.

KARL MARX

W E have to face the fact that this is *Marx's time:* there are few writers of the last century, and of the Italians only Cattaneo,[25] whose pages can arouse the same trembling, angry agi-

25. Carlo Cattaneo (1801–1869) was one the most prominent political theorists and leaders of the Risorgimento. In Milan, his birthplace, he became the leader of the Revolution of 1848. He was a republican and a federalist, a critic of Mazzini's unitarian republicanism as well as of the newly born Italian centralized monarchy. He spent all his life in Switzerland as an exile. His writings are a rare example of clarity and rigor in Italian political literature. He endorsed liberal ideals and tried to ground them in the Italian secular tradition of political thought—that is, republicanism. More or less like John Stuart Mill, he indicated that the seeds of modern liberalism lay in

tation.[26] The pages in which he criticized the petite bourgeoisie ought to be reprinted: they are a critique of fascism! For the utopian and anarchistic communists and the treacherous democrats against whom he inveighed, we could substitute our own indecisive subversives and doubtful social democrats, who instead of a postwar proletarian revolution gave us the revolt of the disgruntled failures and the war veterans. And how often do the maledictions of Marx come to mind as one contemplates the spectacle of Mussolinian intellectuals?

I am drawn to Marx the historian of the class struggle in France and the apostle of the workers' movement. The economist lies dead, along with surplus value, the dream of abolishing classes, and the prophecy of collectivism. In philosophy his Hegelianism marks an advance on Hegel. Historical materialism (without determinism, for that would be a failure to understand the luminous concept of the inversion of praxis) and the theory of the class struggle are established forever as tools of the social sciences and are enough to ensure his fame as a theoretician.

The workers' movement has had a goal and an organizing principle ever since he first sounded his call to battle. It is not true that Marx speaks the language of materialism to the masses, and Mazzini the language of ideals: Mazzini's ideal is nebulous and romantic; Marx's is realistic and applicable.

In Italy, Marx was stuffed away in the attic because of the immaturity of capitalism and of the proletariat. Giolittism[27] was Mussolinism in advance. To rectify the socialism of today by introducing patriotism and democracy into it would be cowardice: the workers' movement will certainly bring about patriotic and democratic results, but to attain its objectives it must follow

---

the republics of early modernity. Cattaneo was an admirer of the American republic and envisaged a "United States of Europe."

26. Original title: "L'ora di Marx"; from *La Libertà*, April 1924; reprinted in *La Rivoluzione Liberale* 3, no. 16 (15 April 1924), p. 63. Translated from *Scritti politici*, pp. 640–641.

27. See note 10.

a policy of intransigence, conceding nothing to the enemies who hope to drain its energy.

Fascism—anticapitalistic and antiworker because infantile —thinks it can dictate the future and keep Italy a political minor, servile and deferent toward its guardians. The fascist parenthesis will probably not be short. But when the avant-garde of workers and the intransigent elites eventually succeed in burying fascism and all its enticements, it will certainly be in the name of Marx.

GAETANO MOSCA

GAETANO Mosca has had to wait quite a few decades to receive the recognition he is due from his compatriots.[28] Vilfredo Pareto died a celebrity, the revered master of a whole generation, to whom he perhaps showed too much indulgence, whereas Mosca, who had preceded him in the most conspicuous findings of political science, remained quietly in Turin in the chair of constitutional law.

Now Gaetano Mosca has been called to the University of Rome, and not to invent theories that justify the winners[29] but to deliver an academic discourse on liberty. It appears that Orlando's former chair of public law will be tailored for him, and he will be the first to teach political science in an Italian university.[30] Thus the battle he began in 1883 at the age of twenty-six to obtain recognition for the science of politics, indeed practically to found it again (in the homeland of Machiavelli), is finally won. Simultaneously the publisher Bocca [of Turin] is reprinting his *The Ruling Class* [*Elementi di scienza politica*], including

28. Original title: "Un conservatore galantuomo"; from *La Rivoluzione Liberale* 3, no. 18 (29 April 1924), p. 71, signed "p.g." Translated from *Scritti politici*, pp. 652–657.
29. Meaning the fascists.
30. See note 15.

the complete text of the first edition (1895) and a second, additional part that represents the writer's new thinking after almost thirty years of political, scholarly, educational, and journalistic experience. It is a book that constitutes the text and virtually the conclusion of his life. It contains the whole man: the thinker, the professor, the cabinet minister.

The first sensation one experiences upon reading the works of Gaetano Mosca is unease, caused by his coldness, his impassivity, and his hermetic acuity. The writer's culture—his determination to remain abstract, doctrinaire, detached from the events of the day and from reference to anything obvious— seems unfriendly to the reader. The tone of the discourse is purposely arid, suppressing sympathy or excitement. Mosca keeps to the high altitude of scholarship, not stooping to clarify or to recognize the feelings that most people have. The questions of the day are never addressed. It would seem that to meet the standards of an observer and a philosopher, he has imposed on himself a species of ascetic refusal of anything too easy or too human. Everything is subjected to strict historical documentation and to scientific demonstration. This writer concedes nothing to the human weakness for personal anecdote, for the emotions, for the things that he holds dear. He gives examples as though he were a mathematician, and looks more readily to Chinese or Babylonian history than to contemporary civilization for the facts to back his assertions.

Out of a world naturally dominated by the heated psychology of resentment and by oratory, he made a bare plot on which to conduct experiments, a source of generalizable conclusions, dispensing with any motivation that was merely personal.

Nonetheless, beneath this skepticism and this apparent impersonality, an observer might, with effort, detect signs, less striking but more telling, of the style and character of the man; indeed, one might even trace the outlines of a frankly conservative psychology, a love for order and clarity, a taste for perspicuous distinctions that in the case of this purebred Sicilian are enough to disprove all the recent legends about the supposed inclination to metaphysical vagueness of the Sicilians, legends built up out of a single example or at best a handful. The born psychologist in Mosca is sufficiently revealed in his great admiration for Manzoni, whom he has taken as a teacher of the art of living, writing lengthy studies that illuminate Manzoni's gifts as an observer of behavior and creator of literary characters. Mosca's lectures on Manzoni, when they are gathered together in a volume, will constitute a most unusual example of politics applied to art and a notable contribution by a diplomat to the re-creation of the world of *I promessi sposi*.

This psychological power attests to an innate latinity of the instincts in Mosca, which has never been attenuated even in his most European and international scholarly writings. No doubt his younger contemporaries may at times feel the temptation to make the same objections to Mosca that are made to experimental psychology, but it would be in bad taste to yield to the temptation, for Mosca has always had the singular courage to modify his theoretical premises on the basis of his study of history. And his historical knowledge is not that of certain low-grade idealists who make use of illustrious names from the past as vehicles for their own schemes and ideas. I mean history in the traditional sense, and for Mosca history *teaches the art of living*. It is the past viewed by a practical man, by a man of prudence; and in his stance as observer you will find the traits of one who knows that he knows the *heart of the human being,* who has sailed in all weathers, and who wants to base himself on dependable precepts in judging another and take that other's measure with mathematical precision. The merits of Mosca's culture lie here, but also the limitations, and although his instinct would be to doubt, the trouble is that doubt is so inartistic and so ill suited to registering the whole range of contradictions and subtle gradations that it resolves itself into a fatal trust on the part of the writer in his own cunning. And then you have the most personal aspects of Mosca's style: his perseverance in unmasking ideas and bringing to light the human instincts and human rascality that lie underneath, and his irony with regard to false idealism.

Hence, although the prejudices of Mosca might be described as positivist in nature, there is conversely a ductility of spirit in him, an abundance of lines of thought and empirical observation, that distance him from the monotony of any school. And against more philosophical objections he is sufficiently shielded by the brilliance of his methodological canon: "Explain past circumstances through present ones, and present circumstances through past ones." Hardly positivism! In an age of erudite scholars and scientific brains, this was truly to sanctify the values of history as human history, with the passion of a Vichian who has not read Vico!

But the most stunning thing is that, in the Italy of 1884, a young man of twenty-six should set about writing *Theory of Governments and Parliamentary Government* [*Teorica dei governi e governo parlamentare*]. While the country was in the grip of a crisis of its institutions and of conscience, Mosca bravely adopted a Europe-wide point of view, making use of data that would have supplied Villari and Turiello [31] with the occasion for regional monographs and protests about current matters, to write a work of scholarship. This is certainly owing in part to his study of foreign writers on politics—Fischel, Bluntschli, Mill, and Taine—but that in turn is another example of how he was one of the first to seriously rejuvenate Italian culture.

His results are never trite; his approach is never generic. Sicily and the evils of life there were close to his heart even when he was engaged in metaphysical deductions, so his work can be understood concretely as a supreme effort by a southerner to

31. Pasquale Villari (1826–1917) and Pasquale Turiello (1836–1902) were two leading conservative scholars and politicians. Their writings on the Southern Question (an expression that Villari coined) had a great impact in Italy. Villari was well known in England as the author of historical works on Machiavelli and Savonarola. He was a friend of John Stuart Mill and an admirer of English liberalism.

think through Italian politics without making national unity into an issue, indeed, by proceeding as though the north and south of Italy really composed a single state.

Seeing the petite bourgeoisie abused by local coteries was Mosca's first political experience: parliamentary deputies who were rotten to the core; parliamentary life bent to serve monopolies operated by provincial magnates; demagogic government ready to sell its favors in order to build a following. And the result of these inducements: everyone on the side of the government. Political parties masked private interests and personal rivalries. The nation was immature, living through all the ambiguities of democracy but not obtaining the advantages because of the absence of objective, economic premises. In these circumstances, being a conservative was a question of being an old-fashioned, honest gentleman, and Mosca did indeed feel nostalgia for the ancien régime, because "those regimes had something paternal about them, and the ancient benevolence of the national character, now largely lost, unfortunately, brought the big people close to the little people and bound them together reciprocally in a system of clientage then almost universal." All these notions would have remained anachronistic, with no glimpse of the future Italy, democratic and liberal, in which the political contest would become a matter of responsibility, intransigence, and Calvinist seriousness, and Mosca would be merely a loyal gentleman of the third Italy rather than a boor from the Bourbon past if the brilliant discovery of the concept of the political elite had not struck him at this point. Mosca's theory of the ruling class is truly one of those ideas that disclose infinite vistas of inquiry to the human mind.

Mosca lifted his gaze from the present corruption of the parliamentary regime and pondered the road to salvation. He posited that the central problem of Italian life, as of every society in history, was the creation of a ruling class able to interpret diffused aspirations and organize mature forces through its political formula, through its myths, as Sorel[32] would say. At first this notion appeared to Mosca to undermine any notion of democracy and all parliamentary systems. The interpretation he gave of his discovery at the time when he first made it was aristocratic. But Depretis[33] was in power, and the socialist movement that was destined to impart a rudimentary consciousness to the lower classes in Italy in subsequent decades had not yet arisen.

Today, in 1924, when everyone is proclaiming the end of parliament and praising the advantages of dictatorship, Mosca is coming to see that the parliamentary system is still the best instrument for forming, refining, differentiating, and finally realizing a select leadership with attitudes shaped in the long apprenticeship of free contest and open criticism. The task of political thought as it carries forward the work of Mosca is to accentuate this democratic and liberal slant and audaciously to harmonize the two notions of the elite and the political contest.

"Elite" in fact signifies *choice,* to be understood not in the sense that an authority is designated to make a selection but rather in the sense that there is a historical process through which the best are revealed. The existence of the chosen ones implies that there are others who are not chosen: not those condemned by nature but those who participate in the process, prepare themselves, put themselves to the test every day, and im-

32. Georges Sorel (1847–1922) was a prominent philosopher and a critic of the Marxist determinism of the Second International. His rupture with socialist politics came in 1901, in tandem with his changed opinion on the Dreyfus case (he was pro-Dreyfus until 1899). He started criticizing reformist socialism and became increasingly critical of Socialist Party involvement in parliamentary elections. He came to see the syndicate as the only political force, because of its direct connection with the sphere of production. Sorel then theorized the "general strike" as the "absolute" and creative revolutionary act par excellence: he assigned to the intellectuals the role of provoking the strike by evoking heroic myths and symbols. His exaltation of violence as the constitutive act of a new political founding had supporters among the Rightists of Charles Maurras and then of Mussolini. Among his writings are *Réflexions sur le violence* (1906 and 1908) and *Les Illusions du progrès* (1906).

33. See note 11.

prove. In this quasi-physiological sense the governors have to represent the governed. There is no aristocracy where democracy is denied.

Mosca, a conservative and a Manzonian, was not able to face up to these conclusions. But the proof of his lasting influence is that we are able to get there, thanks to him.

GIACOMO MATTEOTTI

Intransigent "Subversive"

O n 2 May 1915, three days before D'Annunzio's festival at Quarto, a political meeting was held in Rovigo in opposition to the war, with Dr. Giacomo Matteotti and Aldo Parini as the speakers.[34] The latter defended Missiroli's[35] thesis about democratic Germany—perhaps the only time this ever happened in a public gathering. Instead of a speech, there was a dialogue with the hostile crowd, which distrusted the speakers. Using Christian language, Matteotti spoke out against violence while shivers of D'Annunzianism and petty Machiavellian cynicism ran through the proto-fascist audience.

To speak out for neutrality might have put him in the wrong; but Matteotti was speaking out against the war. They kept interrupting him acrimoniously, but they had to recognize that they were shouting down a faith, not a program. On that occasion Matteotti forecast that the war would be long, hard, and disastrous even for the winners, a thesis he expressed in metaphysical terms: the war was pointless, something that a generation made Nietzschean by its own harsh solitude was merely putting up with.

34. Original title: "Matteotti"; from *La Rivoluzione Liberale* 3, no. 27 (1 July 1924), p. 103. Abridged and translated from *Scritti politici*, pp. 735–739, 747–752. On D'Annunzio see note 54.

35. Mario Missiroli (1886–1974), a conservative journalist and opinion maker, was the editor of several Italian newspapers.

He made the same speech in the provincial council at Rovigo when the war had begun and there was not a single pacifist left who was willing to open his mouth, which led to his trial for defeatism and repeated convictions. Matteotti conducted his own defense in radical terms; far from taking back what he had said, he insisted that its legitimacy be recognized and that his protest against the violence of war was not defeatism but an act of idealistic faith. One has to realize that in Matteotti, jurist, economist, administrator, and practical man, there existed a desperate utopianism, an absolute idealism, an absurd reaction against the philistine narrowness of the false realists. Unwavering, like an apostle, he got the conviction reversed in the highest court of appeal on the grounds that he enjoyed parliamentary immunity while speaking in a provincial council.

His protest had some result: he gained attention as a man disqualified for military service in a cause for which his two brothers had died young, and he was assigned to serve as a noncombatant. They made him undergo the rigors of the officer-training course but refused to grant him a commission because of his crime of defeatism. After posting him to Messina they tried to send him to the front, despite his disqualification, in one of those companies of convicted criminals who were deliberately marched into withering enemy fire by the carabinieri. Matteotti refused, declaring that he was ready to go to the front like a soldier but not to a slaughterhouse like a delinquent. So they interned him at Campo Inglese, together with the son of the brigand Varsalona to spy on him. Matteotti displayed his imperturbable character in the face of solitude, suspicion, and persecution, accepting the consequences of his own actions like a good logician.

We may compare the example of Matteotti the pacifist with the conduct of the more typical representatives of Italian pacifism: fearful and servile, anxious to avoid becoming a target, concealed and silent whether giving orders or taking them, they emulated the nationalists and took shelter in degrading tasks.

Matteotti never deserted, never hid; he accepted the logic of being a "subversive," the consequences of heresy and of going against the crowd. In the battle against the war he was a brave "combatant."

The Aristocratic "Subversive"

Matteotti was never popular. His fellows regarded him with suspicion, and his adversaries hated him with the hatred reserved for renegades. But the truth is that Matteotti was an aristocrat in style, not by birth. His socialism was not a rebellious fling, in the manner of Count Graziadei, who forsook his ancient family line, broke with tradition, and took up the life of a marginalized student with an intellectual lover, the latter becoming in due course the restless wife in a petit-bourgeois family—the typical fate of every proper nihilist, faithful to the demagogic project of "going to the people."

Matteotti, on the other hand, enrolled in the Socialist Party at the age of fourteen, probably without meeting too much resistance from his family. He might not even have known how much money his father had, which in any case was not all that much. His brother Matteo, who preceded him both as a socialist and as a law student, seems to have introduced Giacomo to socialism, despite his own early death at thirty.

His father, whose family had been pot makers, came to Fratta Polesine from the Trentino fifty years ago with virtually no money. He began to save with the constancy and sacrifices of the immigrant, assisted by his wife, Isabella, behind the counter of their little food store. What they made they invested in land with the avidity of the refugee who clutches the soil instinctively, as if to begin the cycle of tradition all over again. The fortune of the Matteotti family, which was in real estate, was valued at 800,000 lire before the war, all of it scattered through the province in small parcels purchased as the occasion arose, year by year, the result of unremitting hard work and prudent speculation. We have to bear in mind this provincial tenacity in order to understand the character of their son: Giacomino was raised with this example, with the conviction that they were not rich people, with the instinct for hard struggle, with a notion of the dignity of sacrifice. At school and then at high school, he had to be at the top of the class, never wasting time, never squandering.

It was on this solid foundation of conservative Protestant virtues that Matteotti became a subversive, an aristocratic one because of his solitude. His interests were exclusively scholarly at first. From the start he preferred the dry study of criminal procedure to quick success at the bar, and although he was already an active socialist, his favorite lecturer was the Honorable Stoppato, a man who represented moderate clericalism. Matteotti's educational path was guided by his own inner needs.

He was one of the few members of a party that remembers the existence of other nations only in superficial speeches at international congresses who had traveled to France, England, Austria, Switzerland, and Germany in his youth. He had studied English in order to read Shakespeare in the original. Once involved in politics, he virtually concealed this bent for philosophy, which sorted ill with the environment in which he had chosen to labor, an environment intolerant of difference and narrowly partisan. But that was precisely the secret of his vitality: if you spent a lot of time in conversation with him and had a chance to observe him, you could sense that behind his actions there lay an inner life of profound and varied drives, of perpetual secret inspiration that he never laid on the line to win one of the little prizes of daily life. This gave him a reserved manner and a cold energy that intimidated his fellows. The rigid public mask of Matteotti concealed private deliberations in which he had exposed his ideas beforehand to all the dialectical torments of his intemperate individualism, so it was natural for him to feel that he had to carry his point inexorably when he took part in debates at the sort of meetings where facile demagogy reigns and there is always somebody ready to come up with a conciliatory

middle-of-the-road position on the spur of the moment. Matteotti's refusal to reconcile would commence with a mocking
smile, followed by perverse, pitiless irony. He always had his
conclusions in mind, not flights of oratory or crowd-pleasing
tricks.

Italian socialism from Enrico Ferri to Bombacci, from Zanardi to Arturino Vella,[36] grew up in a sort of vanity fair, an atmosphere of provincial loquacity and the joy of gathering round the
petit-bourgeois table. Anyone familiar with that atmosphere can
see clearly how Matteotti's intransigence—he once went so far
as to have the doors bolted shut at a meeting because he wanted
to bring the debate to a conclusion before everyone went off to
the banquet—must have constituted a challenge to the easygoing
habits of the jovial types and a break with all the festival traditions of the tender Italian people, the happy good-timers. And
they called him "aristocratic," thinking to isolate him.

Matteotti's Marxism

He made no pretense of being a theorist and used to say frankly
that he lacked the time to resolve philosophical problems because he had to prepare budgets and check the accounts of socialist administrators. This was his way of avoiding any display
of learning. But his Marxism was acquainted with Hegel and
had not overlooked Sorel and Bergsonism; his intransigence was
Sorelian. On the other hand, his reformist concept of gradual
syndicalism was more than a theory; it was the offshoot of everyday experience in a servile country difficult to shake up without giving way to regrettable excesses. He was perhaps the only
Italian socialist (preceded, however, by Gaetano Salvemini[37] in

36. Francesco Zanardi and Arturinó Vella were two socialist leaders.
Concerning Enrico Ferri and Nicola Bombacci, see note 23.
37. Gaetano Salvemini (1873–1957), a prominent historian first of the
commune of Florence in the thirteenth century and later of modern European history, was a charismatic liberal radical and the energetic inspirer of

the Giolitti decade) for whom reformism was not a synonym for opportunism. He accepted from Marx that it was imperative to shake the proletariat up in order to make it envision a life of freedom and self-awareness; he did not even repudiate collectivism, although he had quite unorthodox reservations about it. But he focused entirely on shorter-term, more realistic forms of action, on forming the nuclei of a new society among socialists — communes, schools, cooperatives, leagues — and thus bringing the revolution about as the workers learned how to manage public institutions, not by passing a decree or staging a revolution like the one in 1848. Without this preparatory phase, there would be no vital basis for the eventual conquest of power or for the violence accompanying the birth of a new phase of history. In any case, Matteotti was too intent on defending the workers now to have time to utter prophecies. For him the most important thing was for workers and peasants to become administrators and learn how to run things, so he made a point of attending various communal councils as an alternate councillor, ready to fix their mistakes; but he also wanted persons of low status to learn by performing executive tasks.

But he never complied with the reformist endorsement of protectionism; in fact, he was ready to stand alone with the elderly Modigliani[38] in the stubborn defense of laissez-faire, which for him meant not only denouncing the financial speculations of those who were exploiting the proletariat but also providing training in autonomy and concrete political maturity in his own province.

Everything about Matteotti (his background, his conduct)

---

the earliest antifascist cultural activity in Florence. He escaped to the United States, where he taught at Harvard until the liberation of Italy in 1945.

38. Giuseppe Emanuele Modigliani (1872–1947), a Tuscan Jew and the brother of the painter Amedeo Modigliani, was a lawyer and one of the most beloved socialist leaders. He was particularly active on the committee in charge of uncovering the fascist responsible for Matteotti's assassination in 1924.

was guided by federalist imperatives. From the periphery to the center, from the cooperative to the commune, from the province to the state, his was always an applied socialism, an economic defense of the workers, whether he was recommending "step-by-step progress" in the pages of *La Lotta* of Rovigo or in the league of socialist communes, or addressing the whole proletariat of Italy in the pages of *Avanti!* or *La Giustizia*, or putting the dominant oligarchy of the rich on trial in the most dramatic and turbulent way as rapporteur for the budget committee. The highest proof of his passion for getting concrete and particular things done was the fact that in 1921, instead of going to Livorno and making a splash at that academy of "tendencies" and "factions," he preferred to stay at home and give aid and comfort to the proletariat in the province of Ferrara, where they were having a particularly trying time.[39]

Matteotti's Antifascism

In the Polesine[40] Giacomo Matteotti saw the fascist movement come to life as a movement to push the peasantry back into slavery, as the servile fawning of the frustrated on those who paid them, as medieval cruelty and dark obscurantism in the face of any effort by the workers to achieve their own dignity and freedom. This firsthand acquaintance with what was really happening meant that Matteotti was unable to take seriously the ludicrous theories of the various national-fascists or the mediocre

39. Gobetti's implicit reference is to the congress of the Italian Socialist Party at Livorno, on 21 January 1921, where the communist wing led by Antonio Gramsci and Amedeo Bordiga seceded to found the Communist Party of Italy.

40. The Polesine is the geographical region between Venice and Ferrara, where the Po River flows into the Adriatic Sea. From the end of the nineteenth century that region, then one of the poorest in northern Italy, was the center of socialist organizations and cooperatives; in Gobetti's time it became the area where the landlords started financing and organizing fascist combat groups.

Machiavellian program of Mussolini. There was a fundamental ethical incompatibility, an instinctive antithesis, between him and them. He felt that to combat fascism effectively on the political terrain, it was important to counter it with examples of dignity and unyielding resistance, to make it a matter of character, intransigence, rigor.

He upheld this standard of conduct against all attempts by the government to co-opt him. In 1921 he received a telephone call, at a critical phase of the agrarian struggle, from the prefect of Ferrara, to whom he replied: "Any discussion between us is pointless. If you want to know our plans, you don't need me, because you have your spies. And I place no trust in your words." He was never seen to bend to flattery offered by men in power, and was reluctant even to climb the steps to the prefect's office. Thus the landowners were struck with fear and anger by Matteotti: although they had regard for him, they understood that they had an implacable enemy.

On 12 March 1921, Matteotti was supposed to speak at Castel-guglielmo. The struggle there had reached a pitch of violence in recent months, and the first assassination had occurred in the Polesine. On that Saturday he traversed the streets in a carriage, accompanied by the mayor, Stefano Stievano of Cincara. They were stopped by local men on bicycles who wanted to warn them that the landowners were preparing an ambush. Matteotti insisted that Stievano turn back and went ahead on his own. It was in fact clear that in the town of Castelguglielmo there were hired fascists on the move, forming an armed mob. The workers met Matteotti at the headquarters of the league, and he addressed them calmly, urging them to fight back. When several of the landowners approached and claimed the right to present their side, he refused, knowing that this was an established tactic of theirs when they wanted to create an alibi for their own violence: they would speak abusively to the workers in order to provoke them into reacting and falling into the trap. Matteotti offered instead to go with them and confer at their headquarters. This was agreed to, and he also made the workers promise to stay put in order to avoid more serious incidents.

Maybe his courage and foresight had the effect of provoking the owners, for the moment he entered their premises—and to do that he had to walk between two rows of armed men—they broke their word and crowded around him in fury, revolvers in hand, trying to force him to retract his actions in the Chamber of Deputies and announce that he would leave the Polesine. His reply: "I have only one declaration to make: that I will not make any declarations to you." Though beaten and spat upon, he added not a word, determined to resist. They hustled him by force into the back of a truck, firing into the air to hold at bay the workers who were rushing to his aid. The carabinieri meanwhile stayed inside their barracks.

They drove him around the countryside, their guns drawn, forcing him to hunch up with his knees to his chest and continually threatening to kill him unless he promised to give up political activity. Finally, seeing that their threats were useless, they decided to throw him out of the truck into the road.

Matteotti covered ten kilometers on foot and got back to Rovigo at midnight, where a group of men were waiting for him at the headquarters of the provincial deputation so that the agreement between agricultural workers and bosses could be renewed. Present were the cavalier Piero Mentasti, a member of the Popular Party; the advocate Altieri, a fascist who was there to represent the interests of the small proprietors and leaseholders; and Giovanni Franchi and Aldo Parini, representing the workers. Matteotti arrived with his clothes a little the worse for wear, but he was calm and unruffled. When the other side were out of the room, his colleagues reproached him for being late, to which he replied in dialect with a smile, "They snatched me." Although he recognized some of his aggressors, among them one of his own leaseholders whom he had once allowed to miss payments, he did not want to name them. Instead, he declared that they must have been acting on orders from Commendatore Vittorio Pelà of Castelguglielmo and the Finzi family of Badia, who were relatives of Mussolini's ex-undersecretary.

Since there was talk at the time, and after, of certain unspeakable violations to which Giacomo Matteotti was supposedly forced to submit on that occasion, it is proper to set the record straight here: the ironclad testimony concerning his serene and undisturbed state from the individuals named above who were there that evening allows us to deny categorically that the acts occurred and to qualify the talk as a contemptible fascist boast. The narrative of this kidnapping is striking in any case, and for that reason we wanted to collect all the details of it, based on irrefutable evidence. Until we have the details of the attack on him in Rome, the memory of this ordeal tells us the manner in which he must have met his death. He felt that it was coming.

At Turin, the day Turati was to give a speech, an exile from the Veneto asked him, "Aren't you afraid someone like Farinacci[41] might send a gang after you?" Matteotti's *verbatim* reply was, "If I am the target of further violence, it will be from assassins sent by the landowners of the Polesine or from the Roman gang of the president."

As secretary of the Unitary Socialist Party, he had conducted the fight against fascism with obdurate conviction. In his book *A Year of Fascist Domination* [*Un anno di dominazione fascista*] he left us a complete formal accusation based on a detailed acquaintance with the facts but also on a revolt of his moral conscience. The moment it was suggested that the Confederation of Labor might consider collaborating with the regime, it was Matteotti who quashed the idea. For him collaboration was out of the question because moral repugnance for fascism had overriding force, because it was necessary to show the fascists that

41. Roberto Farinacci (1892–1945), a prominent fascist.

there were still those who would not surrender. As secretary of the party, he aimed to build a network to promote local initiatives and try to tie them into this program. To give an example, he showed up wherever the danger was gravest, although, reluctantly, he had to hide his identity. Sometimes he dared to return to the Polesine in disguise, despite his banishment and at risk of his life, to give courage to those who were carrying on the fight there.

The Volunteer for Death

He remains the man who knew how to be an example. He had solid talent and the confidence for politics; but we can't say what he might have been able to do in the years ahead as minister of the interior or finance; he has passed over into legend.

I received the following letter, written on 16 June, from a worker in Ferrara:

> As you can imagine, we are talking of nothing else here, and the newspapers don't even make it to the piazza because they are grabbed from the sellers and devoured. The grief is universal, and the reaction no longer hidden. It seems as if the spell of fear has been broken, and people are speaking their minds. So his loss will bear the fruits of liberty and civility, and that will bring peace and joy to the spirit of our great man for the sacrifice he has made. Matteotti was a man ready to face death willingly if he thought that was the best means to give the proletariat back its lost freedom.

I cannot imagine a more spontaneous or generous commemoration of Matteotti—as though the workers feel that he personified their mission. Because the generation we have to create now is just that: volunteers for death in order to give the proletariat back its lost freedom.

HENRY FORD

HENRY Ford, as an author,[42] brings Benjamin Franklin to mind.[43] We have a moralist engaged in writing a model life, a representative life. That this biography should be an autobiography was inevitable, and not just to make the theme more convincing or more of an invitation to others to follow in his footsteps. By speaking in the first person Ford is able to present his theories in the guise of a factual narrative: the ideologue stays out of sight behind a parade of the devices of practical idealism.

A Latin readership will greet this compositional technique as a sort of display of cynicism and diabolical energy. But instead we ought to look for traits less envied and more unusual in the author: those of an ingenuous dreamer. Ford's book will have a success as a manual for those with big ideas, and yet such readers, accustomed to view Americanism with the envy of Europeans barred from taking part in really vast projects, are bound by nature to be disappointed.

Ford's commercial and industrial advice is banal. Anyone who has a modicum of experience in business has already discovered his tips without difficulty and applied them with profit. You do not need a budget in the millions to work with; running an avant-garde opposition publishing house is enough to teach you that you should not worry about the competition; that you should not shoot for quick speculative gains but aim to build up the business and improve your product; that the business im-

42. The book referred to is by Henry Ford in collaboration with Samuel Crowther: *My Life and Work*. Gobetti apparently did not identify this book or give any references for his translated quotations; the editor of the *Scritti politici*, Paolo Spriano, identifies the author, title and date of publication (1922), but does not give references for the quotations. I have used the following edition: Garden City: Garden City Publishing Co., 1926. I give the quotations in the original English from that source. [Translator's note.]
43. Original title: "Ford"; from *La Rivoluzione Liberale* 4, no. 10 (8 March 1925), p. 43, signed "p.g." Translated from *Scritti politici*, pp. 819–823.

proves to the extent that you reduce your costs and overhead in order to lower the price and increase the pay the workers take home; that you can take on debt to pay for the initial plant or a new plant but that it is a sign of bad management to resort to credit to cover ordinary operating costs, and even your plant expansions can be done more solidly if they are done gradually and paid for out of earnings rather than with risky expansions of the capital; that you can always simplify your service and make endless improvements to the way work is organized. It is well known that by choosing a product the public needs and applying these and other norms of basic economics, any enterprise ought to prosper.

But Ford's secret is not a commercial or industrial one. A few years ago Fiat sent a team of engineers to America to study the methods used in his factories. Ford gave orders that they should have access to all the data, all the material, all the analyses; that none of the systems of supply, sale, or administration, none of the technical contrivances, should be kept from them.

Ford knows that his secret is a religious secret, a moral system. In the tale of how he began, we note the role of ascetic inspiration. In solitude he nourished his overriding ambition, his idée fixe of becoming a constructor and an entrepreneur, just as a monk in a hermitage devotes himself to meditating on God. In his practical spirit there is a force of concentration as intense as the self-renunciation of the mystic, bringing to mind the religious origins of pragmatism. As a young mechanic, he refused to jump around from one project to another, just he disdained the gambles and improvisations the bankers proposed when he became an industrialist: *worry about one thing at a time.*

In this atmosphere of almost vulgar simplicity the paradox of Ford, his idée fixe, is born: to dedicate himself to making a product that was universally necessary. As a boy, teaching himself about machinery, he works on clocks and makes some for his neighbors; and even at the moment of choosing his future career, he thinks he might try making a serviceable watch for thirty cents, but then he reasons that since a watch is not something that everyone needs, *people in general would not purchase them.* The same reasoning leads him to give up the idea of making farm tractors. (Ford is the son of a farmer, and his solid equilibrium, spiritual independence, and audacious yet dogged firmness make one think of a youth passed in freedom, in the fields, far from school and from the more complex problems of city life. Ford is unconcerned with the city.) He has another idea in the back of his mind, as persistent as the belief that he has a mission: "From the time I saw that road engine as a boy of twelve right forward to today, my great interest has been in making a machine that would travel the roads." Underlying the brain of this industrialist there are the feelings of a farmer: a fascination with the obstacle of distance.

But his concept of mission and here and there his dogmatic, almost proudly nationalist tone should not lead us to classify him as a conventional American type, dynamic and adaptable. In Ford's dry steadfastness and self-possession there is always a trace of intimacy, a glimpse of inward riches: "No work with interest is ever hard. I always am certain of results. . . . But it was a very great thing to have my wife even more confident than I was. She has always been that way."

Some of his aphorisms sound like Protestant clichés: "Life is not a battle except with our own tendency to sag with the downpull of 'getting settled.'" "It is not necessary for the employer to love the employee or for the employee to love the employer. What is necessary is that each should try to do justice to the other according to his deserts." "Let every American become steeled against coddling. Americans ought to resent coddling. It is a drug. Stand up and stand out; let weaklings take charity." But under the clichéd surface there is an alert, lively spirit.

His fundamental idea that everyone has a *service* to perform is Protestant. The way he goes about performing his service by means of a simpler, lighter object, the same for everyone, is Protestant. The period of preparation he undergoes before starting production, studying how to make the product better until it won't have to change anymore, is Protestant. For Ford these are the rules; for us they are organic symptoms of how his mind works. We sense in his imagination a deep well of austere, disguised humanitarianism and utopian energy. His habit of understanding is Christian, as is his need to dream of redemption, which he does with an optimism that to us may seem obsessive. But he knows exactly what he is saying: "The genius of the United States of America is Christian. . . . This carries no sectarian meaning with it, but relates to a basic principle which differs from other principles in that it provides for liberty with morality, and pledges society to a code of relations based on fundamental Christian conceptions of human rights and duties."

This serene dismissal of questions of principle is meant to channel every effort into daily work, and here his tendency to simplify is perhaps too primitive. On the other hand, our own sophisticated civilization does not find it at all easy to meet a faith as candid and straightforward as that with doubts and qualifications: it would be like wounding someone's innocence. Or, rather, we feel ourselves less attached to the present, and our skepticism is a sort of faith in a cloudy future, knowing as we do that we will not be able to receive absolution for our sins except in catastrophe. So we entrust our salvation to the unknown forces of a future society that is not yet on the horizon.

Ford's religion, in contrast, has no need of imponderables. His sense of the sacred is very firm: "There is something sacred about a big business which provides a living for hundreds and thousands of families." "There is something sacred about wages: they represent homes and families and domestic destinies." Work, the right and the duty to work, is the law of Ford's world: it is a *necessity,* and it gives *power.* To obtain a more integral explanation than that you would have to look to the youthful, trusting spirit of the whole race. Have those engaged in dreaming up schemes for Italian industry taken these fundamental ethical questions into account? Will it be possible to wave a magic wand and import such large-scale industrialism into Italy, when it can come into being only by virtue of adaptations and efforts specific to local needs? Have they thought through the problems, conceptual above all [*problemi oltre a tutto ideali*], that arise out of the creation of the Milan-Genoa-Turin triangle of production? This is an undertaking that requires decades of psychological preparation, and that can be realized only very gradually, in an Italy that likes to dabble around with big plans. Whoever wants Italy to have genuine industries, not just gambles for bankers, has a duty to state these doubts publicly.

The fact is that in Ford you do not find merely the outlines of industrial Calvinism; you find an organic structure of activity and personality. Only those who prate about the destiny of Latin culture will make remarks about the absence of poetical genius in this mechanical civilization. Ford's factory is anything but a kingdom of automatons. Ford has not done away with ability. *The truth is that for some people, using their brains is a real hardship.* People like that prefer to be utilized in work that is easy and unvaried, whereas ability always brings a certain degree of commanding and inventive spirit. The types of ability that have no place in Ford's factory are disorderly spontaneity and resourceful improvisation.

In this man of the factory, the imprint of the fields is still there, as strong as it was in his youth. *The healthy sun and the feeling of space on the boundless prairie* constitute the nostalgia of this entrepreneur. He hates high density and is quite sure that the era of big cities is dead; his dream for the future is industry allied to agriculture, with the life of the worker divided between the fields and the factory. These picturesque hopes leave us unmoved, but the secret of American capitalism, its present vitality (and let us add, its present domination of the labor movement), lies precisely in the coexistence, crude as it may be, of the spirit of organization and dreaming idealism. It is as though capitalism, rational, rugged, cynical capitalism, perceives its own original sin and asks for utopian absolution.

ROSA LUXEMBURG

ROSA Luxemburg was in exile in Switzerland before she was twenty.[44] Her fellow Polish socialists insultingly called her *dame hystérique et acariâtre* [a hysterical shrewish lady], rejecting her because she was not patriotic, because like a good Marxist she cared nothing for the reconstruction of the Polish state. Her exile lasted all her life: she saw Warsaw again for a few weeks only in 1905, from the barricades.

But none of her letters [45] betrays regret for her exile. She was a strong woman, capable of working on statistics for sixteen hours straight. She wanted to be, and knew she was, a real revolutionary, above human things like homeland, family, private life. We simply know nothing about her weaknesses, her emotional life, how she dealt with practical things. Gossip could not touch her and was reduced to the facile insult of calling her hysterical. She never admits to the burden of being a woman or complains about the difficulties of her solitary life.

All this might seem too much like a striking ideal, a false and lifeless construct—and yet it is human, as human as the romantic substratum of Rosa's spirit, as the part of her that was still a bad little street girl left to her own devices, as her thoughtless joy in living. The same woman who made firebombs took delight in growing flowers in jail, just as she gave herself over, once she was free again, to those moments of openness when "life wriggles

44. Original title: "La petroliera romantica"; from *La Rivoluzione Liberale* 4, no. 25 (21 June 1925), p. 102. Translated from *Scritti politici*, pp. 847–851.

45. Besides her *Lettere dalla prigione* [*Letters from Prison*], see in the fine series Les prosateurs étrangers modernes published by Rieder: Rosa Luxemburg, *Lettres à Karl et Luise Kautsky* (Paris, 1925). [Author's note.]

at our fingertips and we are ready for any folly."[46] After months
of imprisonment she signs herself "yours, ever and incorrigibly
happy." With naive enthusiasm, when she is forty she begins to
read a book about geology and finds it a revelation, bemoan-
ing the fact that "we have so little time to live, and so much to
learn!" She preserved the exuberance of a young woman to the
day of her death and was a painter, propagandist, writer, economist, speaker, fighter, and translator: at one moment an ironic
observer of detail, at another a subtle humorist; now preoccupied with metaphysical meditations, now intent on revolutionary strategy.

An incurable romanticism gave her the necessary distance
from things, her superiority to circumstances: "We are living
in turbulent times, when everything that exists deserves to van-
ish." Here is her recollection, perhaps her only recollection, of
her parents' home. It is early morning, before sunrise, the most
beautiful of moments, "before stupid, noisy, deafening life starts
up again in the big rented barracks. The august calm of the morning hour extended over the triviality of the pavement; on high,
the first rays of the new sun glinted in the windows, and higher
still, little rosy clouds floated, before melting into the gray sky of
the great city. At that time I firmly believed that 'life,' 'real' life
lay somewhere else, down there beyond the rooftops. Since then
I have wandered in search of it, but it is always hidden behind
some roof. In sum, everything has conspired to mock me, and
real life has perhaps stayed right there in that courtyard where
Antoni and I read *The Origins of Civilization* for the first time."

She felt that this discontent with herself drove her to take
action. And indeed, who can ever survey what they have accomplished without feeling discontent with themselves, "unless it be

46. Gobetti's citations from Luxemburg's letters are all given in Italian
translation, with no further indication of the source than in the previous
note. The English translations here are made from the Italian versions he
gives. Luxemburg's *Briefe an Karl und Luise Kautsky* was published in Berlin
in 1923. [Translator's note.]

a deputy of the Reichstag or a mandarin from the General Commission of the Trade Unions?"

Her pessimism was inspired by idealism and moral grandeur. "I am completely lost in daily misery," she writes during the war years, all of which she spent in prison, "and I find that incomprehensible and insupportable. Look at the icy serenity with which Goethe held himself aloof from things. Imagine what he had to put up with during his life . . . and with what tranquillity and mental equilibrium he continued his studies on the metamorphosis of plants, the theory of color, and a thousand other things throughout that time. I do not ask of you that you write poetry like Goethe, but everyone can emulate his conception of life—the universality of his interests, the inner harmony—or try to at least. And if you should say to me, 'Goethe was not a political militant,' I would answer, 'A militant more than anyone else ought to try to put himself above things; otherwise he will sink up to his ears the first time he has to wade through the mud.'"

Because her politics were serious and ethically motivated, Rosa Luxemburg was able to live her life in jail and in exile. The barricades were her poetry. A Goethean spirit must view life a little bit like that, from exile; and in Rosa Luxemburg the Olympian balance is precisely one and the same thing as the detachment of the exile. These were the grand idealistic motives that sustained her in her Goethean exile.

The Revolutionary

The incendiary lets herself relax in her letters and indulge her feminine aspect: "Women! however sublime their spirit, they notice one's tie before anything else!" "I spoke in the open air in front of two thousand persons in a garden with multicolored lights. *It was most romantic.*"

But on intellectual and party questions she was inexorable. Luise Kautsky, the wife of the "renegade" and therefore an unimpeachable witness, states: "Especially in conflicts among party members she lashed out at any hesitation as pusillanimity, any concession as weakness, any wish to conciliate as cowardice, any tendency to bargain as betrayal. Her passionate nature made her go right to the final limit. She had a horror of all concessions, even when dealing with her closest political friends." "Hence the indulgent Poles called her *dame hystérique et acariâtre;* but the fascination she exercised was owing to the fact that she was always ready to accept the consequences of her positions. When her friends urged her to write from her Polish prison to President Witte or the German consul, she replied, 'Those gentlemen will have a while to wait before a Social Democrat [this was in 1906] asks them for protection and justice. Long live the Revolution!' She begged that no one approach 'Bülow, for example; no matter what happens, I don't want to owe him anything, because in my propaganda I would no longer be able to speak freely, as I must, about him and the government.'"

This woman had the tenderness of a romantic conspirator, yet she knew how to put the problems of the revolution with Marxist realism. After the experience of the first Russian Revolution she was decidedly Leninist, even when she was combating Lenin. Her remarks about 1905–6 are penetrating—for example, "The police are impotent against mass movements." To attain a revolutionary situation, it is necessary that "the antagonism between the classes be deepened, that social relations be accentuated and clarified." Rosa Luxemburg accepted the factory councils from 1906: "Another interesting aspect of the revolution is that in all the workshops elected committees of workers were set up spontaneously to decide on all the conditions of work, hiring, layoffs, etc." She notes how, against the factory councils, the owners even sought a pact with the subversive parties.

With this heroic faith in the masses, with this certainty that they desired their own liberation, Rosa Luxemburg prepared to die on the barricades. She was convinced *that the masses were more mature than their leaders.* "By God, the Revolution is great and strong, unless the Social Democrats manage to undermine it." And in 1917: "The Social Democratic movement here in the superior, developed West is composed of abject poltroons who will sit idly by and let the Russians drown in their own blood."

During four years of imprisonment her reserved character was sustained by the hope of action. She used to daydream about it, the way one daydreams when one has been locked up for a long time. "I would prefer to observe the history of the world otherwise than from behind iron bars," she jokingly said of her confinement. She forgot her Olympian serenity only once, in the passage in which Liebknecht is commemorated with deep emotion:

> But to wander freely out there, through the fields or along the roads, to stop awhile in April or May in front of a garden, watching openmouthed as the poplars, each with its buds formed in its own image, turn green again, and the maple scatters its little yellow-green stars, and the first asters and veronicas peep out from the tangle of grass—this would be a supreme joy for me today. I wouldn't request or appeal for anything more, provided I could pass an hour a day like that. Understand me clearly! I do not mean that I would renounce the active life of thought and confine myself to this contemplation. I mean that I would find my personal happiness that way, and I would then be armed and enchanted for every combat and every privation.

Thus, inside the jail walls, she prepared herself for martyrdom.

BENEDETTO CROCE

The Political Croce

AN unsophisticated observer might think that Croce, as a man engaged in politics and as a theoretician of politics, lacks the sort of passion and experience that drove the great political thinkers like Machiavelli and Treitschke, authors of books that remain historical monuments of their own times and models of philosophical speculation.[47]

Croce has fought in the battle of culture for thirty years, yet seems to have kept his distance from the interests of any party; even his most specifically political acts do not compromise him, leaving him virtually unscathed: he contributed funds to *Avanti!*[48] after Pelloux;[49] he was minister of education under Giolitti;[50] he showed some indulgence to Mussolini's fascism at first, using law-and-order arguments, but subsequently broke with fascism in disgust and remorse. Through all these phases his aim was to offer a concrete example of personal conduct: his actions are matters for his personal conscience, the responses of a citizen, not a politician or a philosopher, to the call of duty. If you look closely at what he tried to do as minister of education, you will find that his constant preoccupation was not to draft a program or reform the institution but to make it function honestly. And therein lies the difference between Gentile, the dogmatic, authoritarian dictator with his provincial self-assurance, and Croce, the political man capable of reflection and doubt, open to every human need, anxious to listen even to the simple voices of instinct and good sense.

In sum, Croce in politics preferred to be a plain human being rather than a sham statesman, for at the age of fifty it was too late for him to learn overnight how to don the mask of a police official or master the low arts of intrigue. But if we absolutely must

47. Original title: "Croce oppositore"; from *La Rivoluzione Liberale* 4, no. 31 (6 September 1925), p. 125. Translated from *Scritti politici*, pp. 876–881.

48. *Avanti!* was the newspaper of the Italian Socialist Party.

49. Luigi G. Pelloux (1839–1924) was one of the least popular politicians of the nineteenth century. As the head of the government at the end of the century, he ordered the army to intervene against the unarmed population of Milan, which was gathering to demonstrate against the imposition of new taxes; more than a hundred people were killed.

50. See note 10.

attach him to one of the parties, although his philosophy served persons in every party, we have to admit that purely by reason of his agreeable, jocose common sense, this indulgent blue blood who chose Naples for his home had to be sympathetic to an honest conservatism, moderately liberal, able to preserve the formalities and—the paramount thing for all those who simply want to get on with their business—the public peace. Because of his enlightened and apprehensive conservatism Croce was against the reactionary trend at the start of the twentieth century; he opposed taking part in the war in 1915, because war depletes the savings and the labor that have accumulated in the economy, as in culture; and today he frowns on the improvisations of national-fascism.

The Theoretician of Politics

Everything of value in the political thought expounded in his scattered notes and in his breviary *Elementi di politica* [51] derives from this moderation, the moderation of a man who is neither apolitical nor a party member, and from his detached, almost indifferent role as an observer. In his thought we find a precise, not haphazard record of the speculative constancy that has undergirded our political life for the past twenty years. At most we might feel compelled to express our regret that Croce has proceeded very summarily, sometimes even too rapidly, veiling (quite deliberately and with trenchant malice) his references to current events. For example, we would have liked to see him use a more leisurely historical approach as he executes capital punishment on certain prejudices and lame theories, illustrating the motives and the psychology behind these errors by alluding to the contemporary situation. Instead, it was enough, for Croce, to make explicit (in a strictly speculative context) the theory of

51. Benedetto Croce, *Elementi di politica* (Bari: Laterza, 1925).

politics that was already laid out in *Filosofia della pratica* and *Materialismo storico.*[52]

Politics deals with actions aimed at utility, and utility is not morality. But it is not simply egoism either, so there is a need to defend the spiritual, and fundamentally valuable, nature of political engagement against all those who dismiss it as completely immoral, the preserve of crooks. So Croce never lets slip a chance to deride and repudiate the abstractionists and hypocrites of moralism. But political sense can't be divorced from juridical sense, meaning that while we shouldn't approach our institutions in the same way as the bigots and vestal virgins do, we do have a right to expect whoever steps into the arena to have a strong sense of tradition, continuity, and legality. Political sense and juridical sense need something further: a clear notion of the state, which is *force* only insofar as it is *consensus* —force not in the vulgar image of "grabbing someone by the neck, bending him over, crushing him" but as the entirety of human and spiritual strength, "including the sagacity of the intellect no less than the vigor of the arm, foresight and prudence no less than ardor and courage, gentleness no less than severity." Thus authority and liberty are indivisible in every state, so we have good reason to celebrate liberty. "Is there any word that makes the human heart beat with greater warmth and sweetness?" Croce concludes, with malicious skepticism, that it is ever necessary to preach the benefits of authority to the people and the benefits of liberty to princes, making it clear that he wants others to decode his message the right way. With the state thus conceived as action, the quest for the foundations of sovereignty becomes an empty one. "In a state everyone is sovereign and subject at

52. Benedetto Croce, *Filosofia della pratica: Economica ed etica*, published in English under the title *Philosophy of the Practice: Economics and Ethics*, trans. Anislie Douglas (London: Macmillan, 1913); Croce, *Materialismo storico ed economia marxistica*, published in English under the title *Historical Materialism and the Economics of Karl Marx*, ed. Michael Curtis (New Brunswick, N.J.: Transaction Books, 1981).

different times. Sovereignty in a relationship does not belong to any of the component parts taken on its own; it inheres in the relationship itself." For all that Croce takes pleasure in satirizing Rousseau and twitting egalitarians, this is still one of the most forceful and radical enunciations of modern democracy.

But the political man is not relegated to, or confined within, the boundaries of the utilitarian field on which he makes his first moves. Politics creates new relationships, becomes an instrument of moral life, goes to the sources of knowledge. The state, participating in the progress of history, is ethical too. But Croce puts us on our guard against those who would confound the state conceived of as morality, as the ethical state, with the political state, and would thence derive the notion that morality is the business of the government, as happened with Gentile, the minister of obscurantist anachronism. The state is, in reality, "the narrow, elementary form of practical life, and moral life bursts free of it and overflows it on every side, scattering itself in copious, fertile rivulets, so fertile that they perpetually unmake and remake political life, and states, by forcing them to renew themselves in keeping with the demands that moral life makes on them." This is a poetical, forceful portrait of the complexity of the real world, which is wholly pervaded by this fundamental distinction.

In *Elementi di politica* Croce also tries to provide a rationale for the validity of political parties, of which he had previously given an inadequate account when he compared them to literary genres. In reality, the importance of political parties lies not so much in their platforms, which are often generic and in any case necessarily no more than a preliminary outline, as it does in the way the party is constituted as a means of getting things accomplished, with its leaders who rise to the top through the vitality of their character and prepare themselves to form the government.

Belonging to a party and governing are not antithetical things: we need to see even in the party politician an example of the action and accomplishment that are the substance of social life, which is the sum total of all relationships and actions.

Croce's whole politics is at bottom an exaltation of the moment of activity and a refusal of abstract cogitation, schematic and generic, and false programs that hide bad intentions. We need to get away from all the pedantry of all the political doctrinaires and confront reality: at that moment of contact, advice and analysis and distinctions serve merely as premises and incitements to deciding and acting.

Croce's Antifascism.

In the wake of the killing of Matteotti, one of the most important facts of Italian politics was Croce's opting for antifascism.[53]

Until last autumn Croce took an optimistic and indulgent view: he had reservations about fascism, but they were moral and pedagogical ones that arose, on one hand, out of his aversion to D'Annunzio[54] and to futurism and, on the other, out of his strong mistrust of all the Italian nationalists, whom he regarded even before the war as a bunch of dangerous political hacks. This tolerant antifascism was not entirely to the taste of us younger people, for we categorized things differently and had a different style, but you could not expect Croce to give up his conservative habits of good taste and cultural moderation. When he did come out in open opposition, his deepest reasons for doing so were still based, to a large degree, on his individual preferences and sensibilities more than on his theoretical appraisal. In his support

53. In 1925, Croce subscribed to *The Manifesto* against fascism, which had a great impact on the new generation of antifascists.

54. Gabriele D'Annunzio (1863–1938) was a poet, novelist, dramatist, and soldier. The sensuous imagery of his poetry displays unrivaled craftsmanship and a subtle pleasure in decadence reminiscent of Nietzsche. His oratory had much to do with Italy's entrance into World War I. In September 1919 he led a march on Fiume, where he established an illegal government. He was an early exponent of fascism.

for the liberal party, to which he has diligently contributed time and effort, Croce is practicing his own ideal Giolittism, which for him means a mental habit of moderation, loyalty, and discretion. When he does deign to take part in the actual political process as a rank-and-file member, he focuses on parliamentary institutions—the traditional means of getting things done, the constitutional and administrative machinery. His attitude is Piedmontese, with an elemental frankness; he is indulgent to theory but insistent on seriousness in individuals and stubbornly faithful to the civic virtues and the historical characteristics of the race. The Piedmontese devotion to the state of such men is devotion to the laic state and combines respect for religion with distrust of priests—a laicism perfectly antithetical to the noisy anticlericalism of the sort of Romagnol atheists who are ready to turn around and fall in love with the Church out of a subversive aesthetics.

But that is not all there is to Croce's antifascism. As a conservative and a commonsense Italian, he has his reasons, but there is also the rebellion of a man of European culture. His conservative commonsense reasons might not always suit our own more combative psychology, but they serve to give his rebellion a proper human dimension, and without them it might risk appearing to be romantic exasperation or prejudice.

We need to bring this European antifascism of Croce to the attention of the Italians: let it be a rebuke to them for their nerves, their hysteria, and their impatience. Croce has found the right tone for rebellion against the present, tackling the decadence of today in the name of the future. For twenty years his work has been the sole Italian example of direct participation in the entire spiritual life of the modern world. Italian provincialism will not easily pardon him for that.

After the infelicitous attempts of the Risorgimento, Croce has been the most perfect type of European produced by our culture. Now, when we are witnessing one of the most radical attempts to break Italy's bond with the European intelligentsia, Croce's cultural stance should become an adamant political stance. His balanced, impartial mind must commit itself rigorously and totally to one side. One is not allowed to be apolitical if one is defending the reasons and the fundamental rights of criticism, thought, and dignity. The poet must defend the freedom of his art, the philosopher the legitimacy of his studies. This is a war for peace in which even the unarmed have to commit themselves to live or die. In this battle, the most vital aspect of the struggle between antifascism and fascism, victory will not depend on militias and youth squads but on confidence in our own intransigence and our capacity not to yield.

Croce can also show the Italians an example of tranquillity in the midst of combat, having carefully preserved a sense of his own limits.

His preoccupations are for the future; in him there is an intense, tremulous awareness that the battle of today will bring grave consequences; the spectacle of civilization in peril he beholds with distress. Croce has thrown himself into a sustained polemic against fascism as though driven by the need for liberation, because no one can fail in his duty. And since his fundamental duty is not to let his own political engagement descend to grubby politics, let him strive to fend off the shadows of a new dark age by continuing to labor at his books and his scholarship as though he were still in a world of civility; after baffling his pedestrian little enemies with fierce irony he will go back to the study of history in his library with a clear conscience.

We feel that Croce is a master precisely because of his impassive refusal to conform.

BENITO MUSSOLINI

Mussolini has been the representative hero of this weariness, this longing for repose.[55] His personification of self-confident optimism, his oratorical tricks, his love of success and of ceremonies on Sunday, his virtuoso command of mystification and emphasis—all these make him deeply popular with the Italians.

It is difficult to picture him in any other guise than that of a daring condottiere leading soldiers of fortune, or the primitive chieftain of a savage band in the grip of a dogmatic terror that prevents them from stopping to think. His victory, amid the disorientation of the rest, is fully explainable if we reflect on his tactical decisionmaking ability.

He lacks the exquisitely modern sense, that of irony; he understands history only through myths; and the critical finesse of creative activity, the principal gift of the great politician, eludes him entirely. His profession of relativism does not even succeed in appearing to be a nimble conjuring trick, because anyone can see all too clearly that it is a panicky, naive hunt for a way to escape from infantile uncertainty and cover misdeeds. Coherence and self-contradiction in Mussolini's case are two different aspects of a political mentality unable to free itself from the old schemas of a moralism for which he has too much disdain to be able to find a real substitute. So he remains divided and wavering between moments of coherence too dogmatic not to appear clumsy and displays of anarchically inappropriate exuberance. What he needs is a world in which nobody asks the condottiere to become a politician. To fight for an idea and work out one's own ideas in the struggle is a luxury and a bore: Mussolini is sufficiently intelligent to apply himself to the task, but

55. Original title: "Mussolini"; from Gobetti, *La Rivoluzione Liberale* (ed. Perona), pp. 173–176. Portions of the text were adapted from articles previously published in *La Rivoluzione Liberale* in 1922 and 1923; see Perona's headnote for details.

struggle pure and simple suffices and spares him the torment of modern critical thought. Only the ingenuous will have been surprised by his recent flirtation with the Catholic Church, for there is no one more removed than Mussolini from the spirit of the laic state, more distant from the old Right of men like Spaventa.[56] There is nothing religious about him, for he scorns the religious problem as such and cannot stand struggling with doubt; he needs a faith in order not to have to think about it anymore, in order to be the temporal arm of a transcendental idea. He could have succeeded as duce of something like the Society of Jesus, could have been an enforcer for some pope engaged in the persecution of heretics, with one single notion in his head, to be repeated and driven "with the cudgel's blow" into "refractory skulls." His articles for *Il popolo d'Italia* were like that: repetitions of a command, dogmas and often mere stereotypes of a monotonous pattern, and so are his communiqués and speeches. As literary texts, they are redolent of military life and of the catechism: the premises are absolute truths, transcendent and crystalline; the deduction is the work of the executioner or the youth squad. In fact the three key moments in the life of Mussolini have coincided with three moments of resolution, enthusiasm, and dogma in recent Italian history: socialist messianism, apocalyptic anti-Germanism, the fascist palingenesis. Is there anyone stupid enough to look for a sequence of development, a reasoned idealism of progress, in the condottiere of these episodes? Why see a political problem when what we have is an instance of the psychology of success and a new economical art of ideas? Would it be a legitimate undertaking to study the political philosophy of Conrad Wolfort, John Hawkwood, or Francesco Bussone?[57]

56. Silvio Spaventa (1822–1893) was one of the most prominent liberal leaders of Risorgimento. He shared an ethical conception of the state and gradually became a nationalist.

57. Gobetti refers here to historical personages and literary characters. Francesco Bussone, for example, was the Count of Carmagnola, a condot-

History will be lenient when it passes judgment on the anachronistic Mussolini, for despite the stiff pride of an unfulfilled petty lord that he displays, he has been humble enough to bow down to it, this belated Garibaldian (like Crispi,[58] but perhaps less stubborn and more malleable on account of his unshakable *arrivisme*): however uncultivated and intellectually impoverished, he succeeded at least twice, by being tough and uninhibited, in helping history to give birth.

The intrinsic weaknesses of his character were revealed when the condottiere had to remake himself as administrator and diplomat. In an international meeting of *inscrutable* individuals, the inferiority of Mussolini—more actor than artist, more tribune than statesman—becomes palpable, because all he can do is reflect himself in the mirror of his own emphasis. His eloquence and forcefulness as a polemicist are unable to cope with irony and understatement; they remain paralyzed as soon as the ground shifts from the electoral meeting and the fencing ring to clever conversation and the nerve-racking, treacherous skirmish of words. Mussolini is at his ease only when he addresses the common folk, gives ear to their desires, and reproves them with an imperious glare for their mischief. Running things day to day, with all its monotony, is another bête noire of the president, and without the amusing diversion of the new sports projects that restore his popularity, the daily grind would be exhausting and barren. In any case, the very essence of dramatic and exceptional governance blocks it off from the world of common necessary tasks on which all the praetorians and subalterns of the revolution in search of sinecures fix their hopes in vain. Pa-

---

tiere of the fifteenth century who owed his fame to Manzoni's eponymous nineteenth-century tragedy.

58. Francesco Crispi (1818–1901), once a follower of Garibaldi, became a conservative nationalist. As head of the government in the 1880s, he pursued a colonialist and protectionist policy and made an alliance with Germany, beginning the antidemocratic trend that would bring Italy to militarism and then fascism.

tience is a better friend of returns and revenges than of improvisation.

Nonetheless, Mussolini has a notable aptitude for holding on
to power amid an enthusiastic population that wants amuse-
ment, a population he knows intimately and on whom he bestows daily surprises (including the telegram to Spalla, the rous-
ing Baracca raid, and his Sunday speeches).[59] Putting aside all
preoccupation with foreign affairs, he has inexorably pursued a
shrewd reactionary strategy of liquidating all the other parties
and all the organs of political life and with the help of the economic crisis appears to want to bring every one of his adversaries to heel. In this experiment too the *trasformismo*[60] of Giolitti has been revived but with more striking theatrical effects;
the gifts of the politician are reduced to cunning maneuvers and
tactical calculations, signs that his arts are entirely humanistic[61] and military. Hence Mussolinism is a much more serious
development even than fascism because it confirms the people
in the habit of paying court and not taking responsibility for
themselves, the custom of expecting their own salvation from
the duce, from the tamer, from the deus ex machina. The political contest under Mussolini's regime is not easy: it is not easy
to oppose him because he shifts constantly, avoiding coherence,
firm positions, or precise distinctions. He is always ready for any
trasformismo. Must Italy ineluctably be condemned by its economic inferiority to this anachronistic brand of courtiership? Or

59. Erminio Spalla, a boxer, was a European champion. Francesco Baracca was an air force officer famous for his undertakings during World
War I.

60. See note 11.

61. Here and throughout, Gobetti uses the words "humanistic" and "hu-
manism" (*umanistico, umanesimo*) exclusively to refer to the movement in
Italy from the fourteenth to the sixteenth centuries that revived the Latin language and the ethos of Greco-Roman antiquity. Gobetti associates human-
ism with empty rhetoric, the behavior of courtiers, and the military culture
of the condottieri—in sum, with the Italian Renaissance, which he detested
and of which he considered Mussolini an epigone. [Translator's note.]

will the forces of the new popular initiative and the sections of the ruling class not yet compromised succeed in setting the tone of our history to come? But clearly, at this point, any forecast on our part would be too partisan and (beyond what derives from the context) falls instead to the reader's initiative.

2 OUR LIBERALISM

OUR FAITH

I

THE misfortunes of Italian public life, the lack of sincerity
and clarity (the main expression of which is Giolittism),[1]
are the result of a tragic contradiction and a disastrous
heterogeneity of methods and individuals, principles and consequences.[2] To resolve the contradiction it will be necessary to get
rid of systems that no longer correspond to reality, and make the
two terms now in conflict combine in a logically complete and
coherent development.

The forms within which our political life unfolds (that is, the
parties) do not allow individuals sufficient vitality; they are looking to practical life for real, concrete ideals able to contain (without stopping at that) their needs and their desires. The parties of
today offer nothing but generic, imprecise formulas from which
nothing can be logically or clearly derived. They claim to represent the interests of individuals, but if we look closely we find
that representing the interests of individuals not only leads to
egoism (which would not in itself be such a bad thing) but leads
us right outside politics—and politics is organization. It shrinks

1. See Chapter 1, note 10.
2. Original title: "La nostra fede"; from *Energie Nuove* ser. 2, no. 1 (5 May
1919), pp. 1–8. Translated from *Scritti politici*, pp. 75–88.

the possibility of concerted action to the point where it almost
vanishes, because it can only arise out of the coexistence, along
with interests, of ideal, theoretical motives that assume concrete
form by becoming political questions.

In the life of the parties at the moment, instead of concreteness, there is only a pernicious circle in which individuals ruin
parties, and the parties do nothing to aid the progress of individuals. Because the parties represent the past, they are a history that people are trying to revise, not concrete actuality. The
central idea of socialism (which is, despite all, a brave, though
isolated and unlucky, attempt to absorb the core of idealistic
morality) has remained a frigid, illusory communism far removed from the thought and the achievements of economic science. The democratic doctrines, which ought to be vitality itself,
giving inner life to history and resolving contingencies, have remained ideologies of the eighteenth century, a crepuscular Enlightenment that has been moribund for more than a century.
The nationalism of men like Treitschke and Naumann, having
failed in the war, can no longer represent anything, since it
amounts merely to ridiculous dogmatism, an ideology springing from the vulgarity of a mean positivism and reduced to pure
imperialism, hence empty, vicious, pointless.

Overall, the ideas that frame and organize forces, the parties,
have remained a century behind. And those involved in them
feel uneasy. History moves forward; individuals move with it.
The schemas cannot remain the same. If they do not subside but
continue to exist, they are subjected, in practical reality, to the
deforming pressure exerted on them by individuals and thus,
though born to organize and systemize, come to promote disorganization and confusion. They persist in name while the internal friction grows, the friction of development, the friction
between the original premises and the subsequent growth. Naturally, this kind of contradiction cannot last long in everyday
reality, but neither, on the other hand, can it ever lead to stable
unification. So we keep on going empirically, temporarily resolv-

ing isolated problems day by day, and each time personal interests naturally win out, ideals are completely lost, and actions are enslaved to an empty nominalism. The best men are inevitably afflicted with skepticism as the level of dishonest activity grows. Take a look at political life from the viewpoint of complete honesty: you will feel disgust, and disgust degenerates into abstention, scorn, indifference for the highest interests. Representative government no longer enjoys popular favor. But what do you want to put in its place—theocracy?

Everyone minds their own business and tries to keep going. The only result is disaster, because the life of the state is life only to the extent that it makes concrete the activities of all the conscientious, active citizens. On the outside, the direction of progress is lost; everything is a detour. And the detour leads to a maze of side roads. The anarchist, who refuses organization; the old-fashioned bourgeois, who sees the state personified in the employee at the tax office; the socialist, who refuses the nation for a larger reality and is left with his *own* individual reality as the only *concrete* thing he has—you see them all fixed and intent on their own tiny personalities, on preoccupations that are not political.

The remedy lies in a healthy rethinking of ideas, in an anxious and careful process of clarification of principles, in a perfect awareness of the many relations that exist between the necessities of life and the ideal principles that transcend it.

II

What logical and practical value can a party have? Only the value that derives from its content, whether that be actual or traditional. And since content today is mostly equivalent to the party's program, the value of a party lies in its formulas. I understand formulas in a broad sense that includes both the value they may have in logic and that which is visible in practice.

It seems clear to me in any case that in the very concept of formula there is a component that fixes and delimits its real range. A formula is a conclusion, a point of arrival, an elaboration that presupposes a whole spiritual process, a whole sequence of efforts in which its justification and its importance lie. It is an abstraction, a symbol of results attained, not the concrete fact of the attainment itself. The value of the symbol will lie entirely in the efficacy that it shows as an expression of the entire implied process. But it remains clear that to understand this value, simple consensus is not enough; it is necessary for every individual to re-create the symbol by going through the process for himself. This means that the party, along with its formula, has to contain another element, has to take on another mission: it has to help the members understand the *history* of its formula. Far from being a resolution, the quietism of the deluded, the party must present itself as a ceaseless process of becoming, a continuous inner struggle, a process of progressive self-awareness. And the formulas will be effective in each person only insofar as they are slowly remade, produced by the spirit of the individual.

This is precisely what I deny our political parties have tried to be. They have offered stasis and consolation to poor, backward folk, and because the formulas were decrepit, to accept them had in itself to be an act of turning back on oneself, a regression. They have remained a tradition that only a handful of scattered people have tried to feel and to continue and that the majority have meanwhile adapted to their own material interests.

Of political education we have not even seen the shadow, as always happens when history is forsaken for abstractions, the dynamic for the static.

Thus the parties have been reduced to mental schemes, a means of classification and, when they do produce actions, of unconscious actions. Missing was the flame that would have catalyzed the formulas, the method, the shared spirit that would have given life to the results. Instead, the formulas were announced, and then individuals capable of spreading them were

sought, whereas the formulas and the individuals to defend them
have to be born together.

The problem of action has become a hard problem. Any advance beyond this point will mean destroying the illusion utterly.
It will mean devaluing the final formulas in order to transfer all
the emphasis onto the methods and procedures for getting there.
To work to bring that about will certainly not be a short-term
project—the results will come slowly—but it is a question of an
entire moral turn. For just that reason we do not advance grand
formulas. We bring with us a new method, a new passion, born
out of a conscious reaction made necessary by the so-called reformers' tendency to simplify, out of a clear insight into the complexity of the problems, the enormousness of the little questions
that can't be resolved by hypostasizing generalities. But out of
our reaction, an affirmation that is our faith and our life is rendered more clear and exact, as we shall see. For now, let us examine the full extent of our negation.

Our adversaries often say that we have come to politics without a clear understanding of the importance of the paramount
problems, without having prepared any solution for them. But
do these great problems really exist? Aren't they instead a more
or less undemanding and straightforward way of grouping together (under the constraint of method and mental habit) a
quantity of other small difficult problems that have to be solved
one by one?

Let us look for a moment at one of these great problems,
a political factor that everyone is talking about these days: the
class struggle. For most people this expression has a certain
fairly clear meaning that has grown by accretion to include the
consciousness of social privilege, the reciprocal hatred that
flows from it, and the need for a resolution in which the hatred
and the privileges that cause it will be extinguished. But this
meaning is so elastic that many people have become convinced
that a coup d'état, a revolution, will sweep away and resolve

everything. Revolution: there you have a very quick solution. And the other is just as facile: conservatism, reaction.

We, in contrast, in looking at this problem, have the presumption to analyze its elements in search of a solution, and underneath the concept of privilege we find legitimate interests that have to be recognized as belonging to everyone and have to be safeguarded. Hatred can be resolved through a clearer appreciation of the necessity of social relationships and interdependence.

It is our view that out of the concept (a necessary and indestructible concept) of equality of chances and variability of outcomes, the concept of social distinction must necessarily arise, whether the distinction is called "class" or anything else you like. Then the problem of how to protect the rights of everyone presents itself in the form of, let us say, the organization of trade unions, becoming concrete in a whole series of technical problems, which very easily lead to complex problems of social assistance, social insurance, popular access to credit, etc. In this manner, not refusing to accept the distinctions but instead working to make them just and legitimate, we resolve the problem every day as it presents itself in new guises every day.

It is not true, in sum, that with us a conception of the state is lacking: we firmly believe that we can impose our conception, and indeed superimpose this general conception, in the current phase of things, which may very well end up being overturned and radically changed, but only through long and patient labor that people will find jarring and that might even alter them a bit. In our action we cannot evade millennia of history, of human labor; it is not possible to deny a tradition that is entirely inside us, that imparts its value and its importance to us. We can only carry it on. And carrying it on means building a bridge between the free thought of the men of today and the legacy of work that they have received. The two elements condition each other mutually and give rise to progress. And I really do not know how an ideology can call itself a general conception of the state anyway when, for all that it is based on certain real presuppositions, it finds a way, with the aid of fantasy and humanitarianism, to arrive at a frightful negation, at a truly grotesque pretense of might.

III

It is part of our general outlook not to believe in the possibility of engaging in a deductive kind of politics. Once again we suffer from our vice of not having the sort of broad vision that perfectly unifies political realities, from our fault of mistrusting ideas that offer vague, general, miraculous remedies to which everything is adaptable and which miraculously justify everything.

It is possible to make deductions on the basis of a unity (individual or universal, it doesn't matter) provided that it is deeply felt. But in practical reality we have a complexity of activities that may very well have equality of nature and possibility but also have deep differences of spiritual intensity, which mean that the effects of the activities almost always transcend their causes, which in turn escape us and cannot be fully analyzed. There is indeed the unification of the spirit that embraces them all and implants in all of them its capacity for life, but this capacity is not fixed a priori, through an act of knowing; knowing develops progressively, together with the outpouring of actions, and cannot anticipate actions through an act of rationality.

Clearly, our skepticism about *general* (generic) *ideas* does not in the least mean that we fail to recognize a rationality in every action, and in the relations between actions a logicality that derives from the unity of the spirit—provided politics is not confused with philosophy. For in philosophy there is a perfect coincidence of thought and action: action is nothing less than the development of the thought of every individual. But in politics the intervention of new elements, new activities, brings the consequence that action transcends every single person's level of possibility, and the forms of knowing are two: the thinking of

reality as actualized or while becoming actual, and the foresee-
ing of events. And when we are in the realm of foresight, we have
to remember that we are not reasoning about philosophy. . . .

We distinguish politics and morality in the same way. Practical activity is involved in the one case and the other, certainly.
But in the moral realm it is the individual who comprehends and
creates his own practical activity, regulates *his* actions in relation to others, in effect makes himself the center of the world. In
politics, on the other hand, the practical activity in question is
that of many individuals aiming at different results, and the overall direction is determined as a function of the various conceptions held by those individuals, some of whom may have taken
into account the general interest, others their own interest, and
yet others some fictitious interest. Therefore, although politics
and morality might join in unity when they are reflected on in
retrospect, inasmuch as they are not in dialectical contradiction,
they are different in the concreteness of the spiritual activity that
produces them. A good politics is always moral too, because it
must attain the general good; but in the world of the contingent
there are people who strive for the general good and others who
do not (fate is nothing other than the meeting of these forces and
their unconscious clash): the essence of politics lies in thinking
through these relationships, these modes in which practical activity presents itself.

IV

Let us return to the examination of parties and their purposes;
here we find another organic deficiency (the absence of intimate
logicality) that adds to and aggravates the other error of method
(lack of development). Let us try to expand the concept with
a rapid survey, noting objections, sketching critiques, finding
salient points to clarify our ideas.

The socialist concept of class we have already analyzed and
resolved into its component parts. It is a dogmatic, absolute ex-

aggeration of a datum factually true: free differentiation among human beings. We all belong to a class, but to the class we want, and precisely here, in seeing that the limit exists and knowing that we have drawn it ourselves, class is overcome, and a more ample reality that contains and transcends it, the nation, emerges in triumph. Here the socialists will object: why not all humanity? But the nation itself is humanity, humanity at a level we can grasp, evident to us as something historically concrete formed by an age-old tradition. The nation may even be contained in the reality of *humanity*, but not through a juxtaposition of concepts, through, rather, concrete historical labor to which everyone brings their contribution of action.

Socialism has not observed this concreteness. It has failed to see it because socialism is an ideology born of the historical environment of the French Revolution and adapted to the pressures of the period that came to a head in 1848. With the passing of those historical conditions the whole of critical communism has ceased to be organic and broken apart; and for the socialists of today there remains the mindset of an absolutely primitive communism combining humanitarianism, love, and equality.

One way or another, socialists have to choose either the scientific dress that Marx tried to give to the old theories, and in that case they have to react to classical economics and to the historical circumstances against which Marx himself aimed his blows; or else the phraseology of equality and fraternity (which, as we will see, disturbs a quite different vision of things: democracy); or else a detailed exegesis in which they make it clear how much they take from Marx and how much from humanitarianism and the Enlightenment.

But the hybrid result that will emerge they must not forget to submit to the judgment of history and perhaps even to that of Karl Marx himself, a master who with all his concreteness would be the first to renounce the moralism and the Mazzinianism of many of his own followers. The dilemma is there in the end, explicitly: with Marx or against Marx.

But just as our socialists have never thought about the relation between the future state, in which the shining reign of justice will commence, and the human iniquity that torments us here and now, they have never faced up squarely to the problem of the exegesis of Marx and the consequent definition of socialism in the present. And a theory that has no continuators can be said to be dead for sure.

Yet socialism lives on in many, or at least enjoys their sympathetic support, because it rides forth as champion and Don Quixote of all opposition to the government and its daily bestiality. But that critical position has properly nothing to do with socialism; indeed, it is our position too, and we are strong adversaries of communism. We do, however, deprecate the way opposition with them has become a habit of being perpetually discontent, thus automatically nullifying itself and voiding any possibility of obtaining concrete results.

There is still the problem of the spread of socialism, of the influence the party currently has. Here we would need to be able to look into the heads of the party members. Never let it be thought that we might wish to devalue a respectable idea like socialism by expressing doubts about their honesty and good faith. The problem we see in socialism now is that of the organization of labor, nothing else. Marx may have posed this problem, but, by God, we will see who resolves it! We are certainly not trying to hide its fundamental importance. But we still stand for a national solution, which can perfectly well be combined with trade unionism. This combination is in fact starting to turn up, in England and perhaps (who knows?) in Germany. . . .

Our national solution has nothing to do with nationalism, which means a collapse to the lowest grade of dogmatism. Nationalism today, in its official form, has no reality and no content other than imperialism. In this case too I would request that its followers make peace with their own consciences. In nationalism there exists the same system of proselytism as in socialism: Do you accept that there is progress? Are you a human being?

Then you are a socialist. And among the nationalists: Do you accept the homeland, the nation? Then you are a nationalist. But once the nation is accepted, there remains the problem of national organization. The nationalists bypass it completely; their sole concern is expansion and the consequent employment of the army. Their sole concern is, in other words, a vicious circle.

I do not claim to deny the concept of struggle, in which activity, the creator of progress, culminates. And in the present state of things the struggle might even take place between armies, but it cannot only be that, because today war would not even have beneficial side effects any more.

There are other forms of activity and consequently of struggle, more actual and fertile, and toward them we have to move and are moving, ridding ourselves as we do so of forms of struggle that no longer correspond to the exigencies of labor and progress. Among these we include *war for the sake of war* as exalted by the nationalists, and in future we may perhaps include every form of war as the confluence of activities that manifest themselves in brutal ways.

For us the whole value of life lies in work, in the intensity of work; and the problem of organization is a problem of the employment of forces that are autonomous and disciplined. But our nationalists are greater simplifiers than we are, or perhaps have more of the superman about them, for they guide industry in whatever direction they wish, and do as they please with it; they even ruin it with protectionism. They do not worry about problems of administration, because the state is there, and it can and should do as it pleases. Forget local autonomy! Truth lies in centralization! Oh, the sublime poetry of having a single man, or a handful of men, to direct the entire nation at home and abroad! And if there really are internal problems of administration, can't the army handle them? If anything, we should organize the whole bureaucracy along military lines. Thus, more or less, do our nationalist friends reason. So we feel entitled to pass on to other, more subtle reasoners.

The Catholic organization certainly constitutes a political reality, at least in the eyes of the people. It has tradition on its side, which it tries to reinforce by exploiting the prevailing sentiments: rigid conservatism and the ideal of love. All the efforts of the Catholic Church have been aimed at gaining control of the universal Christian reality so as to monopolize the private sphere and acquire proprietary rights over it. It is the same system that we have already seen in the case of the nationalists and socialists: they lay claim to a vast ideal domain the more easily to have their own credo swallowed along with it. In this case, the credo would be theocracy. Given the revealed truth of which the Church is the exclusive trustee, there can be no other logical consequence than absolutism. Giuliano puts the matter well: "Every religion, by its very nature and by the very nature of its mission, tends to dominate secular life with all its strength and impose its teaching on it: every religion necessarily becomes a church; and its ideal, no matter how it is camouflaged or modified by historical circumstances, is necessarily theocracy. Even in the eyes of Dante, secular government is a lesser species of the care of souls."[3]

But the very fact that to think does not equal being Catholic, that all men have given and do give a revelation of the truth, amounts to a conclusive demonstration of the aberration of that logic once we accept the act of thought not as an abstraction but as something to be recognized concretely in everyone, just as we recognize in everyone the right to life. Catholicism is a moment of the spirit, not the totality of spirit, for the simple reason that no formula can enfold the totality of spirit, no teaching can determine it—at least for those of us who are not scholastics but who include and justify even scholasticism within our own faith.

---

3. *L'Unità* (1912), no. 36. [Author's note.] Balbino Giuliano (1879–1958), who was associated with Gaetano Salvemini's journal *L'Unità*, translated into the terms of current political analysis the idealist philosophy of Giovanni Gentile. In his early years Gobetti felt a strong attraction to this kind of idealism, as this essay testifies.

And we have a place and a justification for another political reality: democracy, whose very basis is the affirmation of the legitimacy of every form of thought and the negation of all revelations of the truth, because truth is cemented in and created by every individual and is at the same time progress and universality transcending the possibility of each alone.

In this faith, which is simply one way of proclaiming the parity of rights and duties and equality of opportunity, lies the sound part of democracy, which is identical with idealism. But there has been a deeply corrupting injection of eighteenth-century sectarianism into this sound part. Democracy, denying all faiths, all revelations, because it overrides and comprehends all of them, turned into anticlericalism, confining itself to battling against one sect, and so shrank to the point that it took on the features of a sect as well. And in its Rousseauian humanitarianism it confused equality of opportunity with equality of result, opposing a universal, sterile, pacific love against the freedom to develop differently; it allowed healthy tolerance, which was its concrete faith, to degenerate into an indifference on the ideal plane that in practice opens the door to the most bilious intransigence and the most base accommodations.

Out of the affirmation of its own ideals, which was really only a point of departure from which to conduct its activity, it made a doctrine. Radical Masonic phrasemaking has pervaded and engrossed every democratic ideal. The very word has been discredited. Democracy has become a synonym for demagogy; for many it has become confused with socialism, a calm brand of nonrevolutionary socialism full of justice and goodwill—a new revelation of the truth, or nearly so.

V

Yet we do not cut ourselves off from this base, the only one we recognize as healthy and fruitful. We make it the point of departure for our activity too, the form in which to work out our

new passion; only an affirmation of intense spirituality, an idealism that knows no obstacles, can go together with our premise
of democratic faith. But our idealism cannot be limited to theoretical endeavor; it must pervade us and everything with a single
breath of intimate, intense life.

To be ourselves at every moment; to realize every possibility
of action for ourselves and for others at every instant, to feel the
exultant, inebriating throb of life, always, and not as a means
to this or that pale evanescent ideality, but in itself and for itself
as means and end of the very ideality that springs from its own
depths; to attain through this faith the capacity and the force to
renew ourselves at every instant, to view life as humanity evolv-
ing and overcoming itself, weakness endlessly conquering itself,
concreteness in which every humble act gains sanctity, consecration, because it is our act—this is the joy and the significance
of being, the divinity of time as progress in which the obstacle
dies! This vivifying potency of the spirit is suffocated in men by
degenerate habits, hard precipitates in which all ardor is lost,
bestial laziness that can make us fly from fatigue and struggle
but only to find a wearisome peace and quiet in which reechoes
only the sagging monotonous rhythm of the occupations that fill
the daily round.

We need to create a new conquest every day, and since to conquer means no more than to expand one's own limits, we need
to be able to understand ever more clearly the immanence of the
spirit, to see in every fact, in every consequence, a portion of our
own souls.

This profound passion—which does not turn to habit, nor
even to unthinking action, but remains intense normality and
advancing (but not intermittent or fragmentary) conquest—cannot be reconciled with the coldness and indifference that per-
vades and rigidifies life today: malady that wastes and kills,
meanness that snaps our sinews the minute they are stretched.
All of modern life is consumed by this fearful anemia. But we

rebel against it. Here we come back to the distinction between morality and immorality. No one who is indifferent can be moral. To be honest is to have ideas and believe in them and make them one's own center and purpose. Apathy is the negation of humanity, the abasement of self, the absence of ideality. For many it may be the affectation of superiority, the pretense of originality, but we would prefer the intolerant ones, ferocious partisans overflowing with ceaseless hatred, to the whole herd of the vacant. At least the intolerant take a stand and do not shy away from the contest. Wickedness is more human than cowardice.

In the immensity of the world of the spirit we cannot advocate abstention for any form. Every mode of activity is legitimate if it is human. It is honest to recognize a deficiency in one's own thought, but we should not contemn that which we lack. This is the stern sense of responsibility that gives us our faith.

And now is the moment of direct action through which we must give concrete form not just to our proposals but to our entire spirit. To point the way to this goal of concrete achievement ought not to be difficult now. We have to spread our conception of life and vitality and make it be felt; we have to throw into relief the difference that separates the dead schemas of the parties and the potency of the spirit. It is a labor for the long term, that aims to create better, more sincere, stronger men. To attain this better *humanity* we are obliged to devalue and destroy habits, schemas, indifference: for certain, a task requiring muscles and sinews that can bear the brunt.

But as we tear down a world of prejudices and shortcomings we are building a world of concrete reality with ardor and patience. Let us replace the last remains of revealed truth with the truth won day by day through the labor of all, and generic abstractions with patient, open-minded scrutiny of the little problems and the big ones as they arise. Only in this finding of solutions and making them systematic are we really doing politics.

TOWARD A NEW POLITICS

THE democratic idea, notwithstanding all the aberrations of its followers and its adversaries, still lies at the heart of modern society and animates all its healthier notions of the state as an organism with a history and a function.[4] And the political problems that afflict us today are still essentially problems of democracy—problems, that is, that have their origin in the errors and ideological deviations of a unilateral vision of democracy and that will find their solution in a more perfect fusion of the elements that constitute the liberal-democratic state.

The importance of the crisis of democracy cannot escape the notice of any person involved in politics who cares to analyze it. Ostrogorsky, to cite a serious attempt, saw what was amiss as early as 1903 and proposed remedies for the situation with a certain mental firmness notable in arguments as difficult as these.[5] The essential evil, for this writer, was to be found in the unnatural dualism between the state and the individual, which is bridged time and again in another function of practice: the party. But the recomposition can only be ephemeral and in any case ineffective, because it is not recognized constitutionally and because it comes about separately every time, through an empirical fusion of elements that allows one term to prevail over and dominate the other, albeit in an inconsistent and unforeseeable manner. Every element of judgment and practical rationality is distanced, and the struggle occurs between brute forces.

Effective reconciliation could have come about through more energetic and sincere participation by the people if the latter were viewed not as an abstract entity but as a factor in the effort to improve public life; if we had gotten rid of the parties

4. Original title: "Verso una realtà politica concreta"; from *Energie Nuove* ser. 2, no. 2 (20 May 1919), pp. 33–37. Translated from *Scritti politici*, pp. 105–13.

5. M. Ostrogorsky, *La démocratie et l'organisation des partis politiques* (Paris, 1903). [Editor's note by P. Spriano.]

(random groupings of individuals on the basis of interests that are by nature too diverse and sometimes dangerous), we could have had more logical groupings—leagues arising as the occasion presented itself, on the basis of concrete interests and issues and aiming at clearly defined results. Representative government would have come alive and been made to work, with the voters taking sides on the issues and choosing as their representatives (representation in both senses: the choice of the individuals and the delegation of power to them) deputies in favor of protectionism or against protectionism, favorable to centralization or favorable to decentralization, and so on.

In this manner, without giving up on the principle of representative government as hastily as many of our political dilettantes do, Ostrogorsky hoped to see it applied in a way based on competence. His leagues would in fact have increased the sense of responsibility among the electorate, constituting a solid cultural foundation, while the candidates would have gained greater effective competence through the selection of specialists with authority limited to the area of their specialization.

Ostrogorsky sensed the importance of one factor above all in politics: the technical input required for problem solving. Amid the spread of so many *theories* (which still pullulate today, most of them vanishing into thin air because they are never brought up against facts), it is no small merit to have discerned the complexity of the practical world. And we should not overlook his contribution.

But politics is essentially organization, something that Ostrogorsky has not taken sufficiently into account. It is the organization of individual interests, of ideal interests and conceptions, of problems arising from contingent circumstances. A league formed around one issue privileges a single element over all the others. The issue in question is certainly the most important, the most difficult, the one that demands priority. And it needs to be confronted and resolved first. But we cannot just forget about the synthesis that has to follow. There is a moral problem along with the technical one, and a political problem along with the administrative one. We do want to focus on the technical problem, in which all spiritual activity is naturally immanent, but we also believe it is opportune to draw attention to this immanent activity as well, for it animates and unifies all the special problems.

Only on this very complex basis will we be able to link the individual and the state while at the same time bolstering individual values, because only in this way can we make the party into a complete instrument of moral education and the harmonization of legitimate interests. Nor should we forget that the gap between state and individual—which is the weak point of the democracy we have now—will be overcome only by going back to local autonomy, in accord with the notion of Minghetti.[6]

The questions raised by Ostrogorsky, and all the other questions to which we have referred, are given tentative answers by the recent Democratic League for the Renewal of National Politics [Lega democratica per il rinnovamento dell politica nazionale], which is, as we will see, a genuine political organization —in other words, a party. But anyone who has read the long *declaration of principles* published by the league will perhaps think differently, and there is indeed a big difference between the usual proposals that can mean whatever you want them to mean and the solid, concrete language the league speaks in this *program*— if I can use that term.

But we believe that the league is a genuine party for just that reason, a political force capable of growing and rich in genuine content, since it represents ideal interests made concrete in the form of practical interests, an ideal conception realized through a whole series of practical measures. And it has the tradition, and the adherents, to give it vitality and assure its continuity.

When I speak of tradition I do not mean to assimilate the

6. Marco Minghetti, *Discorsi parlamentari*, vol. 1 (Rome, 1888), p. 92. [Author's note.]

league to the old liberal party or anything like it, for although
that would be easy enough, it would also be fairly pointless.
There is another fact that we shouldn't overlook, because if we
do, historical sense and logical inclusiveness will both suffer.
This organization that aims to *renew national politics* was not
simply born out of the mood created by the war or any other contingency of the sort that would limit its range; it will not wither
as soon as circumstances shift. The league has something more
concrete and vital to it. The process of renewal has been purely
internal; it began with a few men of good will who started by renewing themselves through moral and spiritual travail and an
effort lasting many years. Their energies flowed out to the world
in the pages of the two journals most dear to us, *La Voce* and
L'Unità.[7] That is where we have to look for all the concrete labor
that has brought about today's result. Ten years of hard effort
have given us the most firm, solid, effective work that the moral
conscience of Italy has produced since the turn of the century. All
of our finest spirits gathered around Salvemini and Prezzolini;
and in the work that was being brought to those two Florentine
journals and in all the other small individual acts through which
the word was preached, they felt there was really vibrating a new
and unique fervor, a unanimity of conviction and moral direction. All of them felt, unanimously, a need for renewal accompanied by a marvelous clarity of purpose that produced a general
harvest of small conscientious actions directed to the common
goal. And even beyond *La Voce* and *L'Unità*, other moral supporters and inspirers of the new fervor have also completed two
thirds of the work for clarification and national renewal; they
have already wrought two thirds of the new Italian soul.

The league cannot forget this heritage of work, and if it is able
to carry it on and make it a real factor in events as they happen,

7. *La Voce* was a Florentine journal founded in 1908 by Giuseppe Prezzolini and Giovanni Papini. *L'Unità* was a Florentine weekly founded in 1911
by Gaetano Salvemini (see Chapter 1, note 37).

in everyday life, we will certainly have a more intense moral conscience in our nation.

But some people say that they are all generals and ask where the foot soldiers are. So our young people will have to become foot soldiers—those who desire to live, who have fought and who are today tortured by uncertainty, who are awakening only now to the life of the spirit.

The league has given concrete form to its aspirations and convictions, and synthesized the experience of a decade, into a perfect, real order in its *declaration of principles,* in which it takes a stand vis-à-vis the current situation and current aspirations and passes on to the minute examination of the hardest problems in order to sketch a course of action that will lead to solutions.

The concrete breadth of the declaration has avoided at the outset the two common errors that we have noted previously in discussing parties. There is no attempt to lay down general principles and then deduce practical proposals; and there is not the anemia and aridity that suffuse the usual proposals, because here, along with the proposal, mention is made of the hard work that the proposal entails and of the possibility that the proposal may undergo further modification. What we have here is not an abstraction or vague symbol but living history.

There is an overall conception, of course, but it does not in the least constitute a first moment of the spirit, from which the rest is made to flow deductively. The overall conception can be considered only independently when seen in retrospect, and it can be defined as a soundly democratic one, identifiable as idealistic and liberal for the purpose of clarity and in order to distinguish it from a certain kind of radicalism and Masonic reformism.

The democratic idea, in the current state of things, arises out of the dialectic of history itself, and everyone acquires it almost naturally, for it corresponds to the progress made by the spirit in every field. The nation is the legacy of history that democracy takes as its point of departure, not in order to erect imperialistic myths on it but in order to make it the basis of the democratic state. The latter is transformed from abstract entity to life and truth in every individual and is understood rather as the coordination of individual activities.

Now, *coordination* implies that there are free forces to be coordinated; it implies responsibility and the self-aware activity of citizens whose participation through the representative system and through local autonomies invests public life with all of the necessary concreteness. This is where the liberal state finds its justification (and liberal in this context coincides with democratic); it refuses the revealed truth of the theocratic state and views truth as the gradual acquisition of every citizen, as truth that the state has the duty to legitimate, recognize, and protect in every citizen. The state breaks away from the Church completely and addresses openly the problem of its own relationship with the individual.

The notion sketched here makes no claim to novelty; indeed, it is so widespread and prevalent that it would be both difficult in practical terms and pointless to try to assign authorship. That is usually the case with political phenomena, where so-called discoveries turn out for the most part to be aberrations and exaggerations, aesthetic in nature, since the spirit advances through gradual development, not through unexpected revelations.

Hence the practical, concrete problem is that of finding the best form of actualization within the world of contingency, or, in other words, following on from what we have said, that of finding out what the most efficient methods are to further the development of the spirit and the conquest of responsibility on the part of individuals.

To this task the work of the league is seriously and wholly dedicated, because what is at stake is the terrible necessity of construction in face of the simplicities of the revolutionaries and the reactionaries. If the *theory* is in people's hearts, then the pressing need is evidently to foster its actualization, because that has failed up till now, precisely because of a failure to de-

scend sufficiently into the world of contingency and because of
a preference for constructing concepts that have lost all concreteness in their pursuit of universality. Only with this purpose
in mind, and these convictions, can effective, Mazzinian work
of moral education and clarification be accomplished. And this
moral education will bear fruit, this work will not fail, even
should the short-term political achievements be reversed.

The affirmation of the liberty and responsibility of the citizen
is made concrete in the *declaration of principles* through a careful
analysis of, and a systematic opposition to, the privileges that in
the present state of things corrupt and hinder the development
of the powers of individuals and those of the nation. The bank-
ing and industrial trusts that are gradually gaining a monopoly
over national production are privileges, and obstacles, that have
to be broken up and abolished. So are the imperialistic conceptions that substitute slow reciprocal attrition, through forms of
conflict that are inferior by their nature and actually tend to turn
into obsessions, for the gradual development of states. So are the
different kinds of tariff protection, which harm the whole nation
for the profit of a few lucky insiders. The critical thrust of the
document is also directed strongly against those socialist conceptions that are blind to the fact that their own messianic expectation of the dictatorship of the proletariat is preparing an
order of things in which organized minorities of workers will
benefit at the expense of the rural proletariat.

The document emphasizes very strongly the importance of
the problem of the schools and of agricultural reconstruction in
the south, while the ills of the bureaucratic and parliamentary
order are denounced minutely and courageously.

All of this critical work lays the ground for, and illustrates, the
concrete reconstruction that emerges as the nucleus of the declaration. Two principal reforms are envisaged: that of the representative regime and that of the public service. With regard
to the first, proportional representation would permit minori-

ties to take part, it would base the elections on legitimate interests expressed through professional organizations and genuine
differences of conviction, it would bring about the gradual self-
education of the people, and it would reduce the role of personal
animosities in the taking of decisions affecting the collectivity,
while naturally leaving an open field for individuals to prove
their worth.

As for the public service, local autonomy will check excessive interference from the state and thus eliminate the abuse of
power by the higher bureaucracy; and this should make it possible to restructure the functions of the public service in a way
more rational, closer to the needs of individuals, and more technically refined.

Along with these two cornerstones, which provide wonder-
fully well for a system of individual participation in the life of
the state, the *declaration* of the league clearly envisages, and cau-
tiously alludes to, the major problem of trade union organization, on which the future of the working classes and the advancement of labor itself entirely depend. We will in future examine
more closely these problems and the importance of the solutions
indicated in the *declaration of principles*.

But where will we find forces capable of realizing this program right now? Who has an interest in doing so? The league
quite rightly conceives of the state as an organization of citizens in which no estate can take precedence, and of liberty as a
general condition, not a route to domination for select groups.
But the overall state of our culture, the spirit of sacrifice in our
population, are not sufficiently elevated for us to be able to count
on them too much: who will commit to support a program that
offers no one the chance to gain privilege and power over others?
The difficulty would be insuperable if the league had confined
itself to announcing an abstract ideal of celestial justice. But that
is not the case. Liberty, as conceived by the league, is an arduous
step-by-step conquest, not a gift definitively bestowed but a con-

tinuing effort on the part of every individual. The groups of individuals who today are struggling to win independence for themselves, who are frustrated and disgusted by entrenched privilege and feel the need to rebel against the chains of the past and prove their own capacities, are the ones who will join the league and find that they themselves and their own interests are represented in it. In Italy now there are millions of peasants who are just starting to feel like human beings and citizens and who will no longer stand by while their individual rights are trampled. The life of the nation depends on them, provided they organize themselves; for example, the national problem of the south can be solved only by taking account of their needs. The Democratic League for the Renewal of National Politics will have to dedicate its leading members to the defense of their interests.

To bring these new forces into public life will require an immense effort. It will require intense propaganda, conducted with the ardor and firmness of those who know they are working to create the soul of a people. The league has the best men of the nation on its side as active members or sympathizers. But they will not suffice. It needs to reach out to youth, youth, youth, for that is the only way to spread knowledge of, and thus valorize, the intellectual work already done.

The road to renewal is this road that the new organization has chosen. The hour of decision is here; the chance cannot be missed.

Today—or never again.

THE BOURGEOISIE

THERE are a number of hasty and imprecise concepts that are used every day but that are slanted for demagogic reasons to mean quite contradictory things, and no one has any interest in clarifying them, nor any desire to do so; thus they remain sources *of uncertainty, confusion, and political superficiality.*[8] *We shall attempt, in a series of articles, to study a few of these concepts, to fix their meaning, and to delimit their historical and political connotations.*

There has very recently been an attempt, by a legal philosopher no less, employing all the interpretive apparatus of idealism, to define the bourgeoisie. But if we examine the result, it would seem that even this work, by Giuseppe Maggiore,[9] lacks scientific validity and makes do with commonplaces, that, in a word, it ignores the theoretical and historical dimensions of the problem.

The bourgeoisie exists as a reality in the political dialectic, one conceptualized increasingly clearly in terms of the consciousness of the ruling classes and the negation of the proletariat. And since the reality in question is a dynamic one, the concept of it that is being elaborated cannot be adequately expressed in an identically intellectualistic formula but has the value merely of an outline, an approximation that depends upon history for its ideal completion. In examining the concept of the bourgeoisie, we have to recognize, as a postulate of fact and a boundary of theory, the existence of a practical reality that is being created anew every day by individuals, not reducible to schemas and susceptible only of a dialectical interpretation, in which definitions appear rather as myths (to be handled with great care) than as criteria of realistic history.

Maggiore, like a good follower of Gentile, has tried to make himself fully alert to this intrinsic theoretical limit. Social classes, the bread and butter of the sociologist, are for him abstract schematizations that the spirit shapes to classify its own infinite ideal and practical needs and mark their courses. There

8. Original title: "Definizioni: La borghesia"; from *La Rivoluzione Liberale* 1, no. 4 (5 March 1922), p. 13. Translated from *Scritti politici*, pp. 261–66.
9. Giuseppe Maggiore, *Che è la borghesia* (Città di Castello: Il Solco, 1921). [Author's note.]

does not exist a closed and static social class with precise and immutable characteristics: a social class exists inasmuch as the consciousness of individuals posits it and posits at the same time the will to overcome it, the will to liberation. The concept of *class* is inseparable from the concepts of *struggle, movement, development*.

Let us accept this explanation; in the concrete reality of the spiritual act, schemas lose their validity: classes become mere phantasms. The philosopher's task is not to examine them in their empirical consistency but in the eternal process from which they eternally emerge. Nonetheless, the philosopher cannot contest the validity of an investigation that is novel in respect to his own, one that attempts to individuate those schemas in their contingent existence In the spirit, everything is new, everything is in movement; only spirituality itself remains the same, and its dialectical law. But the historian, once he has understood the category that animates the world and penetrated its process, does not halt there, does not construct schemas, but studies the working vitality of all systems. The philosopher attempts to realize the absolute in his system; the historian refuses to recognize the absolute in any system, because he examines each system in relation to a special contingent moment.

Maggiore understands the identity of history and philosophy as a mystical reduction of history to philosophy, of the process to the methodology. His speculation has reached its end in an impotent unity: in idealism unity is a priori (Kant did not write for nothing), but to find it again in the outcome, one must confront and accept dialectically the empirical moment with its contradictions and diversity.

What is the bourgeoisie? Maggiore would answer: A fact of the spirit. In whom ought we to study it? Not in the bourgeois, who have little ideal *awareness* of themselves, but in the proletariat, who have a good *acquaintance* with the bourgeois since they are engaged in a combat with them. This methodological process is a piece of vulgar oversimplification. All it would yield at the end would be a purely abstract concept of the bourgeoisie, because rather than study it in its vitality, one would be accepting the static idea that others have fashioned about it for polemical reasons and whose only value is that of practical myth. A scientist should explain the myth, not accept it. Maggiore instead makes a science of myths. But all that remains of any idea, if we accept the valuation of it provided by its adversaries, is an empty, antiquated schema, which those on the other side have quite naturally shaped in such a way that they can swiftly defeat it. But philistinism and sectarianism have never constituted science.

The bourgeois thus becomes, for Maggiore, a man who has *carved out a place for himself*, a man of the ruling class, a man satisfied with himself. And in substance a bourgeoisie does not exist, but rather the spirit that becomes bourgeois; not a class but a circulation of classes eternally threatened with stasis, the negation of progress, the sterile affirmation of the past. So the bourgeoisie is seen as the moment of inertia and passive acceptance toward which all elites are moving.

Maggiore's definition does not even take the bourgeoisie into consideration, but adapts itself (barely) to the moment at which the bourgeoisie collapses. His formula, *the specter of naturalism*, is an inconclusive philosophical schematization that ignores the real conditions of *today*, in which this specter appears to be bringing about a *predetermined* dissolution. In any case, it is pointless to study its dissolution before one has understood the process of its genesis and its significance.

The whole modern world born of the French Revolution may be called bourgeois in the generic sense, although the word still requires clarification to get rid of misunderstandings and equivocation. What are the differentiating characteristics of the modern world? Its economy is based on the free market, and its politics on liberalism; its philosophical outlook is immanentist and critical, its morality is activist and realistic, its logic is dialectical. Through a process of corruption the free market turns into state socialism, while liberalism turns into demagogic democracy or the nationalism of deal-makers; the critical stance wilts into positivism and sensationism, and the dialectic dissipates its force in eristics and rhetoric. These two moments in the development of one single world can both, and with equal legitimacy, be called bourgeois. That is a precious conclusion, for it means that none of the aforementioned characteristics can be made the exclusive criterion for the definition of the bourgeoisie: we have to return to a more ample concept. The revolutionary principle and the conservative principle are both bourgeois, but each denotes a different phase, a different mode of judging one and the same process, which is characterized by the definition given above.

If the modern world is bourgeois, the ruling class is correctly called bourgeois, not because it is set over against the people but because it is directly or indirectly an offshoot of the people and represents their shortcomings too. Whatever the opposition parties may think, the ruling class is, in every instant of time, the whole people in its creative and political capacity and hence is, with full entitlement, the state. The opposition parties for their part quite rightly resort to polemics and denigration in their holy desire to create a new governing minority. If the task of working out a concept of the bourgeoisie is left to the devices of proletarian writers, it is natural that the resulting concept should be essentially negative, that within the bourgeoisie should be discovered, and theoretically elaborated, all the errors and weaknesses that the modern world encompasses and that belong to the proletariat too—so much so that in the proletariat they give birth to the need for a new society. For the same polemical reason the proletarian analysis of the bourgeoisie was limited to the economic dimension, the one most apt to provoke political demands.

The sense of this bourgeois economy lies in the notion of private property and in the pressure for the citizen to take on the consciousness of a producer and a seller. That consciousness forms in the technician and the worker just as much as it does in the capitalist, so they should all be described as bourgeois in the same way, whatever the logic of the politically engaged may dictate. In fact the struggle of the workers, even at its most revolutionary, is fought on bourgeois terrain and always leads sooner or later to a demand for higher salaries. Further, if we want to call bourgeois those who have the deepest involvement in this society, then the Marxist idea of *ownership of the means of production* can be used to differentiate, not just to describe. Certainly in the modern world it was the owners of industry who came to think of themselves as producers before the workers did. And the revolutionary potential of the workers lies in their capacity to become more vigorously bourgeois (as producers) now that many industrialists no longer know how to fulfill their function as investors and entrepreneurs, because the bourgeois system, with its challenge to Catholicism on the ideal plane and its proven impact on industrial production, is not headed for decline; on the contrary, it awaits fuller realization at the hands of a new elite (even if the new elite should prove to be the dictatorship of the proletariat). This is the irony of history that awaits those who declaimed against the bourgeoisie and announced that they were ready to bury it.

Finally we have achieved some clarity of thought. Classes have value as myths, indefinable forces that are ever renewing themselves and contending for power. The modern political contest is between the conservatives and the progressives, and the task of the historian is to pinpoint the thought of these two contending elements.

Why this clarity was not attained by others before now still has to be explained. It is because these matters were made the objects of dilettantism or polemic, not studied scientifically. The proletariat, because it could form itself only out of the desire to create a better world, has, in a most formidable paradox, theoretically denied its real function in the society of today: in an effort all the more gigantic because it is apparently impotent (given the humble spiritual condition of its members), the proletariat has consented to identify present civilization with the opposing class and has assumed the responsibility of creating a new civilization.

What exactly will be *new* in this civilization is a question that history will answer. Meanwhile, the illusory plans and the sociological claims of socialism and communism will achieve concreteness to the extent that they confront the specific problem of the legacy of bourgeois society. The Marxist myth, with all its temerity, ought to have made the proletarians ready for this task. Because even amid a messianic struggle of two ideal principles, the one a living historical reality, the other in the process of coming to life, history does not tolerate sudden discontinuities, but makes use of myth, faith, and illusion to renew its own eternity.

A TEACHER OF LIBERALISM

THE thought of Luigi Einaudi[10] is taking shape during dark years for Italy, years of crisis that have drained away our creative capacities and to which the people have apparently reacted for the most part by explicitly renouncing their role in Europe.[11] The political contest has necessarily been reduced to the schema of conservatives versus progressives, and liberals faithful to the tradition of autonomy, but with no room for positive action, have to limit themselves to postulating the recognition of freedom as the precondition and necessary premise. On that basis liberal-

10. Luigi Einaudi (1874–1961), who taught economics at the University of Turin, was one of the most prominent defenders of laissez-faire in Gobetti's time. A harsh critic of "parliamentarianism" and protectionism, he was among the founders of European federalism. After World War II, he became a member of the Constituent Assembly and was the first president of the Italian republic (1948–55).

11. Original title: "Il liberalismo di L. Einaudi"; from *La Rivoluzione Liberale* 1, no. 10 (23 April 1922), pp. 37–38. Translated from *Scritti politici*, pp. 322–36.

ism meets, and overlaps with, radical and socialist thought (indeed, Einaudi is a contributor to *Critica sociale*).[12]

But this practical arrangement does not imply any confusion on the ideal plane, for anyone acquainted with the origins of the current crisis. It was in 1900 in fact that Einaudi published *A Merchant Prince: A Study of Italian Colonial Expansion* [*Un principe mercante: Studio sull'espansione coloniale italiana*], the first document of his practical and economic activity, a book that gave solid proof of superior political culture. In it can be found assertions that synthesize all the thought of his later years and out of which it is possible to construct an organic system of politics.

"It is important for our country that the possessors of capital do not just settle back and enjoy the 4 percent return they can get with long-term government bonds or ground rents; they have to take more risk, in enterprises beneficial for themselves and the whole nation. For the good of the country, the ruling class ought to steer their offspring to seek their fortune in the fields of industry and commerce, instead of continuing to steer them toward professional and bureaucratic careers that are already clogged with frustrated aspirants." Einaudi's characteristic style is already there, his way of viewing economic laws with ethical rigor and recognizing that political life has formative value, and likewise the broad coherence of his proposals and his activities, the identity between his thought as a scientist and his thought as an individual.

As soon as you get to know him, the man inspires firm trust. He lacks the decorative qualities and false postures—emphatic or conciliatory—that conventional society imposes on you if you let it. He practices, without theorizing, a morality of antique austerity and elementary simplicity. His ethical vision arises from an almost primitive process and is structured around the affir-

12. *La critica sociale*, the magazine of the Italian Socialist Party, was founded by Filippo Turati in 1891.

mation of the values of the family, which he sees as the anchor of men of character and tireless exertion; and it extends to the *patria* [homeland], the organ of spiritual values and economic activity. More than a theory, Einaudi has a feeling for the *patria;* he sees it as individuals engaged in living: through tradition it confirms in his eyes the continuity of our efforts, the permanent impress left by individual personalities, the vital coherence of the affections. The vision is patriarchal and restricted but fruitful indeed, as long as it remains within the limits of sentimental life.

Hence, with no academic narrowness, his love for devotion to work leads to his limpid vision of the roles of the scientist and the man of action not as distinct schemas but as classical ideals of human vitality. He demands from both the frank simplicity and serene readiness for sacrifice that alone can undergird social responsibility. The devotion with which he carries out his mission as teacher and his assiduous scientific preoccupation with the practical interests and the functioning of the state are concrete examples.

His experience as an educator has led him to a view of the problem of education that fits in with his overall convictions. Einaudi believes in schools as places where ideas may be freely exchanged, promoting the growth of knowledge. That is the real educational value of the schools, their real *utility,* corresponding to an intrinsic necessity. The utilitarian approach to schooling is not schooling at all, and a very bad bargain in economic terms. There is thus an identity of morality and economy that Einaudi goes on to explore more deeply. Professions are not to be studied in the abstract but to be learned in practice; knowledge has to have the value of inner experience, tempering capacity and character; the premises of empiricism, rightly understood, lead to idealistic consequences. Schooling creates liberal values in practice too. It is an ethical necessity that the state not assume the task of organizing the schools; action by the collectivity should not take the place of the initiative of individuals. The schools, as schools of ethics, are an organ of the state, but their ethicality does not spring from the mere fact of their existence: it is the fruit of the creative effort with which individuals will their existence, since every result is worth only the firmness and seriousness that someone puts into its attainment. Hence Einaudi believes in state schools financed directly from the economic contributions of those who use them.[13]

History and Laissez-Faire

As he sees the schools, so he sees the state: as a dialectical outcome of individual wills operating freely. The complexity of this social function sometimes eludes his theory, however, and is grasped in a limited fashion according to partial empirical factors. The reasons for the inadequacy of his overall vision have to be sought in the limitations of his own cultural formation.

Einaudi confesses that in his youth he was "a passionate, almost monomaniacal, reader of English books."[14] A limit was set to this zeal only by the love of practicality, which even in *A Merchant Prince* modifies from direct experience the abstract formulas he had learned. In fact, Einaudi has the ability easily to overcome abstract schematizations because the fecund center of his thought consists of an inner skepticism concerning all formulas (even his own) and an absolute faith in the inexhaustible activity of men. Facts override ideas; in praxis lies the truth. This notion, the natural outcome of the experience of English industrialization, is not simply taken for granted, in the manner of the pragmatists, but neither is it raised to become a canon of philosophical interpretation; rather, it is a truth attached to the individual who has thought it, within the limits of the experience that gave rise to it. A reaction to the claims of the intellectualizers

13. L. Einaudi, *Gli ideali di un economista* (Florence: La Voce, 1921). [Author's note.]

14. Einaudi, *Gli ideali di un economista*, p. 153. [Author's note.]

in the world of economics, it is the necessary premise to a free examination of social phenomena. There is a wealth of interest in Einaudi's attempts to develop this notion in his historical research. His studies on the formation of the British empire are, so to speak, the ideal prolongation of a declaration of faith.

In frank awareness of immanent ineluctable justice, the vitality of England can be thought through only in relation to the part it necessarily plays in international life. Einaudi, as educator, considers the ideal content of the myth of England in relation to the needs of the Italians. Against the literary and academic culture of Italy, ingenuously disdainful of economic values in the name of who knows what disinterested functions of the spirit, he insists on the conceptual grandeur of English utilitarianism, which, assuming for all other peoples the function of saving and investment, with an effort that amounted to sacrifice and heroism, has garnered riches by virtue of endless entrepreneurialism and devotion to work.

And against the mechanical conceptions of our industrialists, *protectionists* because of their *provincialism,* he sets the historical evidence that proves that material fortune, the natural endowment of raw materials, means nothing. "No industry is really indispensable to the life of a country. A society has to keep up with the times and change continually, with the result that an industry that is 'indispensable' in one period can slide without detriment to an entirely secondary level of importance, and perhaps disappear altogether, making way for other 'indispensable' industries."[15] In other words, to translate these assertions into theoretically valid terms, practice creates the ideals and purposes it needs, and replaces and destroys them; the seriousness of the man of action lies in the candid recognition of the ideal dimension that is intrinsic to all facts.

Out of this psychology the English made their empire. They overthrew all the colonial empires that had been built on the

15. Einaudi, *Gli ideali di un economista,* p. 81. [Author's note.]

basis of domination, egoism, and intolerance (the empires of Portugal, Spain, France, and Holland). The first English empire, arising out of the ideal of a worldwide state of nations linked by political and economic ties in a protectionist system, fell. But Cobden and Bright triumphed over Chamberlain. The British empire was born—through a curious irony, since history is not made with words and speeches, but with acts and deeds[16]— under the sign of a policy opposed to imperialism and conquest. The unity of the British empire is valid and effective even today to the extent that the various colonies have remained free and masters of themselves; they have been able to find their own road and their own legitimate historical function amid the dialectic of the forces of modernity through their own autonomous initiative.

The English empire *was born without a theory*,[17] *by chance,* a work of adventure and initiative tirelessly pursued over many generations, creating a higher organism of life not with the force of arms and laws but with the feeling of an *imperial unity.* And here, even in the uncertain language of one extrapolating from economic observations, we find ourselves in the presence of deep philosophical thought. Empiricism, by its very capacity to subsist and continue, is superior to itself: over and above the events of each day, Einaudi discovers the grand design of history. Passionately desiring to discover the inner results of actions, the social psychology beneath the formulations, Einaudi teaches a lesson of profound immanentism. In activity, in the dynamic individual, in spontaneity, there already exists an initial idea, a theory: Einaudi fixes his scrutiny on the relation between the initiative and the result with a solemn ethical consciousness, and in his admiration there is something almost religious.

History eternally teaches the fruitfulness of sacrifice, celebrates the triumph of the spirit, makes use of every type of ego-

16. Einaudi, *Gli ideali di un economista*, p. 85. [Author's note.]
17. Einaudi, *Gli ideali di un economista*, p. 105. [Author's note.]

ism, to affirm the wholeness of society. The prescription of English imperialism rises above the provisional policies decided in a cabinet meeting and acquires validity through its antiutilitarian significance. "The mother country owes everything to the colonies; the colonies must not be obliged to give anything to the mother country." Though this prescription may appear idealistic to nationalists, who make a fetish of egoism, whose egoism is sacred, it is in truth the only *practice* able to define an essentially national course of action. Peoples are great inasmuch as they have great responsibilities, inasmuch as they live and work for those who do not work, suffer for those who are content with peace and mediocrity, spend their force to impress a new direction on events, to enrich society with their efforts.

Einaudi wants, realistically, these ideals to guide our own policies as a great nation, our colonial policies. The moral values of religiosity, autonomy, and dignity do not hold sway only in the world of the individual. Einaudi is able to apprehend them, with exquisite tact, in their social and national significance; he knows that great peoples respect them even in savages.

Socialism and Initiative

Einaudi's laissez-faire convictions, which he modestly prefers to limit to a descriptive or autobiographical account of psychological experience, rather than rigidify them into a theory, are in logical consequence frankly antisocialist and antidemagogic. He detests the rhetorical abuse that a host of scribblers, deficient in intelligent economic or technical experience, make of ready-made phrases, of the magic words "liberty," "progress," "democracy." He likewise detests their refusal to search for any sense beneath those ready-made phrases and their opposition to any attempt to explain or justify them.

Einaudi critically examines state socialism and collectivism (especially in his article "Il governo delle cose" ["The Government of Things"]) with perfect irony and the precise and pene-

trating style of a great writer; indeed, his hatred for empty decla-
mation makes him go too far in one-sided rejection. Marx, for
Einaudi, is never anything more than an example of the bad re-
searcher, the sloppy collector of data who generalizes without
sufficient analytical grounds, the economist who through naïveté or bad faith clings to the simplistic demagogic notion of *surplus value*. And a political movement inspired by such a bad scientist arouses a circumspect distrust in Einaudi. Nor from the
economic point of view can we gainsay him; indeed, if his anti-
Marxism is intended to teach a few solid lessons in economic science to the presumptuous apostles of new pseudotheories who
in the name of Marx abandon Smith, Ricardo, industrial progress, and common sense, then we willingly side with him. But
perhaps he goes astray by seconding the prejudices of Marx's
own unreliable followers and thereby regarding Marx as an
economist when he was in fact a philosopher, historian, prophet,
political agitator—but not an economist. Economics deals exclusively with reality and the past; it is the art of government—
and is always ignored at the start by great movements that arise
in the name of an overriding sense of urgency. The oversimpli-
fications of Marx the economist favor the greatness of Marx the
constructor of myths. And even if we do condemn the myth, we
have to understand and admire his concrete endeavor to show
the way to its realization by making it a problem of will and
force. Would Einaudi not agree that, if we look closely, an ideal
likeness (the one that unites all the great undertakings of history)
can be found between the effort leading, in full liberty and independence, to the creation of the British empire and the free initiative from which the workers' movement arises in correspondence with the real needs and the real aspirations of modern
civilization, apart from its generic dogmatic postulates? Is Marxism not also, like English liberalism, a formal faith, an interpretation of the world, a method that cogently opposes all forms of
utopian communism precisely because it denies their moralistic
formulas? The workers' movement is also a notable example of

laissez-faire; it is also born without a theory. And it is our belief that the failure to recognize this fact (not so much in daily experience as in his historical interpretation of the modern world) is the basic fault of the political vision of Luigi Einaudi, who often stops at offering useful technical advice when the problem at hand was one of political strength and popular experience. No doubt his opposition has been more effectively useful to the proletariat than a lot of orthodox chatter; indeed, I think that precisely because of his stimulating polemics the problems of investment and skilled labor (problems the old socialist demagogues looked down on) have become a preoccupation and a topic of research for the communists of Turin. But perhaps a little more open sympathy on his part would have made matters clearer and helped them to understand.

Having identified the workers' movement with its static collectivist proposals, Einaudi discussed it as though it were a form of state socialism. He might have been warranted to do so by an assessment of some of the empirical results of socialist action, but he unwarrantably disregards the autonomous, antibureaucratic spirit that is guiding the reawakening of the workers.

Certainly the ideals of state socialism can quite reasonably be defined as the *ideals of incapacity.* Einaudi dislikes above all the way this doctrine discourages moral education: its reformist quietist utilitarianism, its refusal of the spirit of responsibility and of any real differentiation and specialization among the productive energies. At a lower stage of social life, and granting the incapacity of individuals to think for themselves, a way of governing that—as if to fashion a model—forced the masses to do the work of social assistance, organization, and solidarity might have provisional value. But if the hard alternative is posed —England or Germany, liberty or organization—then Einaudi opts for the first horn of the dilemma. Undeniably we see here a residue of the abstraction of the "passionate, almost monomaniacal reader of English books," since an alternative posed in such sharp terms becomes more a question about words than a question about society. Liberty and organization are correlative terms that do not cancel one another out but fuse in a higher synthesis, and they cannot be hypostasized or practically identified with two different nations where the same word has a different history and where the relations between two identical names are profoundly different. The "liberty" of the English is not a synonym of the "liberty" of the Germans, in fact it is more a synonym of "organization," and vice versa.

Einaudi's own explanation for his preference follows shortly thereafter and is theoretical in nature. "Historical experience proves that it is impossible to govern according to 'reason'; and it is an incontrovertible fact that human sentiments, passions, and even prejudices are a force of great power, which the science and the art of government always have to deal with."[18]

His *laissez-faire* lies substantially here, in this recognition of praxis. It is a faith, not a doctrine, and hence intolerant but not dogmatic. From his point of view, free-market economics, though it sometimes remains abstract and limited, tends to pass over into a higher spiritual laissez-faire. "A condition of free exchange arrived at after experiencing the errors of protectionism is greatly preferable to free exchange imposed on barbarian nations by civilization." The intimate spiritual nature of Einaudi's laissez-faire ideas succeeds finally in expressing itself in precise and adequate theoretical terms, overcoming the barriers of his antiphilosophical prejudice, in his lucid, stirring profession of faith: *toward the ideal city.* Here we have the myth of order, authority, discipline, and dogma set against the myth of struggle, disorder, the disunion of spirits. There are even flashes of Hegelianism, independent of Hegel and aware of their own importance, that are very surprising in such an empiricist: "The idea is born of opposition. If no one tells you that you are wrong, you no longer know that you possess the truth. . . . On the day of victory for the unique ideal of life, the struggle would begin

18. Einaudi, *Gli ideali di un economista*, p. 212. [Author's note.]

again, because it is absurd for men to content themselves with
nothing. . . . History teaches the decline of every state that ever
tried to impose a single pattern of life." And if order (dogma)
could be the kingdom of felicity, Einaudi sees the negation of it
in the European war, its incompatibility with the concrete responsibility of mankind. So, he remarks, "millions of men died
to remove the bitter cup of happiness and spiritual unity from
Europe." You could find no more explicit and solidly grounded
critique of all the forms of dogmatism—from the Catholic to the
democratic.

The State

We may now examine the theory of the state to which the
thought of Einaudi leads. The state as conceived by the moral-
ists is denied in the name of a more profound national ethicality.
From Treitschke he accepts the exigency of the state as force and
accurately adds the gloss "not physical force as an end in itself,
but force used to protect and promote the highest human good."
He then criticizes the absence in Treitschke of a positive ethical
ideal, attributing that to a lack of the philosophical spirit. Here
Einaudi's critique is incongruent, and the lack of philosophical spirit he reproves is in fact the negation, quite conscious on
Treitschke's part, of any philosophy of being, of any nondialec-
tical philosophy. The ethical stance of Treitschke is exactly the
same as the one adopted elsewhere by Einaudi, a formal ethics,
an ethics of activity (Kant versus Christian morality).

The state for Einaudi is moral inasmuch as it coincides with
the moral activity of the citizens and repudiates any function distinct from that of individuals, any abstract task of elevation and
enlightenment. He reveals the partisan motives and sets forth
clearly the empirical consequences of the latter theory of the
state. For him the state is conceived as "the entity that guarantees the rule of law over men, that is, the rule of a purely formal,
external norm under the protection of which men are free to

develop their own qualities, however diverse, and can contest among themselves for the supremacy of their ideals, however diverse."[19] "We want unity, but it has to be won by living and suffering, raising us above materiality and brute pleasure." When he wants to be even more explicit, unity is myth and ideal, "the rule of law as a precondition for the anarchy of individual spirits." Force resides in extrinsic life, whereas unity is limited to the forms and conditions of life. Given this dialectical and relativistic vision, the criterion of every test is in the inner struggle: the democratic state can no longer be taken in the sense of government by numerical weight, by majority vote; instead, Einaudi takes it to be the result of a perennial conflict in which the majority subsists as a function of a minority. That is the meaning of his polemic against every kind of obstacle to free discussion, which leads him to accept even the filibuster (not from empty libertarianism).

Anglophilia and Piedmontese Tradition

Having explained and expounded organically the living part of Luigi Einaudi's Anglophilia, we still have to make some observations about its limitations and draw attention to its weak points and contradictions; otherwise, our vision of the man will be incomplete.

The contradictions emerge whenever the psychological ideal becomes a conclusive, explicit political ideal. Anglophilia, the notion that the English way of life should be culturally accepted and assimilated, is fundamentally wrong for the backward Italian economy, where it turns into a transcendent ideal, an inappropriate guide to action inasmuch as the forces that make it a living reality in its place of origin do not exist among us. The aristocracy that governs England, bourgeois and technologically advanced, has barely begun to develop here, and when Einaudi ad-

19. Einaudi, *Gli ideali di un economista*, p. 345. [Author's note.]

dresses himself to this nascent chrysalis exclusively, paying no attention to the other forces of modernity, his words are tragically destined, in the general Italian situation, to turn into *sermons* with no effect. Sometimes we hear the echo of Ferrara.[20]

Indeed, Einaudi's position is historically close to that of Ferrara and Cavour. The problem Ferrara set himself, to re-create within the little state of Piedmont the English science of modernity, was an integral part of the progress of our science and our industry. Einaudi's long and loving study of Piedmontese economic life and his firm understanding of what Cavour empirically wrought both aim to give to the problem, theoretically stated, a practical concreteness adequate to our tradition. Let me try to put this point in starker terms. Within Einaudi the historian battles with the economist, the practical man with the scientist—in sum, one kind of laissez-faire with another: Cavour with Ferrara. Einaudi would overcome the internal conflict if he were able to raise his judgment of the personality of Cavour above the level of the intentions and prejudices of the man himself and succeed in understanding all of his actual accomplishments on a new basis. As long as he evaluates Cavour through the eyes of Ferrara, several of the inner drives of the Italian Risorgimento will inevitably escape him, and his traditionalism, his historical politics that aims to advance on the basis of "concrete and precise national requirements," will be suffocated by his abstract Anglophilia. There was in the humble reality of nineteenth-century Piedmont (from which Italy was born) something more than just a strain of English culture.

When Einaudi turns to large international problems, he, by adopting an English perspective, sometimes forgets for a while the most cherished aspects of Piedmontese tradition, including

20. Francesco Ferrara (1810–1900) was the first prominent economist to support the theory of the free market and was the leader of the libertarian polemic against economic revisionism during the 1870s. His works had a great impact in the first generation of Italian liberals, in particular Camillo Cavour, the architect of Italian unity.

the most vigorous one of all: the idea of a strong monarchy, as the House of Savoy was in the seventeenth and eighteenth centuries. These errors arise out of the notion he has fashioned for himself concerning the function of England in the modern world. Einaudi is disposed to see the imperial nation as the peaceful unifier of peoples, the herald of the fellowship of nations. But England has a function only as long as it performs it anew; England is a product of history, and its worth will be estimated by future historians in relation to its will and to unforeseeable events, not on the basis of a preset metaphysical scheme. Einaudi himself taught us this lesson, for when he lamented a naval disaster suffered by England as if it were a savage crime, we might have pointed out to him, virtually in his own words, that England is immortal as long as it is able to be, and need not fear naval disasters as long as it possesses a function in history—but its downfall would not be cause for lament, if others were more fit to discharge its obligations.

His sympathies for English federalism and for the fellowship of nations arise from the same premises as the theory of Norman Angell, but Luigi Einaudi is less dogmatic and only rarely given to abstractions. Even when he identifies his own bias, one feels that he is trying to go beyond it, to keep his thoughts from hardening into commonplaces.

If the autarkic state is economically inconceivable in modern society, then according to the economists, the old model of the sovereign state, absolute and independent within the limits of its territory, ought to be equally outmoded. Out of an economic schema came a generalization that took the place of a concrete political experience with a rich history.

The constatation is true as far as the economy is concerned; and the actual technological conditions of world production are bringing, and must bring, this about. Laissez-faire economics is perfectly valid and reliable on this terrain. But the political consequences that it has been forced to yield amount to generic aspirations and literary rhetoric. Einaudi strove to embody these ideals in a concrete political organism, but he got no further than indications of functions common to other states and preferences in foreign policy. When he understood that the fellowship of nations falls apart in the face of concrete national individualities, the theorist of England in him gave way to the historian. The fellowship of nations became for him the overarching formula for a realistic politics to be actuated in relative, practical terms: recognition of the interdependence of the nations in the economic field, free trade, productive collaboration. Thus he clearly surpassed the abstract phase described above, which remains as a historical example of theoretical uncertainty.

Economics and Morality

The ultimate instance of this uncertainty (which never varies and to a large extent makes Einaudi what he is, a restless spirit rich in problematic complexity, remote from the dryness of the technicians of economics) is not, strictly speaking, relevant to the theme of this essay and will be lightly touched on here to portray the friction between the scientist and the politician, between the moralist and the observer of economic facts. The solution is given by the philosophy that defines science and morality as *formal* values, as absolutes that govern the world of the spirit or, rather, that can properly be called the description of the world of the spirit and its process. This philosophy considers politics and the empirical world as the results of the free endeavor of individuals elicited in each moment by the total historical realization of the past. The laws of morality take effect in political facts but do not determine the content of those facts a priori. Einaudi is correct when he says that "economic science is subordinated to the moral law, and no conflict is possible between what their own long-term self-interest counsels men to do and the dictates of their conscience regarding the duty they owe to future generations." And certainly, without claiming to pass judgment here on Einaudi's scientific contribution, his true importance in the history of doctrine consists essentially in his having brought the study of finance back from the disorganized multiplicity of fact collecting to a condition of organic unity in which the motives of action and the genesis of economic reality are explained through a process deriving from the dialectic of society.

This formal analysis of economic facts is the only one that can justify the belief that economic science need not surrender to arbitrary empiricism. But although this science rises above empirical events, it neither controls nor predicts them, and any judgment it claims to pass a priori about individual facts will have purely abstract exemplary value. Any rigorously deductive forecast would be ridiculous and erroneous; the isolated fact, if deduced from a law, is no longer an isolated fact but a scientific fact. An economic concept, which is a concept precisely because it lacks full contingent specificity, applies to individual cases but is not a penetrable social law. In sum, practice is explained but not created by the theory of practice.

Einaudi has seen this problem more clearly than anyone else, with his formal identification of economics and ethics (leaving aside further qualifications that research may introduce), but he does not always rigorously abstain from making predictions about social reality with the aid of his economic science—hence his *sermons* and his disappointments.

Firsthand experience has given him, in an almost tragic manner, a sense of history as becoming, superior to all laws, coherent only with itself. The universal external object of knowledge lies only in this coherence—hence the sureness and serenity (rare in an economist) shown by Einaudi in his judgments of reality and of his own efforts in recent years. The a priori study of individual facts in the practical world is still a single practical fact; the inquirer becomes, must become, a human being, coherent with himself; but all of his knowledge thereby acquires the additional value of mere individual experience. We cannot demand infallibility of the inquirer. The praxis of the man of science would appear to contradict Einaudi's theory. History alone makes both moments true, incorporating what was formerly a single unrealized fact, invalid except as psychological fact, into the laws of an eternal process. A theorist who has heeded his own responsibility and the categorical imperative that impelled him to action must be satisfied with this higher coherence, without other intellectualistic preoccupations. Luigi Einaudi has helped all scholars to resolve the problem, confronting it in its moral aspects and resolving it independently of philosophical antinomies.

A MANIFESTO

La Rivoluzione Liberale grounds its position on a global and vigorous interpretation of the Italian Risorgimento;

against the abstractions of the demagogues and the false realists, we examine current problems in light of their origin and of their relation with traditional elements of Italian life;

and recognizing the truth of the empirical and individualistic foundations of classic English laissez-faire, we stand for a modern consciousness of the state.[21]

THESE programmatic formulas, which impose on us a specific responsibility vis-à-vis our readers, must be developed in frank and concrete detail. And since initially their rationale and their significance reside in our individual experience, let us try to clarify and define this premise.

In 1918 the first number of a biweekly periodical was published; it had a generic program (*New Energies*), and its collaborators were obscure young men who stood apart from the lively scene of relentlessly turbulent activism on the part of the political sects then flourishing.

They lacked the slickness of clever modern people, but neither were they so virginal as to make senseless professions of

21. Original title: "Manifesto"; from *La Rivoluzione Liberale* 1, no. 1 (12 February 1922), pp. 1–2. Translated from *Scritti politici*, pp. 227–40.

newborn purity. They believed that through realism they could best express their rigorous idealism.

This intention did not lack an element of ingenuousness, but as I think back on it, that urge to act (which we still feel) freed us from any debt to the aesthetes and made us see political *practice* as the realization, the natural extension, of our own personalities. History drove us, as individuals, to assume attitudes and posit exigencies that were not unique.

What others saw as ingenuousness was perhaps instead a creative attachment (culturally ill-prepared) to history. And if we lacked a sense that there was *a time and a place for things,* that was part of our strength.

We faced the postwar crisis without the prejudices that afflicted *combatants and defeatists.* We saw immediately that to indulge in sentimental gratitude or remorse when the consequences of the war were following their own rough practical logic and creating absolutely novel concrete circumstances would mean abandoning the effective political participation that we had awaited for so long and transforming a state of personal psychological fatigue into a general crisis of inertia that might in fact mean vanishing from history altogether.

The problem of the war, studied in hindsight, embodied a moral problem—not because there was a widespread, confused desire for peace and justice but because the war might become the first moment of a process that would finally bring hidden forces of the nation into political life, forces that had acquired an elementary awareness of their social roles through the creative sacrifice of their personalities during four years of discipline.

The demagogic illusion cast no spell on us. Our spontaneity sought other spontaneous forces with which to join—individuals of vitality, whatever their purposes. We wanted to be part of the movement of *spontaneity* in history and thus found ourselves confronted with the unsolved central problem of our life as a modern people: *unity.* Seeing how uncertain the efforts of workers and peasants to gain popular autonomy were, we were led to seek the wider and deeper reasons for that in our tragically constrictive conditions of organic weakness and historical immaturity.

Italy's inability to achieve organic unity is essentially the inability of its citizens to form a consciousness of the state and to make their own practical contribution to the living reality of organized society. A historical investigation, of which we will offer a sketch, will have to account for:

1) the absence of a ruling class as a political class

2) the absence of modern economic life—in other words, of a technologically advanced social class of skilled workers, entrepreneurs, and investors

3) the absence of a consciousness, or the direct exercise, of freedom

Deprived of freedom, we were deprived of an open political contest. We lacked the first principle of political education, the selection of the ruling classes. But the vitality of a state, assuming that the citizens have any sort of role in it, is based precisely on the capacity of everyone to act freely and in this way to carry out the necessary work of participation, review, and opposition.

The medieval Italian communes gave birth to the elements of modern economic life, through a revolution more formidable than France's. But the elementary spontaneity of their action necessarily made them refractory to any form of discipline. They had autonomy, but they did not have any formal guarantee of autonomy.

Far from restoring Roman harmony, the communes were in practice opponents of the Church and shared in the latter's sin of exclusivism. The individual has a counterpart: the idea of humanity. But there was no progression from individual activity to system: we had the explosion of the passions, not the organization of initiatives. Thus the achievement of the communes did not lead to a moral and national civilization, in the way the Reformation did, but to a civilization of aestheticism. By that I mean that they escaped from Catholic dogmatism only by throwing themselves into incoherent effort; they did not make their opposition organic.

Our equivalent to the Reformation was Machiavelli, a man apart, a theorist of politics. His ideas were unable to find any social terrain in which to take root or individuals who would live them out. Machiavelli is a modern man because he founded a conception of the state, rebelled against transcendence, conceived of an *art of politics* as the organization of practice, and professed a religiosity of practical life as spontaneity of initiative and economics. But in the immaturity of the situation, these concepts were distorted into empirical schemas and particularistic pettiness. Two centuries later, the ideal conclusion of Machiavelli (Vico), found no echo in the practical world.

The people had no role; revolution was imposed on them from outside. Only Piedmont, which suffered rough travail through a disorderly interplay of forces and labor, was capable of realizing its mission. At the end of the eighteenth century, the complex demands of modernity characterized the social life of Piedmont more clearly than elsewhere. Cut off from any rhetorical tradition (it was a stranger to literature), Piedmont was wholly focused on economic life, which was being organized on laissez-faire principles. The peasants were in revolutionary ferment as they attained consciousness of themselves as *producers*. The feudal class, which had specialized (so to speak) in fulfilling the military function, was aware of the inadequacy of the old methods in politics and openly favored reformist programs. With Radicati,[22] criticism of the Catholic Church noisily commences.

22. Alberto Radicati (1698–1737) was a political minister of the Kingdom of Piedmont. He was forced into exile as a consequence of his disagreement with the king and the Church; he became a Calvinist and lived in London and Holland. He was the first Italian philosopher of the Enlightenment and an interpreter of the liberal implications of Protestantism.

In this regional movement, the essentially negative work of Vittorio Alfieri[23] had a unitary function. His polemic against dogmatism, his pragmatic readiness to endorse the validity of any movement for autonomy, his opposition to the French Revolution (which, despite all the enthusiasm for the Enlightenment in Italy, turned to *tyranny* as soon as it was exported here), his elaboration, partly intentional and partly indirect, of the concepts of people, nation, and liberty—in all these respects he overcame the limits of the Piedmontese movement and reconnected with a tradition, creating the basic core of the revolutionary myth that guided our Risorgimento.

An aristocracy capable of taking positive political action on the basis of Alfieri's program (and here it is not important to scrutinize the degree to which that was consciously expressed by Alfieri) had barely begun to form when the turmoil of the French invasion intervened and impeded its organization. And at this point the general uncertainty produced a weak result: the formation of two vague currents of thought and action. On the one hand, the adherents of the revolutionary movement confusedly sought an ideal consistency outside Catholicism and tried to rouse the people to desire freedom of culture and of labor. On the other hand, those in government put their trust in reaction and, clinging to the revealed truth of absolutism, opposed the order of the past to the new movements, which they saw as anarchic and random.

These two movements were not what they seemed. They did not succeed in transforming their opposition to one another into

23. Vittorio Alfieri (1749–1803), one of Gobetti's heroes, was a Turinese tragic poet whose predominant topic was the overthrow of tyranny. He wrote poems on American independence and the French Revolution, whose tyrannical and imperialist evolution he strongly criticized. He was the author of inspiring tragedies, like *Antigone, Oreste,* and *Saul.* His *Life* (1804) was loved by English and American Romantics. Ralph Waldo Emerson was among his admirers.

the ideal logic of liberalism against Catholicism, state against Church, modernity against the Middle Ages. The result was theoretical confusion, irresolvable struggles, unreal misunderstandings, and illusory political differences.

The first attempt to found a ruling class and a state after the French Revolution occurred in 1821 in Piedmont, where, as we have seen, the old government was solid and active in the Prussian manner, despite the torpor and simplistic views that reaction was propagating, and served as the primary model and the primary teacher (through *antinomy,* not *on purpose*) of political experience.

The new ideal content, apart from these traditional elements, came to the revolution from romanticism. This idealistic romanticism reacted against sensationist and intellectualistic systems, affirmed the values of history, on them founded the concepts of national tradition, political realism, progress, and gradual development. This nucleus of romantic thought took shape in Piedmont during the Napoleonic domination, though it lacked reflexive consciousness and was hampered by its implicit contradictions.

The anti-Gallism acquired from Alfieri took concrete form in the affirmation of the concept of independence and went beyond the bounds of Alfieri's own thought to induce a violent polemic against sensationism (the essential character of France being identified with sensationism). The libertarian teaching of Alfieri likewise led to a rethinking of the concept of liberty itself, purged of its materialistic residues. The defect of romantic spiritualism lay in the limits set by Catholic tradition, which, like all systems founded on the principles of theocracy and transcendence, made orthodoxy paramount. Hence our romantic movement never succeeded in fully releasing its own intimate vigor and did not have the political and philosophical vitality of German romanticism.

The most intense effort to throw off the chains of age-old

tradition was made by Luigi Ornato,[24] the thinker behind the upheaval of 1821 and the most daring representative of the assault on dogmatism. Ornato's dim awareness of the contradictions that were tormenting Italy during its birth as a nation led him to elaborate a spiritualism that split off from Catholic belief and its religious need and its fervent wish for more intimate life through a Platonizing Christianity. Ornato's mysticism, culminating in the supreme concept of liberty, sanctified every form of spiritual ardor and voiced the demand for a religious life able to achieve full clarity and to resolve itself entirely into moral and philosophical life.

But with Santarosa[25] the clear consciousness of Ornato was already dwindling into a dogmatic, dualistic spiritualism, and the expression of the religious urge was mingled with submission to the Church. No wonder: Christianity—in the beginning, ardent sentiment, ideal moment of natural anarchy, heresy, deed surpassing all facts, violent affirmation of spirituality against all that is given—cannot last and be really complete unless ardor hardens into organic structure, unless abstract purity of aspiration gives way to the solid order of practicality.

The romantic religious currents did not have the power to create a religious reform out of the pristine Christian impulse, and so they were absorbed by Catholicism. The romantic cult of history supplied the traditional content of this reversion to Catholicism. The revolutionary fertility of Ornato's thought was repressed by conservative moderatism. The man of the hour was now Balbo,[26] the new religiosity was that of the neo-Guelphs, and

24. Luigi Ornato (1787–1842) was a philosopher. He introduced German Romanticism to Piedmont and participated in the riots of 1821 for a liberal constitution.

25. Santorre di Santarosa (1783–1825) was, along with Ornato, one of the leaders of the 1821 riots. To escape the death penalty he left Turin and went into exile in Paris, where he became a follower of Victor Cousin. He died fighting for Greece's independence.

26. Cesare Balbo (1789–1853), a Catholic historian and a moderate sup-

liberalism and Catholicism became inseparable terms. Theocracy succeeded in turning the arms of the liberals, their spirituality and their faith, against them to crush any movement for genuine renewal.

With the young aristocracy of 1821 destroyed, the new aristocracy continued to be the instrument of government from on high, the expression of an external dominion. The turmoil of 1848 was a revolution only in appearance, for the mixture of liberalism and neo-Guelphism had lost the consciousness of its own historical significance. The same equivocation persisted in liberal Catholicism. Submission to the Church strangled the ethical will from which the new state might have been born. The dominant strain of liberalism developed out of the ideas of Santarosa, not those of Ornato, and saw state and Church as mirroring the dualism of body and spirit. It stripped the function of the state of any ideal significance and reduced it to mere administration, leaving the care of souls to the Church. The libertarian psychology that prevailed in these years could accept a traditional power like that of the Church out of pure inertia, but had no contribution of vitality to make to the creation of a new state. And since in this phase the dialectic of European history overrode the contingent will of the majority of Italian citizens, the external appurtenances of the liberal state, its machinery, were installed, but there was no flame of inner life.

Only a few theorists were even conscious of this degeneration and immaturity, chief among them Giovanni Maria Bertini,[27] Bertrando Spaventa,[28] and the Hegelians of Naples. Bertini, having lived out the Christianizing elements of the Revolution of 1848 and having vigorously defended the best traditions of Ital-

---

porter of the Risorgimento, theorized a combination of Catholicism and liberalism and a revival of Guelphism (see the introduction, note 13).

27. Giovanni Maria Bertini (1818–1876) was a Turinese Catholic and a spiritualist philosopher who tried to reconcile reason and faith.

28. Bertrando Spaventa (1817–1883) was the leader of Italian Hegelianism. A Neapolitan, he was the ideal inspirer of Gentile's neo-Idealism.

ian thought against the sensationism and skepticism of France, came, through inexorable logic, to see the role of the new state as opposition to everything the Vatican did and to religious transcendence. But he was not equipped by disposition to turn his ideas into political organization, nor was the moment propitious after so many compromises. The handful of isolated Hegelians forgot the formidable struggles of Spaventa against the Jesuits and the liberal Cavourians and mingled with the conservatives. Thus was formed the Right: it had a political theory but no capacity to realize it. Gioberti,[29] who had caught a glimpse of the process theorized by Bertini and Spaventa, was forgotten in these years. Mazzini, the creator of the first impulse to autonomous liberation, remained alone and misunderstood.

The endless debates that took place during the Risorgimento around the question of schooling reveal that there was a practical awareness of this immaturity (nor have the echoes and consequences yet died out: this is a current problem that we will try to shed light on by reviewing the necessary historical antecedents). Practice, the value of consciousness, broke through the limits of theory. Education for the masses appeared to be the only way for the people to attain the power of willing. The new state had to make itself function as one, but before it could exercise its function, it had to create elements capable of operating and understanding the significance of conditions—hence the implicit rift within our liberalism: it cannot be content to express the result of the dialectic between the political forces; in-

29. Vincenzo Gioberti (1801–1852) was a philosopher and a politician of the Kingdom of Piedmont and a proponent of Italian unity. He became a priest and was professor of philosophy in Turin. As a philosopher he was one of the main representatives of post-Kantian Idealism. The *Encyclopaedia Britannica* (1999), s.v. "Gioberti, Vincenzo") notes that he coined the term "palingenesis" to indicate "the return of human concepts to the essential centre of being from which they become divorced" because of rationalism and scientism. The reunion of the ideal and the real was at the core of his Christian idealism, which he defined as a pure actualism, providing Gentile with the main inspiration for his own neo-Idealism.

stead it has to renounce immanence and impose one element of the process over the others. The government, having inherited the legacy of Catholicism, retains an abstract ethical function of democratic egalitarianism: the Risorgimento forgot the rules of liberalism and became democratic—in order to continue the patriarchal traditions of theocracy. The democratic myth, however, was triumphantly penetrated by the element destined to dissolve it, because it represented the ineluctability of modern progress. The Catholics had to identify themselves as liberals; the government made concessions to Catholicism only in order to indulge the people. The Casati law,[30] which (all of its technical errors notwithstanding) imposed on the state the duty to conquer illiteracy, constituted the violent superposition of a transcendent principle on autonomy and initiative arising from below, but it laid down the basis on which to bring the people into the world of modern consciousness, from which they had been excluded by the ingrained malady of feudalism. And yet, right at the start of the process, there arose another internal opposition to negate it. If the operation took place autonomously within the framework of old structures like the commune and the region, it would lead to an outdated federalism. You overcome federalism by suffocating the initiatives of the indeterminate myth of unity. Here lies the origin and the rationale of another challenging modern problem: decentralization. This is the road we will follow as we study the essence of the problem and the solution.

For all these reasons the Piedmontese government and the Italian government that succeeded it had to be a form of *state socialism*.

Just as Lassalle, on the basis of realist thought, leads to Marx, so Cavour leads to Mazzini. Mazzini and Marx (leaving to one side the different ways their myths were expressed) lay the revo-

30. The Casati law of 1859 (from the name of the minister Luigi Casati) instituted the public system of education and made going to elementary school obligatory.

lutionary bases for the new society, and although the notions of national mission and class struggle are quite at variance with one another, both men assert an idealistic (or, if you prefer, voluntaristic) principle that locates the function of the state in the free activities of the people arising out of a process of individual differentiation. In this sense, Mazzini and Marx are the two greatest liberals of the modern world. But from 1850 to 1914 the Catholic legacy and the conditions of social disintegration in Italy (the problem of the south) forced the new state to grow in obedience to an abstract function of morality that corrupted the activist (laissez-faire) principle into a democratic conception of tired, mean utilitarianism. This is the validity and the task of Italian reformism, which our socialists think they invented, when in fact it arose with the first attacks on the Jesuits over the question of schooling for the people.

Social evolution after 1850, when an element of economic reorganization was introduced into Italian life with the creation of a new industrial base, has substituted economic reformism for the legislation on schooling of state socialism.

The reconstruction of schooling might, as a moral revolution, have produced the embryo of a governing class, but it showed itself unable to create a politics that would stimulate the powers of every individual. In fact, the first moment of the organization of popular consciousness was to be primarily an economic moment, the elementary affirmation of autonomy and liberty.

The work of the Left (as economic reformism) was the logical outcome of our impotence to make a revolution, the dialectical result of two inert forces incapable of expanding. Theocracy lived on in democracy and reformism, while liberalism was reduced to an opportunistic administrative function. In substance, there was an attempt at reconciliation that transformed the initial equivocal relationship between Church and state into an equivocal relationship between the people and the government.

The ideal at which the government aims is at bottom the state socialism of Lassalle (according to Missiroli, the ideal of Giolittism was *socialist monarchy*).[31] But our legacy of failed revolution means that the Italian reform (later, socialist) movement cannot develop within the framework of a state in which the people do not believe because they have not created it with their own blood. German socialism coincides, in its ethical value, with the significance of the state; it represents the realization of the idea of the state in the consciousness of the citizens. The practical struggle is reduced to economic matters because both sides are already imbued with a common principle, which is in fact nourished by economic progress.

But in Italy a tradition that, if not liberal, is at least individualistic, irremediably saps the vitality of any system that ignores free initiative and makes of the state an activity distinct from the activity of the citizens.

State socialism, of which we have traced the origin and development, is therefore a passing moment, representing a compromise that has to be superseded. Once we get to the field of social legislation, politics turns into perpetual blackmail, with endless concessions leading to endless demands, while no principle of responsibility and moral education enters into the political contest.

The state is corroded from within by antagonism between government and people: a government without validity or autonomy because it is divorced from real conditions and founded on compromise; a people habituated to materialism, without consciousness and will, engaged in a perennial anarchic challenge to social organization. This contradiction, which erupted with the failure in Africa,[32] is the most cogent critique of the

31. See Chapter 1, note 35.

32. The Italian government began colonial expansion in Africa in the middle of the 1880s, going to Eritrea (1885–1896), then Somalia (1889–1905) and Libya and the islands of the Aegean (1911–1912). The Eritrean campaign took several failed attempts before the final occupation and showed the

nationalist program. Imperialism is a puerility as long as the most challenging problems of existence remain to be dealt with. The practice of Italian politics, after the era of the Left, inevitably culminated in Giolittism.[33]

The European war came at the height of our crisis of unity and overturned all intentions and opinions, creating dialectical solutions where the problem was insoluble. After centuries of compromise and reformism, after fifty years of social peace, it flung us into a whirling crisis that was, ultimately, the hard exercise of freedom. The present civil war is putting all the parties and all the forces to the test; it is the highest expression of new needs and new energies.

In this crisis our own work must play a clarifying role and elaborate a line of thought incorporating the need for unity. History is presenting us again, in the world of today, with the basic themes that we have already noted. But to the extent that our theory conjoins with all the experiments in autonomy, it becomes a practice and sets itself the task of clarifying, assisting, and renewing the movement for the redemption of the people, following the logic of empirical development.

Those who understand this position cannot accuse us of being too abstract. We would be guilty of that if we proposed a line of empirical action that adhered to the illusory schemas of the political contest the way those lost in current prejudice see it; that would only make the confusion worse. Our central thought postulates the truth of a new concrete approach that will generate the new history that it already knows deep within itself. Thus our precise task becomes the elaboration of the ideas of the new ruling class and the organization of every practical effort that will lead to that end.

Sentimental myths with a patriarchal vision of human so-

---

weakness of the liberal state ambitious to compete with more powerful European countries in pressing colonialism.
33. See Chapter 1, note 10.

ciety have failed; social discipline will have to be expressed through the state as an *organic structure:* not the merely potential indeterminacy of the nation, no more the egotistical triviality of the *patria,* but a new life through which the individual remakes his own life. In the state I affirm humanity, no longer as *loving affection* but as *rationality;* I annul my egoism to declare myself a man in society, the organ of an organism. The soul of this organism is, in Mazzinian terms, the people as the expression of a value and an activity, as the accomplishment of a mission.

But the instruments of this activity, the fleeting empirical forms of this mission (the parties), were born in the past and are unclear in the present situation: the conflict that they are undergoing compels us to draw a distinction between their work of interpreting the real and their praxis. As organs of the interpretation of the real, they have been destroyed by new, unforeseen realities. The political contest no longer gives the measure of the social struggle.

Liberalism is dead because it did not resolve the problem of state unity. Anyone who wishes to assume the heritage of liberalism will have to go back and think through this problem, because it creates exigencies that lead to a whole new economics. The noblest attempt to make liberalism self-aware in recent years was *L'Unità,* the periodical of Salvemini, which in the present crisis represented a clear torment, the precursor of a new time when individual effort will be ideally and historically mature.

Catholicism killed the liberal idea, but it was intimately debilitated by liberalism in its turn. The Popular Party that arose within Catholicism, however serious on the ideal plane, is aiming at a conservative result through a demagogic praxis. The champion of dogmatism and incivility in the modern world is arming hordes of peasants to strangle civilization because of its own theocratic logic.

Socialism, because of its lack of preparation, has fallen apart just when it should have succeeded. In Turati[34] it has declared its impotence. Instead of remaining faithful to the logic of political autonomy, it has accepted the legacy of parliamentarianism. There still remain a few communists (not the Communist Party) clinging to a Marxist vision, or rather an Italian Marxist vision; spellbound by Lenin, they see the revolution as the test of the political capacity of the working classes, of their readiness to form the state. But at present, with the unity of the popular movement broken, these ideas are not able to inspire the *masses* with any discipline. The great revolution is only half complete. The workers' movement has in recent years been the first laic movement in Italy, the only one able to take the modern revolutionary importance of the state to its ultimate logical consequence and express its anti-Catholic religious ideal, its denial of all churches.

The impulse was not converted into something durable because the healthy part of our ruling class was unable to recognize the *national value of the workers' movement*. For their part the leaders of the socialist movement failed in their duty because they were afraid, but flattered at the same time, to be part of government. The unitary politics of Serrati[35] is a pernicious Giolittism (without Giolitti's genius) and reveals the most barren incapacity to bring clarity to situations. Truly, it is only struggle that can lead to unity. Failing ethical unity between the people and the state, only the government can address the unitary function, and to keep out of the fray becomes its true morality. In

34. Filippo Turati (1857–1932) was the founding father of the Italian Socialist Party. His name is associated with that of Anna Kuliscioff, the Russian exile who became his companion and a leader of Italian feminism. Turati was one of the most important leaders of the Second International. A moderate reformist, he was unable to understand the character of the new mass dictatorship and unwilling to defend himself and his movement against fascist violence. In 1926, Carlo Rosselli organized his flight to Paris, where he died six years later.

35. Giacinto Menotti Serrati (1876–1926) was a member of the Socialist Party and then one of the founders of the Communist Party. His radical maximalism encountered the hostility of Gramsci.

the thought of Serrati the conflicting aspirations of peasants and workers became embroiled before they were even fully articulated. For each to attain his deserts, it is necessary instead that declarations from below should proceed autonomously, as if obeying a law of *separatism*. The parties must lead the struggle: the government has the higher duty of reconciliation, of making sure that the struggle does not alter the normal development of the necessary exigencies of equilibrium. To affirm this result a priori means nullifying the free forces right at the moment of their birth.

Implicit in the socialist movement, quite apart from its abstract plans for socialization, there was the possibility of a new economy that would finally resolve the insoluble contradiction between protectionism and the free market. In examining this problem we must not forget even now the fertile debate on the factory councils. What is needed is to get past the abstract formulas of laissez-faire and make the new economy grow out of the matrix of the workers' movement and the agrarian movement. The free market is arising in Piedmont and Tuscany as the economic structure that suits the flourishing agriculture of the small proprietors there. But industry has to flourish in Italy too, along with agriculture, and Italian industry is divorced from the liberal movement: the protectionist preferences of the workers themselves and the new possibilities opened up by Taylorism both shed light on this. We are preparing a factory economy that will develop along laissez-faire lines as far as trading goes, while the internal relationship between employers and workers is rigidly disciplined.

It is our firm belief that the ardor and initiative that led the workers to undertake the occupation of the factories have not been extinguished forever and can in no wise be soothed by the seductions of social legislation.

The new basis for Italian life will have to be found in the creation of two intransigent parties opposed to reformist programs and revolutionary in their self-consistency: the workers' party and the peasants' party. The initial nuclei of these two tendencies are already at work in the reality of the nation, even though they do not yet have any parliamentary representation: they are the Communist Party and the nascent agricultural organizations in the south, supported by the Sardinian Action Party and now reaching the other regions ready to receive them. These are the only forces on the horizon capable of taking up the legacy of the petite bourgeoisie, which is by now thoroughly bureaucratized in every respect.

The frank recognition of these two realities must not lead us to take sides with either one, precisely because we believe in the validity of each and because our liberal revolution encapsulates a vision of both elements in contention. Ours is a liberalism of potentiality; it must not steer us into the work of compromise (for then we would deny our own autonomist premises), but it ought to make us support both initiatives.

A precise technical task awaits us: the preparation of free spirits capable of abandoning prejudice and joining with the popular initiative at the decisive moment. We have to enlighten the necessary elements of the life of the future (industrialists, investors, entrepreneurs) and train them in this new freedom of vision.

Let one guiding idea bond us together politically in this action, this contest: let the myth of the revolution against the bourgeoisie lead, through the dialectic of history, to an antibureaucratic revolution.

That proposal has characteristic significance in our thought and may perhaps become the ideal around which the activity of the Italians will organize itself in the years to come.

LIBERALISM AND THE WORKERS

I s there a contradiction between our belief in the unforesee-
ability of history and our revolutionary work as liberals who
perceive autonomous action by the mass parties as the culmination of the national formation of the state?[36] This interesting
question is put by a friend of ours who writes for *L'Unità*[37] and
supports our cultural work and who has doubts about the validity of the direction we are currently pursuing. He asks:

> Will it be possible to get the people to rally to the state, the orga-
> nized structure of social life, as long as you are still operating
> with a conception of the liberal state that the workers have been
> raised, until now, to consider as their enemy? Will these workers
> be attracted by proposals for economic freedom, when what they
> have been taught up to now is that economic freedom is the
> source of their exploited condition, that freedom allows those
> who are rich already to hold on to, even increase, their gains,
> that it may permit those luckier or less scrupulous to rise from
> poverty to wealth, but that it can never lead us to the regime of
> economic and social justice for all to which the proletariat as-
> pires?[38]

Rather than answer this question, we prefer to ask a different
one: Is it necessary in principle that they should rally in this way?
Do the ideas of a mass movement (that is, a nonscientific movement) lie in its formulas or in its praxis? The process of achieving
self-awareness and liberation for the workers has to follow its
own path. The important thing is for them to feel that political
action is necessary and for them to believe that their salvation
will come from taking action, not from living in hope or cultivat-

36. Original title: "Liberalismo e operai," a section of an article entitled
"Esperienza Liberale [I]"; from *La Rivoluzione Liberale* 1, no. 7 (2 April 1922),
pp. 27–28, signed "Antiguelfo." Translated from *Scritti politici*, pp. 301–2.
37. See Chapter 2, note 7.
38. Giannotto Perelli, a collaborator of *L'Unità*. [Editor's note by P. Spriano.]

ing abstract justice. If they need the help of myths and abstract programs to impel them to take up the struggle, then let us by all means embrace the ones that historical experience shows us a priori to be galvanizing illusions. There is no need for them to be attuned to history in the same sense as we are. The important thing for us is that their free, revolutionary wills be unleashed, with whatever degree of messianism that may entail. In fact, we fully recognize, without waiting for the outcome or even anticipating it, that they are *accomplishing* liberal work *even now* simply because they are pursuing a process of autonomy and liberation and translating their initiatives into political discipline. That is the substance of our liberalism, and it is diametrically opposed to any conservative practice.

LIBERALISM AND THE MASSES

THE political problem of the future, thinking along lines suggested by Luigi Albertini,[39] is not whether liberalism will be able to bring the *masses* over to its side—a question already answered at the moment it is being asked—but to determine *which masses* it will be able, and want, to bring over.[40] The question appears genuinely *problematic*, not a project or a fantasy; let us try to explain what we mean.

It is hard to discern the differences between the terms *liberalism* and *democracy* if we analyze them by looking back to the environments out of which we have seen them arise, just as it would be a strained rhetorical exercise to distinguish between the two "historical" concepts of *equality* and *liberty*, with a meta-

39. Luigi Albertini (1871–1914) was an opinion maker and the editor of the newspaper *Il Corriere della Sera*. A liberal conservative, he was an energetic opponent of Mussolini and was expelled from the *Corriere* in 1925.
40. Original title: "Il liberalismo e le masse [I]"; from *La Rivoluzione Liberale* 2, no. 9 (10 April 1923), p. 37. Translated from *Scritti politici*, pp. 477–79.

physical disquisition. But if we shift the historical focus from the eighteenth to the nineteenth century and from Europe to Italy, we might say that democracy came to us as an attenuated form of liberalism, that it was the remedy sought by the Italians against the misunderstanding that they had challenged in vain, and that the replacement of the myth of liberation by the myth of equality would signal the withering of the spirit of initiative and struggle and the prevalence of dreams of regeneration and utopian tranquillity.

A liberal party that is not dominated by a *passion for freedom* is nothing more than a party of government, a diplomacy for initiates that exercises its role of guardian by deceiving the governed with compromises and with the artifices of social policy. The practice of Giolitti can be called liberal only in this conservative sense, and the collaborationist approach recommended by the newspaper *La Stampa* did not save liberalism, but the established institutions; it was tailored to the petit-bourgeois spirit of the Socialist Party and took no account of the workers' movement. In the face of the historical problem, the formulas of both socialist democracy and consumer liberalism are conservative to the same degree, merely configured somewhat differently because of the different psychology of the two cities, Turin and Milan, in which they originated.

Since the era of the demiurge Cavour, Italy has had no liberal tradition, because the problems of the workers' movement are not dealt with in the logic of the liberals, and the workers' movement is the only force that could revive a myth of liberation by transforming the social equilibrium.

But the liberal leaders, from Sonnino[41] to Giolitti,[42] when they do not simply deny, in the name of reactionary absolutism, that a social problem exists, treat it as one of charity: they talk about assisting the *masses* so as to reduce their suffering and also the pos-

41. *Rassegna settimanale*, 1878. [Author's note.]
42. On Sonnino and Giolitti see Chapter 1, notes 15 and 10, respectively.

sibility that they might revolt. There have been a handful of heretics who, in writing about the notion of the right to strike, moved on from that to a more complex analysis of political action; almost the only two that come to mind are Francesco Papafava[43] in his newspaper articles and Luigi Einaudi in his early writings.

Economists and politicians have always preferred to concentrate on the figure of the consumer, a mere logical construct, vulgar, parasitic, and apolitical. The efforts of the free-marketeers to create a consumer consciousness were bound to come to nothing, because the consumer is a cipher, not an individual capable as such of political consciousness.

Luigi Albertini is right to call for a revival of the liberal spirit in opposition to fascism. The morality of liberalism is heroic and realistic, productive through a process of ascesis, whereas fascist morality aims for social peace, the renunciation of any initiative, and surveillance by a paternalistic government. Liberalism is rigorist and favors autonomy; fascism is socialist and utopian. The antithesis could not burst forth more vigorously. Luigi Albertini is right to subject fascism to the same criticism to which he subjected Turati's conduct. Mussolini doesn't really have too many incongruities between his present and past positions to answer for. Despite his illogical, intuitionist temperament he has remained a social reformer infected with the extremism that Lenin talks about.

But to make discourse about liberal action possible, Luigi Albertini will have to address the dilemma we put to him: either accept the class struggle and summon the workers to the myth of liberation or put up with fascism, collaborationist regeneration, and social-democratic morality.

43. Francesco Papafava was an economist and a contributor to the *Giornale degli economisti*.

AGAINST THE APOLITICAL ONES

THOSE who identify liberalism with tolerance and with problem-oriented technique have no understanding of what liberalism is.[44] Liberal tolerance is a matter of moral education, and it has a meaningful part to play among civilized nations. In an uncivilized country like Italy—where those in power tend automatically, accordingly as they feel more or less sure of themselves, to behave like animal tamers and treat those they govern like undernourished beasts to be domesticated—the only way to defend tolerance is with the most inexorable intolerance. Granting for the sake of argument that it is possible to participate in politics as a mere sophist or technician, it is clear that even Prezzolini, Missiroli, and Petrini[45] will have to fight tooth and nail, with long-forgotten, prehistoric savagery, in defense of intelligence and decorum, if they do not wish to become mixed up with the totalitarian palingenesis of the courtiers.

If you are in politics, you are a combatant. Either you pay court to the new bosses, or you are in opposition. Those in the middle are neither independent nor disinterested. The regime welcomes skeptics. All it asks of the citizens is to surrender their dignity and their political rights: there is a man in Italy who is taking care of things, so let everyone else admire him and get on with their own work, or have fun at the festivals, or hide themselves away in the library.

Faced with these options, one should not even pursue literature without engaging in combat: those who fail to heed the call become political minors. For the rest, even in this kind of infighting, superiority of manners and morals will always distinguish

44. Original title: "Guerra agli apolitici"; from *La Rivoluzione Liberale* 3, no. 10 (4 March 1924), p. 40, signed "p.g." Translated from *Scritti politici*, pp. 625–26.

45. On Missiroli see Chapter 1, note 35. Domenico Petrini (1902–31) was a literary critic.

our own political intransigence from the grubby politics of traf-
fickers.

   We are preparing a more cultured governing class, a stronger
awareness of political problems, and working for the future, for
a secure future in which our realism will make sense and will
harmonize with the whole tone of Italian life. But all this other
stuff is just frippery, alibis for deserters, cowardly hypocrisy, as
long as it cloaks itself in the claim to be apolitical. There is no
such thing as *preparation* that is not at the same time actual
struggle; it is no use thinking that today is a time for study, and
tomorrow will be a time for action. Unless you are stiffening into
eternal antiseptic opposition, you have no right to make plans for
tomorrow's political contest. You are refusing to fight that contest today. We agree with Petrini: *this Italy is not yet our Italy.* But
only because *our* Italy is already inside us, and we are opposing it
now to Mussolini's Italy. Ours is an opposition without illusions
and without optimism; but those who are skeptical in a different way, who claim to be apolitical, are not just men of letters or
rhetoricians, they are deserters and accomplices of the regime.
Let me make it clear that I do not level this accusation against
my friend Petrini, who does define himself as a skeptic but only
after stating frankly that he is on the side of the opposition. My
words are aimed at a whole Italian disease; let those willing to
understand do so.

A COMMENT TO A PRELUDE

W E are not the editors of *L'Impero*,[46] so history is not some-
      thing we use as the basis for more or less amusing intel-
lectual games.[47] Nor do we ask Machiavelli to be the interpreter

----

   46. This short essay served as an introduction to excerpts from Machiavelli's *Discourses,* each of which was used by Gobetti to comment upon articles published in *L'Impero,* a new fascist magazine. For instance, Gobetti put
a excerpt from *Discourses* 2.2 under the title "Dedicated to Mussolini: Lib-

of our faith: too many centuries and too many ideas lie between him and us. Modern democracy follows in the wake of the Protestant revolution and the great absolutist monarchies. Machiavelli was impervious to the former and had only a presentiment of the rise of the great modern states, for his experience was still tied to the city-state.

And yet the Italians of today still have something to learn from the Florentine secretary. There is in Machiavelli a faith in the power of the people, a consciousness of the people as the foundation of the state, and this is not just an offshoot of his birth in Florence, or the republican passion of the Savonarolan years of his youth, or humanist enthusiasm. To go back to the Machiavelli of *The Prince* today, forgetting that the utopia of *The Prince* proved to be an absurdity even for the period in which the book was written, to believe that the rudimentary state of *The Prince* might be the modern state, would mean not only ignoring the European history of the past four centuries but announcing that one was less contemporary than Machiavelli himself.

DEMOCRACY

A Portrait of Servile Intelligence

FASCISM has beaten the democratic movements without even having to fight.[48] There could not be any more grievous insult to the Italian democratic movements than certain terms like

---

erty and the Empire," and one from *Discourses* 1.6 under the title "Dedicated to the Empire: Democracy and Imperialism." Gobetti's references to the *Discourses* were meant to be polemical against Mussolini's appropriation of *The Prince,* in particular chapter 26, where Machiavelli called for a "redeemer" of Italy.

47. Original title: "Commento a un preludio"; from *La Rivoluzione Liberale* 3, no. 20 (13 May 1924), p. 77, unsigned. Translated from *Scritti politici,* p. 673.

48. Original title: "Democrazia"; from *La Rivoluzione Liberale* 3, no. 20 (13 May 1924), p. 77. Translated from *Scritti politici,* pp. 674–78.

"pro-fascist democrats" and "democratic fascists" now widely used to quantify and classify them. The fact that such conjoined terms are gaining acceptability would seem to indicate that a failing grade is both legitimate and inexorable: the democratic movement in Italy has not had members who have really studied seriously.

Just as it put up with Giolitti,[49] the Italian democratic movement would put up with Mussolini or even a government by the army general staff. It is fighting fascism to defend its old politics, the politics of bloc voting, to defend its chance to make a deal with the government of Mussolini. By saying as much we provoked a grave scandal. But the very fact that the only preconditions stipulated by the democrats are liberty and the national militia proves that within certain bounds of space and time, they are prepared to come to terms.

To tame fascism seems democratic. First they tried to set the revisionists against the local warlords, the Mussolinians against the fascists. Now we are told that fascism must become the captive of its own majority, trapped by its own legality.

Eugenio Rignano has written a book to illustrate this new approach, which is encapsulated in the very title: *Democracy and Fascism*.[50] This is a book that will be popular. The author courteously lectures the fascists; who knows, perhaps they will listen to deluded elders instead of wayward sons. The good sense of Rignano is so lucid, his objectivity so refined and so self-satisfied, his international culture so calm and convincing, that his democratic pedagogy may very well be to the taste of tamed Italians. At heart the Italians are all fascists and democrats like him. Fascism exists, so let's derive some benefit from it, let's temper its impulsiveness by electing fascist deputies to parliament. Fascists become democrats: that's how revolutions are legalized.

49. See Chapter 1, note 10.
50. Eugenio Rignano, *Democrazia e fascismo* (Milan: Casa editrice Alpes, 1924).

The Italians have already accepted these conclusions as a resource for their innate courtiership, though Rignano himself
reached them by following the high road of his own puritan optimism. But we may wonder whether he is applying English methods of inquiry and appraisal to a phenomenon that in England
would be literally unthinkable. He cites John Stuart Mill; he proclaims himself a positivist and an experimentalist; he is a Protestant without religion, a philosopher of biology. If he failed to
acknowledge the merits of Mussolini like a reasonable man, he
would feel that he was not being sufficiently positive. His objectivity teaches him to see a degree of reason on each side. He
hasn't an inkling that when one side has nothing reasonable
about it, the judgment of Solomon is absolutely tendentious.
He stands above the fray, serene, disinterested, apolitical. He
doesn't see that apolitical people are always wrong. Their apolitical stance is partisan; they are defenders of the status quo, an
inert force that tilts the balance in favor of the regime and conservative interests. Reactionary governments have always appreciated the special utility that the class of the apolitical people
have to offer. Today the majority of the Italians are like that:
scrupulously objective persons who don't want to go against the
trend, ready to make peace with the regime so as not to disturb
national order and concord. All they ask of Mussolini is the opportunity to work with him the way they worked with Giolitti.
They thank him for having delivered them from Bolshevism and
for giving them order and hierarchy. This is an opposition plead-
ing for the liberty to serve.

Mussolini flatters these disinterested people; he appreciates
the fact they are apolitical. Subjects are subjects, scientists are
scientists, and politics is the business of the one who rules.

The Equivocation of the Moderates

The theories of democratic moderates like Rignano are estim-
able, and for our part we are quite ready to admit that J. S. Mill,

Taine, even Spencer and Comte, have suffered undeserved neglect. But we do not like their history. Every time you look
closely, what you find beneath the surface is a reactionary, a disappointed intellectual.

Rignano's democracy is the democracy of the positivists: a
static concept of social harmony based on a biological analogy,
with a bias in favor of gradual evolution, placidly welcomed.
Democracy for them is a fait accompli, but for us it is still a goal.

Rignano talks about a "natural evolutionary process, irresistible and preordained," about the "tendency of an ever larger
number of members of society to regain the freedom of thought
and action that nature gave them as soon as the conditions of
existence of society itself—represented by the level of social solidarity that has been attained—permit and to the degree that they
permit, at which point they become members of society through
free assent and consent instead of external compulsion." Underneath the surface of this Spencerian philosophy of solidarity lies
an equivocation, the same equivocation that underlies Gentile's
liberty/authority! If we do not accept historical materialism, we
will have a *guardian* to assess the *level of social solidarity that has
been attained.*

Rignano exalts the advantages of liberty: different interests
assert themselves, mistakes are corrected through mutual criticism, the human personality acquires dignity, the tenor of social
life improves. But when the dilemma of liberty and solidarity is
posed, his nostalgia for the old regime surfaces. Liberty is sacrificed to authority and order. He is a Gentilian positivist!

Italian democracy has never succeeded in overcoming this
difficulty: lack of preparation has always worked in favor of the
prejudices of the conservative and the moderate slumbering under the skin of the democrat. But as long as this fear of anarchy and this sluggish reluctance about extreme measures persist, there are no real democrats at all.

Marxism Against "Popular Education"

The only way to conquer the obsession with anarchy is to accept the cult of the class struggle. Instead, the Italian democrats have sworn the most implacable hatred of Marx. They conceive of society as harmony, not as conflict, so for them the risk to democracy is "the danger that a given class with the strength of numbers, of organization, of collective consciousness, and of its essential role in the national economy may be led astray by erroneous doctrines propagated and taken to heart in good faith, may lose the sense of social solidarity that links them to the rest of society, and, by elevating their own class antagonism above the general interest (though that is where their own supreme interest lies), may threaten society with dissolution." The democracy of the moderates has a remedy to hand: culture for the people. We have to educate them and teach them solidarity, with libraries and universities for everyone. Libraries on one hand, the fascist club on the other: the democracy of Rignano is not very much more liberal, nor does it have much more understanding of history, than fascism, and in the one and the other there is the same fear of politics. Mussolini ought to make Rignano a senator.

Rignano, like the entire Italian middle bourgeoisie, has promoted fascism through his uncontrollable, overpowering hatred of Marxism. Marx's order that there be no retreat, his invectives against the weaklings who desire a peaceful, idyllic social life, turned out to be too harsh and untimely for a people like ours, accustomed to smudging sharp angles, overcoming intransigence, and reconciling opposites. Choosing Mazzini over Marx was racially instinctive for them, and even the old guard of the workers' gospel, along with the rest of the socialist supporters of unity, have adapted to that in the end.

It is not so much a question of theory as one of national psychology. The prevalent habit of attributing the weakness of the Italian state to the defects of the common people overlooks the

guilt of the false intellectuals. In fact, the separation, so notice-
able in Italy, between the people and the intellectuals is the
strongest proof of our democratic impotence.

Italian individualism has no confidence in itself; it lacks the
courage for extreme statements. It seems that the mind of everyone here is haunted by dread of a tradition of sedition and factious unruliness, so they think that public order might be in peril
every single day. Well brought up persons who have studied
medieval history in their school textbooks and acquired an illusory belief in progress are by nature enemies of anything new
that might happen without warning, any irruption of new forces
into reality. In secret, underneath the veneer of national pride,
they are afraid of the desperate outbursts of their race, afraid
that the masquerade of a serious, tranquil way of life that they
have forged out of the hypocrisy of the years since national unification may be undermined—hence the hatred between the intellectuals and the people. The former tend to set themselves apart,
splitting off responsibilities by taking an apolitical attitude. They
are content to preach solidarity the way one might preach obedience to slaves, and are preoccupied with making sure that the
people recite their catechism.

The economic reasons for this psychology have been repeatedly explained in these pages. Italian pauperism justifies the subversive attitude of the plebeians and the philistine, courtly balancing act of the elites.

These are the conditions to be overcome. For that reason a
real democracy will have to originate in the historical terrain
of Marxism; and the Italian democrats who, in the style of the
good Colajanni,[51] rail at Marx are pure reactionaries. Culture for
the people is a piece of foolishness outside the political contest;
there is no culture without initiative, conquest, and direct exercise. The fact that the people read and love Mazzini may be of

51. Napoleone Colajanni (1847–1921) was a positivist sociologist and a
leader of the Socialist Party.

interest to dilettantes in search of new forms of philanthropy. But clearly this kind of facile philanthropy is just one more indication of a reactionary spirit.

The sense of social solidarity can come only from the exercise of individual rights, which are naturally bounded by the similar rights of everyone else. Those who preach abstract solidarity are ripe to become servants at court. Order does not exist as though it were some sort of biological given; order exists as autonomy, and the only possible preparation for it is the exercise of intransigence, active participation in political life.

Democracy will come about in Italy as a consequence of capitalism becoming mature and an open contest among the political parties. Today the parties that are fighting fascism relentlessly and aim to bury it are the ones that can lay the groundwork.

OUR PROTESTANTISM

W HAT do we mean when we say that Italy did not have a Reformation of its own and that the absence of a religious protest here accounts for Italy's political and ideal immaturity? [52]

If this observation is understood to refer only to a problem of criticism and religious freedom, if the purpose is merely to set up the modern Protestant nations as a model, then it would be nothing more than a heretical stance by historians, and Catholics could quite rightly defend Catholicism as the instinct of the race.

A Protestant movement in this county has to try to meet a more painful predicament, a problem absolutely central in Italian life. The ascendancy of Catholicism, the conservative and re-

52. Original title: "Il nostro protestantismo"; from *La Rivoluzione Liberale* 4, no. 20 (17 May 1925), p. 83. First published in the Protestant journal *Conscientia* in December 1923. Translated from *Scritti politici*, pp. 823–26.

actionary practice accompanied by demagogic trickery that re-
curs in our history, is inevitable as long as the traditional—and
actual—economic conditions prevail. The most serious attempts
at heresy in Italy took place during the period of free and pros-
perous economic activity by the communes of the Middle Ages.
When the nations fronting on the Atlantic gained historical importance and the New World was discovered, the Italian economy entered a period of stasis: trade declined drastically; agriculture, naturally poor anyway and hindered by the presence
of noble and ecclesiastical feudal tenures held under the bene-
fice system, did not have a class of hard-working cultivators; and
artisanal manufacturing did no more than provide some relief
in a few northern cities. In these general conditions of life it became possible for the Counter Reformation to celebrate its triumph.

Against pagan Rome, against the barbarians, against the
modern state, the best weapon of the Church has always been
generalized poverty. Impoverished plebeians were Catholic because of the lure of charity; and thus dogmatism held sway over
their humbled and submissive minds.

The twinning of Catholicism and fascism is perfectly logical
once you recall that fascism gained its foothold during a crisis
in Italy characterized by widespread unemployment; and its reform of the educational system, impeccably reactionary, makes
use of religious instruction precisely to eliminate any tendency
to rebellious insubordination among the common people.

It is evident that all the Protestant revolutions in Europe
proved their vitality through the creation of new moral character; without a moral revolution, free inquiry would be mere literature.

Luther and Calvin heralded the morality of work entailed by
the nascent democracies of production. They offered the Anglo-
Saxon peoples a religion of autonomy and sacrifice, initiative
and investment. Capitalism was born out of this individualistic revolution of consciences trained in personal responsibility,

in the taste for private property, in the glow of dignity. In this sense the spirit of the Protestant democracies is identical with the laissez-faire morality of capitalism and the urge for freedom on the part of the masses.

The factory is a precise reflection of the coexistence of social interests, the solidarity of work. The individual becomes accustomed to feel himself part of a productive process, an indispensable part, but, at the same time, not a sufficient part. Could there be a more perfect school of pride and humility? I will never forget the impression I had of the workers when I had a chance to visit the Fiat plant, one of the few modern, capitalist, Anglo-Saxon production facilities that exist in Italy. I sensed their attitude of control, their unfeigned self-possession, their disdain for every kind of amateurishness. Those whose lives are centered on the plant have dignity in their work and the habit of self-sacrifice and fatigue. The rhythm of their lives is strictly based on a sense of tolerance and interdependence that disposes them to punctuality, rigor, and continuity. These capitalist virtues suggest a sort of arid asceticism, but in compensation, the repression of suffering fuels with exasperation their courage for the fight and their instinct to defend themselves politically.

Anglo-Saxon maturity, the capacity to believe in definite ideologies and face danger in order to make them prevail, the hard will to take part in the political contest with dignity, are all born in this novitiate, which signifies the last great revolution to occur after the advent of Christianity.

The European war has shown how the work-based democracies thus nourished are the ones readiest for battle, the ones most zealous in defense of the national life, the ones most capable of the spirit of sacrifice: and anyone who has read Calvin could have predicted as much. The religions of individualism have always been heroic.

But historically in Italy the typical traits of those engaged in production sprang from the compromises to which they were driven in the hard battle against poverty. The artisan and the merchant went into decline after the age of the communes. The agriculturalist was still the ancient serf, working the land on behalf of a master or the Church, defended only by his permanent leasehold [emphyteusis]. The civilization most characteristic of Italy became that shaped by the princely courts or by office work, and the habits it formed were those of cleverness, the balancing acts of diplomacy and adulation, the taste for pleasure and rhetoric. Pauperism in Italy coincides with the impoverishment of conscience: those who do not feel that they have productive roles to play in contemporary civilization will neither have faith in themselves nor a religious devotion to their own dignity. That is the sense in which the Italian political problem — in a setting of opportunism, the shameless hunt for a job in an office, and self-abasement before the dominant social class — is a moral problem.

Protestantism in Italy has to battle a parasitical economy and petit-bourgeois unanimity and seek the cadres of heresy and democratic revolution among workers acculturated to free struggle and the morality of work. That way it will cease to be an imported ideology and will become the authentic myth of an Italy trained in dignity, the myth of citizens able to sacrifice themselves for the life of the nation because they are able to govern themselves without dictators and without theocracies.

3 SOCIALISM AND COMMUNISM

THE SOCIALISTS

Reformist Premises

SURROUNDED by liberalism, with its ambiguous art of governing, by nationalist demagogy, and by the clerical threat, the Italian Socialist Party never even came close, in its logic or its praxis, to looking like a political phenomenon connected with the history of Marxism in Italy.[1] Marxism teaches direct popular initiative and the formation of a worker aristocracy capable of promoting the rise of the working class through the experiment of daily struggle. In Italy only a few solitaries, like Antonio Labriola and Rodolfo Mondolfo,[2] have thought it through with any degree of originality, while syndicalists, like Enrico Leone and Arturo Labriola,[3] have occasionally made

1. Original title: "I socialisti"; from Gobetti, *La rivoluzione liberale* (ed. Perona), pp. 77–91. The text was adapted from its first publication in various issues of *La Rivoluzione Liberale* in 1922 and 1923. See Perona's notes and her textual introduction for details.

2. On Antonio Labriola see note 28. Rodolfo Mondolfo (1877–1976) was a leading socialist intellectual and a professor of philosophy at the Universities of Bologna and Padua. Against the deterministic interpretation of Marx then popular, he opposed a historicist reading stressing the role of consciousness and the will. He provided a theoretical foundation for reformism and criticized Leninism and Sorel's irrationalism. He tried to combine the thought of Marx and Mazzini. As a consequence of anti-Semitic laws, he left Italy and taught in Argentina for the rest of his life.

3. Arturo Labriola (1873–1959) was a Neapolitan economist who, in spite

use of it to invigorate their critical arguments. The experiment launched by the *Ordine Nuovo* in Turin was the only people's initiative that grew out of Marxism.[4]

Born as a supposedly revolutionary party, socialism settled for the tactics of economic betterment and cooperativism and ended by swelling its membership with all the malcontents of the middle bourgeoisie, whose concern was to create parasitical clienteles of their own through the practice of reformism.

It is no wonder that the institutional problem should be ignored or forgotten when economic life tends naturally to broaden political education by shifting the focus from formal and individual elements to the requirements of production. But it is a sign of political and legislative insufficiency when no one dares, whatever the circumstances, to raise questions about our *Statuto*,[5] which is characterized, because of the very circumstances that brought it about, by an anachronistic spirit that is infringed every day; on top of that, the ups and downs of daily life after national unity have continually made the Italians feel their humiliating lack of liberty and security.

The urge to be free, in a country in which the concern for liberty has perpetually been stifled by the concern for unity, remains strong enough to justify the persistence of a fake radical party, a party reduced to adopting heroic poses from the French Revolution and masking with Garibaldian and Mazzinian affectations an underlying corruption and infantilism.

For these reasons thirty years of socialist propaganda were

---

of his socialist ideas, drew close to Pareto, with whom he shared strong antiprotectionist and antistatist beliefs. Within the Socialist Party he opposed Turati's reformism and drew closer to Sorel's revolutionary syndicalism, sharing the same view as Enrico Leone (1875–1940).

4. See the next essay, "The Communists."

5. The *Statuto* was the liberal charter that Carlo Alberto of Savoy, king of Piedmont, endorsed in 1848. After the unity of Italy a revised *Statuto* became the constitution of the new liberal state. The *Statuto* looked to a liberal representative state and reflected the spirit of European liberalism of the nineteenth century, which was deeply antidemocratic.

muddled and deranged by the rhetoric of principles and utilitarianism in action. In order to keep their revolutionary premises unsullied, the socialists refrained from discussing practical problems and political reforms, and when they were forced eventually to come to terms with reality, they saw no reason to be intransigent. Their reformist practice was illuminated neither by culture nor by technology, and when they preached revolution, they got drunk on their own words. It was only after two decades of useless effort that the friends of Bissolati[6] grasped the ambiguity and tried to resolve it in themselves and clarify the situation by engaging in reformist criticism of the government. Unfortunately their generically humanitarian approach was not grounded on any prior analysis, and the experiment came to no more than an imitation of the French.

Salvemini

In the history of Italian socialism the experiment of Salvemini[7] is more interesting with regard to the clarification of its program.

Salvemini's intellectual position from 1900 to 1910 appears analogous to that of Sorel,[8] provided we bear in mind the specific limitations imposed on the political contest in Italy as a result of historical and economic immaturity. Nor should the reference to Sorel make the reader suspect rigoristic premises or mysterious mythic initiation rites, because our attribution of Sorelism to Salvemini is not based on the hypothesis that he read him directly or received any specific influence, and has no dogmatic significance. What we are trying to do is make a precise histori-

6. Leonida Bissolati (1857–1920) was among the founders of the Italian Socialist Party. He gradually became a nationalist and a statist and supported Italian colonization of Libya and Italy's participation in the First World War.
7. See Chapter 1, note 37.
8. See Chapter 1, note 32.

cal analogy with the critical function Salvemini had vis-à-vis a socialist movement that was degenerating into reformism and parasitism.

If we should wish to reduce the comparison to a question of political style, we would have to conclude definitively that in Salvemini there is no real trace of the Marxist mentality, even if critical considerations enhanced by the authority of Marxism quite rightly give him the edge in his debate with Turati.[9]

It is not hard to demonstrate that the leading ideas of Salvemini come from a quite different background and aim at different goals. By unmasking the verbose revolutionism of Enrico Ferri [10] and demonstrating that since objective conditions were inexorably against the revolution, the best counsel was to undertake a determined struggle to obtain political reforms, Salvemini was really only continuing the battle the socialists had fought from 1892 to 1901 to free the citizens from the yoke of the state and irrelevant parliamentarianism and to promote purposeful initiatives rather than demagogic actions by reminding them of their responsibilities.

In his critique of reformism, state socialism, and cooperative parasitism there is an implied stance of simple political realism, not Marxism, related to a radicalizing brand of liberalism with hints of solidarism. It is the same surge of emotional involvement that later inspired him to research the Southern Question.

And in fact, all he sees at times is a question of morality and upbringing. In other words, the pure Marxist frame of reference escapes him completely: in these cases his Marxism amounts to no more than basic antipathy for ideological superstructures, a love for the factual that he inherits directly from Cattaneo.[11] But the lessons in realism that Salvemini has given the Socialist Party were never limited to a fetish about facts and the morality

9. See Chapter 2, note 34.
10. See Chapter 1, note 23.
11. See Chapter 1, note 25.

of solidarity or to his ongoing preoccupation with the Southern Question.

Indeed, he joined the socialists in the first place for reasons with no more ideological content than the desire to wage an effective campaign against privilege of all kinds: the same motive accounts fully for his divorce from them. For if we dare to broach the delicate subject of personalities, it has to be said that just this solemn moralism, while it constitutes his most appealing trait, also seems to be the key to his ineffectiveness. Excessive moralism, the absence of ascetic detachment from the individual and pessimistic aspects of the problem, set limits on his action: characteristically he showed fierce intransigence when everyone else was giving up and displaying their debased tolerance through accords and appeasements. Too apt to clarify and schematize, closed off from the sense of imponderable factors, he is too much a man of suffering to succeed as a militant. It is easier for him to describe a phenomenon than it is for him to adapt to the subtle play of dynamic forces.

When he did break away from socialism, without recrimination or drama, he made it clear how his own Enlightenment values were really a problem-based approach [*problemismo*]: not a faith but a descriptive canon, a method of understanding. He hunts for the objective fact, leaving out the subtleties, ignoring the illusions that govern deeds. His rationalist conception resolves into an effort to enlighten and to persuade, and these may be useful contributions to cultured society, but not to a party. This constitutes the elementary preparation of a serious ruling class, but it doesn't solve the problem of persons and initiatives, because it doesn't give the sense of action.

Bound by theoretical and moral preconceptions, he never escaped schematism in assessing individuals and confined himself to fighting a twenty-year crusade against Giolitti,[12] who, as government leader, had the same ideas, methods, and prejudices as

12. See Chapter 1, note 10.

Salvemini but deployed them with the cynicism of the animal tamer rather than with the enthusiasm of the apostle. It was the Socialist Party that was, until 1911, the vanguard of the reforming action of the government, and it was Salvemini who saw clearly the methods and who detailed the ideas behind this practice, with the clarity that only a fanatical adversary can achieve. Later the split with the Socialist Party drew him to overly specific regional interests and to a role as a sort of preacher, and this greatly reduced his political acuity and capacity to evaluate the forces and the limits of concreteness.

But in the period of his socialist critique, before 1910, we find that his style was much more complex, and his will much more involved in the rhythm of social dialectic. One can still reread with surprise and delight his critique of the ambiguities of anti-clericalism, and we are certainly in agreement with him when he states that "the working class has to create itself on its own, with its own forces, its own rights," or when we see him noting, almost religiously, that "the multitudes have an inexhaustible well of mysticism and aspiration for the good," or when he ruminates on "the marvelous force of moral expansion encapsulated in the formula of the socialist ideal." Over against utilitarian expectations trusting in government largess he set the "true practicality of great, apparently disinterested initiatives."

There is no denying that the reasons for his opposition to ministerial reformism were very much deeper and more varied than this cordial sense of humanity and historical experience. His anti-Giolittism, which may now seem almost quixotic and which history facetiously confuses with his sense of irony, had tragic and heroic meaning because of the religious dimension in which Salvemini always viewed any popular movement. In these illusions and myths there resides a profound capacity for realism. How could we not prefer him in this first phase, in the battle against state socialism, when Salvemini was totally bent on finding ways to prevent aristocracies-turned-oligarchies from being co-opted into supporting the government, thus dispersing the combative vanguard of the workers' party and indeed class unity itself? In the later phase, all his complaints were limited to questions of justice. There is no doubt that the former was really the high road of genuine political action, inasmuch as it met the tactical necessity of gearing the pace of the vanguard to that of the bulk of the army and took the most obvious precautions against the formation of a reign of mediocrity in place of the true worker elites. When he gave it up, Salvemini passed from Marx and Cattaneo to democracy. The most valid of the themes he preached remains his strong stand for unity with regard to the Southern Question: a frankly laissez-faire stance incapable of leading to action because of his persistent moralistic solitude.

In reality Salvemini's fault was that he did not elaborate his critique of revolutionism into a decisively revolutionary stance, and that remains the weak point of his laissez-faireism and his regionalism.

The concessions of universal suffrage and proportional representation were an irreparable defeat for him. His instinctive moralism stayed rigorous as long as the role of victim befell him, but his campaign of epuration and moral uplift had a flavor of irony and lacked compelling power when it was waged in the Chamber of Deputies. The rhythm of action, while directed at concrete goals, has to aim beyond them at a transcendent illusion or an ideal of infinite autonomy; the attainment of freedom through juridical institutions or even through political reforms is only a spur to action and signifies nothing without the force of the initiatives. The lucid rationalism of Salvemini tended instead to view the initiatives as satisfied and effected the moment reforms had been won, which meant that the most realistic lesson of the workers' movement escaped him: a liberal imperative of intransigence.

Still, Salvemini represents a characteristic and central moment in the work of the Socialist Party: the constitutional opposition. As long as the Socialist Party was content to rehearse the romantic theme of vindication for the oppressed, it was able to represent peasants and workers at the same time, act in both revolutionary and conservative ways. And as it gradually shrinks to a party of the middle class, with a typical consumer psychology, its fight against protectionism (the route indicated by Salvemini and adopted by Modigliani)[13] might certainly seem the most coherent one to follow and the only one likely to have a formative influence. Gradualist, integralist, syndicalist, anarchist, and revolutionary proposals were all articulated in unreal terms: ragged echoes of concepts and theories legitimate in other countries, vain attempts to hide the underlying ambiguity.

The incapacity for revolution became more and more evident as the northern organizations prevailed and as socialism in the north was transformed into a virtually hegemonic party, analogous in its corruption to the southern democracy that was supported by the very middle bourgeoisie that had always stifled the attempts of the agrarian proletariat to win advancement, and that had been the target of the harshest criticism of Salvemini and other intellectuals dedicated to the socialist cause. At that point Salvemini abandoned the party and tried to make it clear that his action was a liberal defense of the peasants.

Reformist Equivocation

Socialist reformism was the logical consequence of the premises and the psychology manifested in the first unruly striving for liberation on the part of the lower classes in Italy.

The equilibrium of the Italian political contest was severely altered by the aftermath of the Risorgimento, which had created a specific revolutionary situation without being able to bring it to completion or to satisfy it and which, although it remained potential while the technicians and diplomats were striving to create the Italian state as a work of art, became turbidly explicit when the completed state revealed itself to be void of ideal sig-

13. See Chapter 1, note 38.

nificance and incapable of receiving life from the masses. Meanwhile, outside the government, there was a domain of more or less "intelligent" mediocrities that professed a priori their function of assisting and helping the people and tried to undermine any kind of direct action through reforms and the work of reconciliation, beguiling the rebels with peaceful proposals that preserved their own role as enlightened preceptors.

The Socialist Party failed to discern this game and allowed another form of the inescapable antithesis that separates the people from the government in this immature country to occur within itself as it was infiltrated by conservatives. The accord it reached with the liberal conservatives and the radicals was justified by the need to defend the most elementary freedoms against Crispi and Pelloux.[14] But when that danger was past, the socialists were no longer able to distinguish themselves from Giolitti except through more intense demagogy. The unity of the party, which is vainly discussed and proclaimed, actually conceals the most contrasting tendencies, which reproduce in semi-extremist language the various themes of the other Italian parties, from the conservatives to the radicals. The course of action is the same; it is not diverse principles that clash, but diverse individuals.

Hence Bissolati has been more coherent and sincere than Turati in accepting a government responsibility that was inevitable given the ideal premises. The party's antigovernment poses became the party's government positions, parliamentary maneuvers. Leaving the piazza for the Palazzo di Montecitorio [the Chamber of Deputies], the revolution turned into diplomacy. Election rallies were now no more than props with which the new chieftains maintained the illusion, gave themselves an outlet for their instinct to posture as tribunes of the plebs, and systematically reinforced their personal sway. Concern for the unity of the movement, more than cohesion of ideas, came to domi-

14. On Crispi see Chapter 1, note 58; and on Pelloux, Chapter 1, note 49.

nate; because it was necessary to make it look as though they represented a strong organization, they maintained a veneer of unity by resorting to all the intellectualistic eloquence of concealed ambition. The vacuous disputes of the party congresses about the denial of tendencies (Imola, Bologna), integralism (Rome), reformism of Right or Left (Florence, Modena) hid this recondite calculation. The efforts of the masses to win autonomy escaped the attention of the party chieftains; the desire for autonomy fermented vainly in search of expression and surfaced finally in the most confused manner after the European war appeared to have brought new nuclei of workers and peasants to social responsibility. But when the dissension between reformists and revolutionaries was made clear, Livorno was the squalid outcome of an ambiguity that had lasted thirty years, and the uncertainty of Serrati disorganized the popular forces for good.[15]

Turati

Through all these vicissitudes one man remained on the field, constant and never self-contradictory because never decided, the inspiration of an entire political tradition, though disinclined himself to assume the responsibilities of a warrior chief: Filippo Turati.

And yet what value should we place on this thirty years of coherence in political life? The problem would seem to be confined to the psychological realm, and, for that matter, all of Turati's admirers adopt the same justification. But linear coherence, oneness of word and thought, firmness of character, are here the heralds of a sentimentally dogmatic outlook, a premature conclusion that remains one-dimensional but considers itself perfect.

And anyhow, what is the speculative nature, the ideal core, of

15. Gobetti is referring to the communist split from the Socialist Party during the National Convention of 1921 in Livorno.

the commonplaces that Turati goes on repeating? Marxism has not penetrated his spirit, nor has he fed on the real experience of leading political troops into battle. Turati's ideology is not redeemed by open and vigorous humanity; it is limited to a typical moment of Italian history: the absence of struggle.

Turati's moral education distanced him notably from problems of culture and historical realism: from his first juvenile writings, his spirit developed in the intellectual atmosphere of positivist sociology, and the humanitarianism that made his propaganda spellbinding among the masses has a utilitarian hue and takes over the patriarchal functions of the lay brother in all too self-interested a fashion. From Anna Kuliscioff he acquired a romantically tinted Marxism; from Enrico Ferri he took the optimism of the indulgent scientist and the missionary habit of the defender of the poor;[16] and from Bissolati the concern to find a few easy formulas of sociological sentimentalism and apply them to political problems. His morality has nothing rigorous about it, being merely the *defensive function of life and development,* a mean particularistic atomism that reduces the problems of force to a *tactics* of economic cleverness when applied to the field of politics.

Besides, even when he accepts the need for a (gradual!) conquest of power by the masses, his objective is to arrive peacefully at *radical economic change.* Here the weave becomes exceedingly tortuous, and the problem of the relations between economics and politics that Marxism forcefully posed is naively handled by a mind foreign to the more subtle aspects of historical dialectic and the realism of praxis. For Turati it is enough to keep alive his prejudices, which incline to optimism, and his tolerant notion of progress: the class struggle and the ideal importance, for the renewal of the active rhythm of history, of the conquest of power on the part of the emergent working class escape his purview.

16. On Kuliscioff and Ferri see Chapter 2, note 34, and Chapter 1, note 23, respectively.

Compared to the great importance of critical communism and the revolutionary discipline it has restored, the reformism of Turati reveals its sterility and capacity to corrupt.

Another ambiguity in our political nonculture for which Turati is responsible lies buried in the interminable discussions on the dilemma between the *minimal program* and the *maximal program*. The minimal program is a government program, a technical expedient for the exercise of state power. But it is not the job, and has never been the job, of a mass party to elaborate such a program, which can contribute only partially at best to the political contest and, in any case, only through highly evolved methods similar to those proposed by Ostrogorsky,[17] hence far beyond the range of a demagogic party. The action of the people at the present historical moment can develop only along the guidelines of a maximum program, a conception of life and reality elaborated as a myth to inspire deeds; and any interest in practical reforms has to remain an interest of an administrative order, a tactical measure to get past contingent obstacles. But the preparation for victory in this great battle that recommences eternally can come only from the choice of a strategic plan. Strategy resolved into tactics in the last decade of the past century, when Turati and the early Italian socialist movement had their most vivid political experiences. Once they had solved the material problem of existence, in fraternal accord with the radicals and anarchists, they found they had no more coherent long-term goals. Against Crispi and Pelloux, Turati was able to wage the battle with singular diplomatic skill and great generosity. He succeeded in preserving the individuality of his party even while profiting from the decisive support of the conservative elements he could not do without. But in this compromise, all the intellectual originality of the Italian socialists was consumed. The contrast between them and the syndicalists and the anarchists signified that in

17. Gobetti discussed Ostrogorsky's ideas in "Toward a New Politics" (see Chapter 2).

practice they were conservatives. Their gradualism attenuated any opposition to constituted power. The internationalist idea was maintained out of humanitarian and positivist prejudice or, in the case of Treves, out of a crude messianic racial imperative. Giolittism signaled the collapse of this ideology because the government showed itself more enlightened and humanitarian than the party.

While Salvemini chose to engage in opposition inspired by practical motives arising out of the squalid living conditions of the rural proletariat of the south, and so redeemed himself through the effectiveness of his criticism, Turati and the other northern socialists in parliament gradually reduced themselves ever more miserably to silent complicity with the dominant bourgeoisie and salvaged their own personal integrity by professing a simplistic rhetorical pacifism and a democratic philosophy through which they hoped to acquire for the organized working classes of the north the privileges the dominant class enjoyed. It was pure timidity that prevented Turati from following out this collaborationist logic and assuming governmental responsibility. In fact, the ideas and reforms he preached to the masses with demagogic emphasis were those Giolitti was enacting in government. His pose as a revolutionary served electoral purposes and corresponded to the psychology of restlessness that the modern city nourishes in individuals who come in from the countryside unprepared for the tempo of industrial life, dreaming of adventure.

The Tragicomedy of Indecision

After the war, as soon as the people became aware that they had been left out of the making of the nation and had been steered by the reformists to exploit the state anarchically for twenty years, they sought a code of their own that would overturn the order imposed on them by traditions not their own. Then Turati found himself speaking the language of reaction, with the choicest

messianic turns of phrase. His skepticism about any organization of forces and his faith in Giolittian diplomacy turned out,
in a solemn historical moment, to be gravely corrupting.

Government action might have been effective, and socialist
democracy might have been able to join forces with tired bourgeois democracy; but individual men proved unable to act. By
now we can assess the phenomenon of collaborationism with
perfect objectivity, but the conclusion has to be that after the experiences with Giolitti and with Nitti,[18] it brought nothing new to
our national life. It could have consolidated, in opportune fashion, a state of affairs already irreversible and brought a sense of
reassurance to the middle classes perturbed by the demand that
promises made during the war be kept. Since it was beyond them
to play an inspiring role in this situation with the enthusiasm of
an epic initiative, the socialists should instead have dominated
events with administrative expertise and a spirit of orderly dis-
tributive justice. For a genuine conservative policy it was important to locate the point at which the interests of the rich and the
pressing demands of the lower classes could meet and establish
reciprocal tolerance. The innovations of wartime and the policies of Nitti had effectively paved the way for the two sides to
coexist with the aid of a program of legislation able to convert
the opposing claims into new juridical relations. The authority
that Filippo Turati and his friends would have been able to confer on the government by taking part in it would have guaranteed
the continuation of this equilibrium, and the people would have
survived to fight another day.

But instead the trade union aristocracies found themselves
drained of all political consistency, victims of systematic corruption and the hunt for government handouts. Their greed was no
use to them in the task of diplomatic reconciliation. The socialist political machine was the victim of its own success, which

18. See Chapter 1, note 15.

had produced bureaucratic bloat. The horde of malcontents who had joined the party kept it from being able to shift its ground adroitly. Instead of being a disciplined vanguard, quick to maneuver, like an army, the card-carrying membership reflected the uncertainties of the Italian situation, divided as they were between a nucleus of workers who were shaped by the life of the modern city and a crowd of peasants enfeebled rather than enfranchised by their brief bewildering experience of life in the factory. The participation of groups of actual rural cultivators, exasperated by the war, augmented the confusion, because no one knew how to get them to stick to their assignments like trained troops.

This is not the place to point out the mistakes inherent in the diagnosis of the situation made by the revolutionaries. But it has to be said that the reformists were unable to respond to the revolutionaries with clear original thinking. They were unable to confront them with an organization of their own. The work they did was corrosive. Instead of assuming their responsibilities outside the party, they behaved like advance sentinels of a tactic that enjoyed the confidence of the industrialists, adhering to the revolution in word but boycotting any attempt to clarify the situation with their deeds. They remained in the party purely to keep from losing their parliamentary influence, which would have reached its apotheosis if they had ever succeeded in handing over to Giolitti or Nitti the gift of an acquiescent, tame proletariat. But that very goal was pursued with the infantile methods of an organization of carbonari. Playing the role of tribunes of the plebs had killed any diplomatic sense in these men. The days of July 1922 will remain the most transparent example of a battle fought with every intention of losing. The immediate possibilities of the situation all came down to collaborationism, but the socialists let themselves get caught up in a parliamentary crisis. They had the most inopportune scruples at the moment when their contribution was needed and could still have saved the proletariat from an openly violent reaction. They demobilized their forces by defining a strike as being within the letter of the law when it was actually the last chance of winning the battle, and ended up by laughably presenting themselves as candidates for government when the bourgeoisie, having evaded the peril, had no more hesitation in rebuffing them with insults. The historian of this droll episode, which was the first unlooked-for victory of the fascists, will not be able to salvage either their minds or their characters: even in the fable the part of the fox who gets tricked is never a sympathetic one. Turati, Modigliani, and the trade union mandarins deluded themselves that throughout Italy there existed the same state of optimism and good-natured complicity that obtained in Milan. In their electoral districts, as in parliament, they never succeeded in acting out that life of passion and exasperation that they had been incapable of finding thirty years earlier in the works of Karl Marx.

Still longing for the fulfillment of their hopes, the proletariat by now had not even a flicker of interest in the reformist experiment. The tone of Italian life was coming from a different quarter, and the reactionary resolve of more skillful groups took advantage of unoccupied intellect and unemployed muscle to try an offensive in grand style which wrapped itself, as often happens, in the rhetoric of patriotism. When you think about it, it was nothing but the second term, identical albeit reciprocal, of the collaborationist aspiration: we should not be surprised that the foot soldiers of the reaction turned out to be the same people who had waited for an offensive from the Left, nor that when new leaders took the place of the old they turned out to be, to all effects, their twins in belief and illusion—in sum, that the fascists should find themselves proposing, with merry effrontery, the palingenesis of collaborationism.

Except that the fascists were warriors as well as tribunes, and as it turned out, they were not disposed to perform the tragicomedy of indecision for us again.

THE COMMUNISTS

The Factory

THROUGH the efforts of an intelligent nucleus of captains of industry (the only bourgeois that Italy has had), there was modern industry in Turin, initially at least, before the European war.[19] The war enlarged it: through the work of Giovanni Agnelli[20] an industrial organism was created around the Fiat plant that altered the entire profile of activity in the city.

A communist writer described it this way: "We are dealing with a gigantic industrial apparatus that corresponds to a small capitalist state, that is indeed a small capitalist imperialist state, because it lays down the law to the mechanical industry in Turin and because it tends, with its exceptional productivity, to overwhelm and absorb all its competitors; and this small absolute state has its own autocrat."

The importance of the Fiat plant was not reducible to technological or economic progress but depended on a specifically modern situation. In a great city, the first model industry to create a new psychology of the citizen was developing.

Turin was thus the modern city of the peninsula, the seat of an aristocratic industry concentrated, through the selection of personnel and ability, in the hands of a few exceptionally clever men, an industry that became the first cell of a complex economic organism in which the coordination of the elements and the experience of new systems of production nourished a social consciousness in individuals. Only these characteristics can explain the originality of Turinese political life, whereas in Milan commercial dilettantism gave rise to a reformist psychology

19. Original title: "I communisti"; from Gobetti, *La rivoluzione liberale* (ed. Perona), pp. 92–112. The text was adapted by Gobetti from its first publication in *La Rivoluzione Liberale* 1, no. 7 (2 April 1922). See Perona's headnote and her textual introduction for details.

20. Giovanni Agnelli (1866–1945) was the industrialist who founded the first modern Italian industrial plant, the Fiat factory in Turin, in 1899.

contrary to the intransigent politics of the industrial city. The fact is that in Turin industrial concentration was creating a concentration of workers. The selection of management personnel promoted the selection of workers with intelligence and the refinement of the virtues of the laborers. Nor could these coefficients of technical progress fail to lead to political consequences.

By following its own logical ideal to the limit, capitalism, in a process that appeared to validate Marx, forced the workers' movement to return to its own ideal premises and organize itself around the center of its daily life; capitalism directly helped the workers' movement to express its own rebel logic.

The old myths of Italian and foreign social democracy (fragile documents of revolution or reform according to the different temperaments that revived them) collapsed helplessly in the face of direct experience. Within the political frame of reference of those who believed them there remained the dilemma between confused demagogic agitation (Bombacci)[21] and the fearful conservative retrenchment of reform.

Those who took note of the new demands of the lower classes and tried to study them could discern that their structure was fundamentally changed. Here and there vigorous minorities of workers were emerging who had achieved their own class consciousness and deduced from that, with infallible logic, the practical decision to resist. The ideal of a working-class aristocracy conscious of its own strength and capable of renewing itself and political life, once a flash of lightning in the historical vision of Marx, and the intuition that for us remains the living part of Marxism, over and above his creaky economic constructs, found the concrete resonance that gave it a seminal role in the development of the Italian economy.

The quasi-Taylorist specialization of labor roused the worker to an awareness of his own indispensability. On the other hand, contrary to the humble American and Protestant ideal of labor

21. See Chapter 1, note 23.

reduced to a pure mechanical fact, complex demands of production that enabled an ever-growing nucleus of the elect to share in the secret and in the difficulty of highly qualified work generated an obscure sense of aristocratic idealism in the wage earners that fermented into a need for power.

Thus two of the essential forces of modern civilization met at precisely the most troubled stage of their ascent. Around the nucleus of workers with the most foresight and around the similar nucleus of entrepreneurs there grew up cohorts of followers who brought their own complex needs to the struggle.

The city became the center of the lives and aspirations that surrounded it, and obliged the newly arrived immigrants (manual workers and petit-bourgeois merchants) to accept their place in the front lines between the contrasting drives of a dialectic that towered above them.

In the face of Italy's indifference to this turbulent, impromptu process, Turin, it seemed, would have to assume the burden once again of conquering the peninsula for European life.

The theory of this new economic reality was sketched, in a fragmentary and incomplete manner, by the young men of the *Ordine Nuovo*. Out of the political experience that they saw unfolding before their eyes, they worked out the idea of an organism that would encompass all the legitimate productive efforts, conforming plastically to the reality of the historical forces and freely ordering them in a hierarchy of functions, values, and necessities. The factory council—in which the needs of investment capital, the enterprise, and the work force were organized according to the particular responsibility of each, measured by the activity discharged—was their new, precise idea, and in the name of that idea they attempted to gather the workers together and endow them with a political personality.

Meanwhile, along with and against this typically Turinese experience, there was the muffled resonance of a new international situation that elicited complex ideals in the travail of difficult an-

tinomies: the revolutionary vanguard in Turin found itself faced
with the obstacle of new problems of tactics, theory, and popular
psychology created by the general situation. The international
revolutionary crisis, a mixture of unsatisfied messianic aspirations and the poverty and impotence in which the majority of
the people lived, became the very antithesis of the aims and the
actions developed out of the unusual autonomous experience of
the proletarian aristocracies. The problem on which the Turinese theorists of the factory council spent their energies in vain
was how to relate and coordinate their own concrete revolutionary instinct and the confused uncertainty of the inner drives that
predominated in the popular masses of the nation.

Gramsci

If we want to penetrate the intimate cultural profile and psychology of the group that directed the communist movement
in Turin, we have to go back to the history of socialist journalism during the war years. In 1914 socialism in Turin had the
same lack of preparation and provincial superficiality that were
characteristic, as we have seen, of the whole Italian movement.
Instead of a politics of ideals, capable of having a formative influence, instead of at least organizing their ideas around the abstract and yet noble banner of internationalism, most of the
workers professed a mean-spirited neutralism in imitation of
the Giolittians, an arid utilitarian position devoid of spiritual
content, scarcely justifiable in a party in government and utterly
repugnant in a party of the people.[22]

This absence of ideals and intransigence in the Italian Socialist Party corresponded to the absence of a core of educated,
hardworking leaders. The physiognomy of old-style socialism in
Turin was essentially a product of the Cooperative Alliance, a

---

22. The Giolittians were the liberals of the prewar generation who set
the model for political action even for the socialists; see Chapter 1, note 10.

large economic entity that had demonstrated its ability to meet the competition from the retail trade in providing for the needs of the consumer but was a breeding ground of collaborationism and the bureaucratic spirit when it came to politics. Nor could any current, even if it became dominant within the party, break away from the alliance in local affairs, because it was the real base of party finances. The leading figures, the ones most popular in the rudimentary psychology of the masses, were Nofri, the technician of cooperativism (within which he made sure of a sinecure for himself); Casalini, the missionary of hygiene, the doctor of the poor, who satisfied all of his own philanthropic ideals by working in his own city; and Morgari, the popular apostle of the fight against abuses and privilege. The "Marquis" Balsamo-Crivelli, with his refined erudition, Pastonchi, noted for his historical studies, and "Professor" Zino Zini added the requisite romantic tint to the portrait, with their philosophical and aristocratic support for the cause of the humble and the oppressed.[23]

That the background and the intellectual profile of Antonio Gramsci were very different from these traditions was already evident during the years in which he completed his literary studies at the University of Turin and joined the Socialist Party, the latter probably for humanitarian reasons colored by the pessimism he felt as an isolated immigrant from Sardinia. . . .[24]

As a writer for the *Avanti!*[25] Gramsci was a revelation. On

23. Gobetti is giving Turinese examples of socialist models that were popular everywhere in Italy, particularly in the central and northern regions: cooperatives of distribution; neighborhood medical centers for workers and their families; popular apostles (as opposed to the Catholic ones) of the socialist cause; local teachers; philanthropists and good Samaritans, and so on.

24. At this point in the book *La rivoluzione liberale*, to which this chapter belongs, Gobetti inserted a sketch on Gramsci, which I have omitted here and included among the biographical essays in the first chapter of this anthology, since he later revised it and published it separately in the journal *La Rivoluzione Liberale*.

25. See Chapter 1, note 48.

the page devoted to the local news of Turin he had a column of
his own, *Sotto la Mole*, filled with destructive polemic and acer-
bic satire. In his prose one was immediately struck by the ferocious, insistent, dialectical style, brusque yet serene: the lucid
catastrophic desperation of Marx blended with Oriani's [26] vision
of historical dialectic, and an art of balance and harmonic construction derived from the classics.

But his activity as theorist of the revolutionary process began
with the work he did for *Il Grido del Popolo* [*The Cry of the People*],
the small weekly propaganda paper of the party that became
a journal of thought and culture in 1918. It published the first
translations of Russian revolutionary texts and offered a political interpretation of the actions of the Bolsheviks; and though
the name on the masthead belonged to another, it was from
the brain of Gramsci that the inspiration for these researches
flowed. In the figure of Lenin he saw a heroic drive for liberation:
the ideal motifs that constituted the Bolshevik myth, burning
secretly in the popular psychology, should act not as the model
for a revolution in Italy but as the stimulus for a free initiative
operating from below.

The antibureaucratic thrust of the Italian revolution had
been noted by Gramsci as early as 1917, when his autonomist
thought took concrete form in a special issue with the pregnant
title *La città futura* [*The City of the Future*], published as the
prototype and manifesto of a periodical devoted to worker political culture.

Ordine Nuovo

In 1919 *La città futura* became the *Ordine Nuovo*, the only example of revolutionary and Marxist journalism with any claim to
ideal seriousness to have appeared in Italy. In the *Ordine Nuovo*

26. Alfredo Oriani (1852–1909) was a well-known and admired opinion
maker and a critic of the decadence of public spirit in Italy.

the tragic dissension afflicting every political action in Italy—ineluctably torn between the drive for autonomy and the reformist tradition—was evident from the very first issues in the contrast between the ideas of its founders. They deserve to be remembered for the singular work into which they threw themselves: besides Gramsci there were Tasca, Togliatti, and Terracini.[27]

Terracini's temperament was more political than theoretical; he was systemically averse to demagogy; aristocratic; an opponent of oratorical vehemence; a subtle reasoner; determined to the point of monotony and stubbornness when engaged in debate and action; unconstrained by moral prejudice in his assessment of ideas and ready to treat them as forces when that seemed opportune. He was the diplomat, the Machiavellian, but so lacking in sympathy and ability to inspire others that when at last he stood alone in the breach, none of his diplomatic qualities enabled him to break out of the desolate circle of solitude and make plans for action.

Togliatti, finding himself, like Terracini, in a position of responsibility, became the victim of his own uneasiness, an apparent cynicism, inexorable and tyrannical, that is really indecision, that was judged to be equivocal and is perhaps only a hypercriti-

27. Angelo Tasca, Palmiro Togliatti, and Umberto Elia Terracini were the leaders who, along with Gramsci, organized the communist group in Turin and who, in 1921, founded the Italian Communist Party. Tasca (1892–1960) spent many years in exile and dissociated himself from the communists when Stalin opposed the Weimar Republic and started imposing a forced collectivization of the land in Russia. Togliatti (1893–1964), who spent several years in Moscow during the fascist period, went back to Italy in 1944 and organized the strategy that would create the provisional government of southern Italy after the total collapse of the monarchical state after Mussolini's regime and the alliance with Germany came to an end. Togliatti was a member of the Constituent Assembly that wrote the democratic constitution of Italy and the general secretary of the Italian Communist Party until his death in 1964. Terracini (1895–1983), after ten years spent in a fascist jail, was an exile in France and then a partisan in the Italian resistance. He was president of the Constituent Assembly and a prominent constitutional law scholar.

cal impulse he cannot suppress and about which we ought in any case to refrain from passing objective judgment.

The real dissension arose between Gramsci and Tasca and was the trial by fire that showed that the former was the one who had reached a mature understanding of the new problems. Angelo Tasca came to political activism with a primarily literary education and with the mindset of a propagandist and apostle. When he joined the *Ordine Nuovo*, he viewed it as a journal of ideas that was meant to take up the problematic of Antonio Labriola[28] and trace a revision of Marxism and the history of the socialist intellectual movement. He began with a series of studies on Louis Blanc, written with the bibliographic scruple of somebody writing for the *Giornale storico della letteratura italiana*. His main interest, other than in getting his quotations and his references right, was in the problem of small landholdings, of which he took a sentimental view verging on the petit-bourgeois: something patriarchal, a blend of Bakunin and Turati, remained in his thought.[29] This was the socialism of a man of books, of a messianist who conceived the redemption of the people as enlightened rebirth; who drew a veil, that of his own petit-bourgeois dream of the virtuous worker, over modern civilization; who thrived on the moderate habits of his forebears, on the tranquil composure of house and garden. In him the fantasy of the intellectual never ceased to clash with the equilibrium of the cultivated Latin, and Christian messianism sometimes overruled the calculating imperturbability of the Piedmontese.

After the first tentative months of existence, emphatic but sterile, in which the only lively things in the *Ordine Nuovo* were

28. Antonio Labriola (1843–1904), the first Italian Marxist scholar, provided an original interpretation of Marx's philosophy. He taught at the University of Rome and wrote seminal essays on Socrates, Spinoza, and Vico. He enrolled in the Socialist Party and began a rich correspondence with Engels, Kautsky, Liebknecht, Adler, Bebel, and Lafargue. He was deeply critical of Marxist revisionism and developed the notion of the "philosophy of praxis."

29. See Chapter 2, note 34.

a few brilliant cultural commentaries that revealed the caustic side of Palmiro Togliatti, Gramsci made the debate on the factory councils into the central theme. According to him, they were to be the cadres of the new worker state and, during the period of violent struggle, of the revolutionary army. In place of abstract propaganda exercises, concrete action was needed: the workers had to get used to real discipline and the conscious exercise of authority, taking on the mentality of producers, of a ruling class, through contact with the organizations in which they worked. Since working life is lived in the factory, the workers had to organize their resistance against the industrialists in the factory. The new state, born not in the name of the abstract rights and duties of the citizen but for the purpose of furthering the industriousness of the workers, had to adapt plastically to the structures within which their activity took place and come to an understanding of their needs and investigate their problems within that context.

Whatever we may think of the practical validity of these formulas, at last there was a concept of revolution before which all the claptrap of abstraction and reformism simply caved in. The syndicalism of Tasca, who accepted the councils, like the unions [*sindacati*], as vehicles for propaganda work, was shown to be inadequate to the workers' consciousness. He remained an outsider to this new experiment in class struggle.

Ordine Nuovo became the center around which the most aware groups of proletarians clustered and by whose influence they were guided during the fiercest struggles and the most doubtful moments. The occupation of the factories and the electoral campaign to win control of city government were the culminating episodes in a proletarian offensive guided by the same men who had laid the theoretical groundwork.

But the effectiveness of the new aristocracy was hampered by the dead weight of the socialist heritage, the incapacity of the leaders of the labor confederation, the utilitarian ideals with which the mass of the petite bourgeoisie had been raised, the reactionary spirit of the peasants who had confusedly flowed into the Socialist Party, and finally the shortcomings, the narrowness and impotence, of the leadership itself, who failed to divide responsibility among themselves and find suitable new recruits while rampant personal ambition suffocated a movement that had grown up too fast. Amid all this friction, the work of the *Ordine Nuovo* proved insufficient to make its agenda prevail.

The Struggle for the Councils

Throughout 1920 the factory council was the focus of revolutionary activity, the touchstone that set the various trends within the workers' movement apart from one another, and the organ of the struggle against the associations of the industrialists. Faced with these last, who in various local situations showed that they were ready to fight and viewed themselves, morally and intellectually, as the leaders of the nation's industrial development, the writers at the *Ordine Nuovo* realized in turn that they would not be able to fight back with the old principles peculiar to the debate on unionism, nor rely on the purely economic tactics of the General Confederation of Labor. The movement needed personalities on its side who were fully and unremittingly committed, and the general struggle had to take place along a unified front of action.

Mario Guarnieri, a reformist, has left us the documents (extremely tendentious ones because of their ostentatious eclecticism) concerning the early working-out of this analysis and the initial discussions between supporters and opponents of the councils. But the theoretical and practical dissension raises much more complex issues than that of personalities and correlates to distinct regional differences produced by conditions of more advanced technical progress and a more keen grasp of the politics of class relations in the realm of production.

In August 1919 the worker groups at Fiat central, with whom Gramsci was closely involved in discussion and collaboration, envisioned the creation of the new instrument of struggle and proletarian organization based on a preexisting institution, the internal [factory] commissions. These had been in existence for some years in the city without notable opposition on the part of the industrialists and were intended, in the eyes of the peaceful Colombino, to constitute a new kind of trade and technical school and, in the unspoken intention of Buozzi,[30] might even have served to increase the rate of production.

The plan was to renounce the agreements explicitly or implicitly in place with the employers, which placed limits on organization for economic purposes, and make the internal commissions into political organs, able to exercise power along with, and counter to, the power of the employers. They would be expanded until they had the structure of real, proper factory councils, able to impose their own discipline on the workers and to organize them in accordance with the natural hierarchy of production.

Experience soon showed that while the internal commissions might make a good point of departure, because of a sort of psychological tradition, the functions of the new council had to be kept separate from the old ones of the commission, or at any rate, new commissars had to be appointed in every department to direct the workers' movement.

Ordine Nuovo, flanked by the Turinese edition of *Avanti!*, which Ottavio Pastore[31] allowed to become a sort of natural extension of the thought of Gramsci, assumed the control and the preparation of the economic structures and the political work. It highlighted the originality of the new movement of the councils and the need to keep them separate from union activity. Indeed,

30. Bruno Buozzi (1881–1944) was a union organizer and the general secretary of the General Confederation of Labor. He was killed by the Nazis in 1944. Emilio Colombino was secretary of the union of Fiat workers in Turin.
31. Ottavio Pastore was one of Gramsci's closest friends and followed him when he left the socialist newspaper *Avanti!* to found *Ordine Nuovo*.

the union is an organ of resistance, not of initiative, one that tends to promote the consciousness of being wage earners in the workers, not the dignity of being producers; that accepts their status as slaves and seeks to improve it in reformist and utilitarian terms rather than change it. But in the council the worker would sense his full dignity as an indispensable element of modern life, associated with technicians, intellectuals, and entrepreneurs, and would focus his aspirations not on his own particular advantage but on an ideal of progress and autonomy; thus he would reinforce his own aptitudes, seeking to create a practical organization through which his class might come to power.

The plan of action was no longer democratic in the broad sense, nor was it pedagogic: the new society to be created would not be the society of the people as an indistinct populace but that of the people as proletariat. The government would be an aristocracy risen from below, able to take up the burden of the effete ruling class.

Far from an organ of collaboration, the council was seen as the first cell of the economic and political organization to come and as the army of the united front of struggle in the period before the conquest of power. At the head of this movement were groups of workers who in the myth of the *Ordine Nuovo* felt their own freedom. There were examples, young members of the proletariat dedicated to revolutionary propaganda, without messianism or humanitarian hopes, who spoke the language of Hegelianism without knowing it and placed an arid and austere ideal of the state over and above their own thoughts. And since the masses were unable to understand and participate willingly in the new ideas, the leadership assumed the burden of guiding them to the destination they could not see and making them face up to events that would compel them consciously or not to take specific actions. At Turin in April 1920 they in fact succeeded in organizing and staging a general strike for ten days that did not advance the usual wage demands but had a purely ideal purpose: the continuation of the councils. The strike failed because the national council of the Socialist Party wanted it confined to Turin and because the industrialists, intelligently led by Olivetti[32] (who had studied the thought of the new revolutionaries and grasped its spirit and the dangers it posed), fought back very hard. Still, the defeat was one of those stern lessons that put firmness of will to the test and enable an estimate of relative strength. It did not shatter the discipline of the workers; indeed, it revealed a singular capacity for sacrifice on their part. It showed the ineptitude of the Socialist Party for any direct action and brought an understanding of the need to endow the movement with a national political structure able to command from all workers the support necessary for the defense of the more progressive groups who found themselves in the vanguard of the revolutionary movement.

The dissension between the *Ordine Nuovo* and Serrati came down to this: for the former the united front of proletarian action had to be the most advanced outpost, and for Serrati[33] it had to be several trenches to the rear. Serrati saw the seizure of power as the crowning moment of the general improvement of the masses (a Mazzinian utopia, abstract and indeterminate), while Gramsci believed in the seizure of power only as the means of elevating the masses. Between these two mentalities, the one democratic and the other Marxist, there was clearly an antithesis after April 1920, and the effective constitution of a Turinese Communist Party distinct from and opposed to the Socialist Party dates from that period.

And the baptism of the new party was the occupation of the factories in September—its revenge for the battle it had lost in the spring, the trial by fire of the maturity of the Turinese workers. And yet its victory signified at the same time finality and decadence, because it demonstrated the impossibility of extend-

32. Adriano Olivetti was a creative Piedmontese industrialist and the organizer of a center for social and political research. The Olivetti computer factory is still active.
33. See Chapter 2, note 35.

ing the movement to all of Italy, both because of economic obstacles and because outside Turin there did not exist a mature
worker leadership.

Faced with the magnificent movement for workers' councils
we have described, a liberal cannot assume the purely negative
position of Luigi Einaudi and Edoardo Giretti.[34] We are in the
presence of one of the most genuine phenomena of political autonomy to have achieved realization in modern Italy. All party
prejudice aside, anyone who ponders the effects of the postwar
crisis, which is a crisis of will, of coherence, of liberty, and still
believes in a revival of the revolutionary movement that was in-
terrupted in the Risorgimento, a revival capable finally of penetrating the spirit of the popular masses and awakening them to
liberty, ought to see in these feelings and in these trials the high
road of the political contest of the future. The Turinese communists had gone beyond libertarian, demagogic phrasemaking
and set themselves concrete problems. They defended free local
initiative against the trade union bureaucracy. Moving out from
the factory, they took up the specific legacy of the bourgeois tradition, proposing not to create a new economy out of thin air
but to take up and continue the progress in the technique of production already achieved by the industrialists. They well knew,
contrary to abstract plans for socialization, what importance to
attribute to the factor of investment in industry and what role
belonged to the entrepreneur in production. The factory council as conceived by its theorizers could also satisfy the demands
of the white-collar workers, not in their role of petits bourgeois
but in their role of employees, elements in the process of production. We can say in conclusion that their concrete experience of
political action liberated the young Turinese communists com-

34. On Einaudi see "A Teacher of Liberalism" in Chapter 2. The laissez-
faire economist Edoardo Giretti was, along with Einaudi, one of the liberals
whom Gobetti appreciated for his honesty and his consistent opposition to
the statist liberals. Gobetti did not, however, share Giretti's opposition to
workers' organization.

pletely from the illusions and the commonplaces of the old socialism and internationalism. They perceived a laissez-faire aspect of the workers' movement. Though their experiment failed,
it still remains one of the noblest efforts ever made to bring renewal to our political life.

The Communist Party

Faced with the desperate movement instigated by the communists, Giolitti resorted to his tried and true tactics and was able
to tame the rebels, handing them over inert to the vendetta of
the petite bourgeoisie, who could hardly believe that their worst
nightmare, the slogan "Those who don't work won't eat" bla-
zoned on the flag of their executioners, had vanished. It was in
these circumstances, after the decline of the ideal of liberty that
the vanguard of the proletariat alone was still fighting for, in
this crisis of will and this depletion of strength and character,
that fascism, the avenger and consoler of the terrified middle
classes, could emerge, armed with its patriarchal violence and its
D'Annunzian rapture. Mussolini's tyrannical dream, no different
from the pleasing dictatorship of the bureaucracy and the trade
unions contemplated by our social democrats, just more Italian,
more humanistic, amateurish, and theatrical, represented precisely the renunciation by individuals of their responsibilities,
the renunciation by the social classes of the forces they had mo-
bilized. It was a palingenesis of decadence in which the most
combative and worthy minorities were prostrated by an economic crisis of unemployment that was stronger than their
power of will and fatally propitious for the return to an economy
of slavery invoked by rhetoricians.

In these conditions, all that remained for those who had lost
at Turin was the duty of resistance. Since the ruin was irreparable, the vanguard would have to separate their own responsibilities from the bent and broken masses and restate their firm,
vindictive intention as solitary heretics of the future. So it was

that in great haste and without pause to reflect on whether it was opportune or tactically wise the Communist Party was founded.

It is perfectly clear why the real Italian revolutionaries could no longer place any faith in the Socialist Party, which had been incapable of really accomplishing anything because of its bloated bureaucratic structure, because of the priority it gave to unity, and because its collaborationist tactics had implicitly saddled it with governmental responsibility. Now it stood impotent before the armed offensive of the seekers of peace and quiet and recreation. The party had put itself at risk by gradually, empirically adapting itself to the old regime through its defense of cooperativist privileges and acting as a conservative force, without introducing either a new idea or a new impetus into national life, content to accept the Giolittian heritage. If Serrati, a man of truly generous heart, had also been a great politician, the battle to keep the party united might at least have had formative value; and more would have come of the effort to give the united movement a hardworking and free executive that would arouse the popular forces, instead of waiting for them to wake up, and that would have aligned the work of the party with the ideas of its more active, coherent revolutionary minority.

Instead, Serrati's unity was vitiated by a quietist and democratic prejudice, for as a result of the generically messianic propaganda of the Socialist Party, elements from the bourgeois strata of society and from the peasantry had gradually joined, hoping for economic betterment, lacking any political preparation or will to liberation, and unwavering in their generic anarchic hostility to the state for utilitarian reasons. The psychology of these neophytes was to emerge as the most insurmountable obstacle to clear political differentiation. Democratic voting would result in this unprepared horde gaining control of the movement; and with no capacity to exercise control or take initiative, they would end up following demagogic stratagems and condottieri.

Like Serrati, the communists were lacking in diplomatic

skills and chose to take a stand on a modest question of sincerity. So the separation became inevitable; the problem of obedience to Moscow was merely the occasion for the conflict of two systems and was willingly accepted by the reformists, who needed to make up for quite a few sins of internationalism to be able to side with the government.

The sequel of events has shown that the communists in fact sacrificed their political future over this question of sincerity. They dreamed of being a party acting in isolation, intransigent and inexorably ready to seize dictatorial power when the moment came for them to launch an offensive in grand style. But when it came to resisting fascism, a united proletarian front, which they later vainly called for, would have been much more energetic and effective. Machiavellian tactics of a quite different kind would been more favorable to an intransigent politics: the job of the communists was to make all the forces serve the resistance. Naturally the party would have freed itself of its less intrepid components, eliminating them and leaving them far to the rear, and we would have been spared the spectacle of a group going into the most difficult and decisive battle with an improvised army of uncertain troops and no officers.

The fact is that the face of the new party showed the admixture of discordant and immature elements—messianists of revolutionary propaganda like Bombacci and Misiano (decorative elements of the extreme Left) alongside a theorist of the catastrophe of the bourgeois economy like Graziadei; the abstentionist fringe of Bordiga, promoting with meridional exuberance a bureaucratic revolutionism that managed to turn into state socialism, all the while reducing politics to the hermetic dogmatics of theory, alongside the subtle schemes and historical improvisations of Tuntar[35]—the characteristic result of a strong

35. On Bombacci and Misiano see Chapter 1, note 23. Antonio Graziadei (1873–1953) was an economist who abandoned the Socialist Party to become a communist; he went into exile in France. Amedeo Bordiga was, along with

talent for criticism applied with arid intellectualism in an international setting in which three civilizations meet without creating a new civilization, producing only the pathology of restlessness. Amid these frictions and shades of difference Gramsci
might have seized command if unemployment had not unex-
pectedly reduced the number of disciplined troops needed for
the fight. Thus the communists were lonely heretics instead of a
typical vanguard in the play of forces. They shut themselves off
from all communication with national life, limiting themselves
to declarations of their surviving faith in an internationalist foreign policy. Their plans and their practical activity remained tied
to an abstract theoretical coherence built on purely dialectical
and syllogistic calculations.

Since the Socialist Party had failed because of the absence
of structures adapted to the social strata involved in production
and able to function as the framework of the new state, the new
Communist Party, according to Gramsci and Bordiga, ought to
organize itself as a movement with rigid internal discipline: the
people would sense the superiority of this guiding minority and
accept its direction. The trouble was that ideologies like that lost
any potential to gain a foothold in Italian economic life when the
problem of the factory councils became definitively insoluble.
It is curious to be talking about organic structures and organic
unity when there is nothing there to be fitted into the structure.

In three years of existence the party has wrapped itself her-
metically around a problem of tactics, of which the disconcerted
proletarian army has barely caught a glimpse. With the disap-
pearance of both the practical and ideal consensus, personality
conflicts became dominant.

At this point the critique we wish to offer of the process, theoretical and practical, that has left the communists in a state

Gramsci and Giovanni Sanna, a founder of the Communist Party of Italy in
1921. He led the maximalist fringe and was expelled from the party in 1930.
Giuseppe Tuntar was first a leader of the Socialist Party, then a leader of the
newly constituted Communist Party.

of prostration diverges notably from the objections commonly heard. It is true that the elaboration of their practical ideas and empirical problems remained rather nebulous and contradictory, but we know that an opposition party needs two practical programs: one mythical, promising renewal to weary combatants here and now, filled with Christian longing for the kingdom of peace, even while they negate it with their own restlessness; and one political, which will reveal itself only at the hour of victory. This curious irony lies in wait for the revolutionary movement: when the endgame arrives, the revolutionaries find they have to fight against themselves first. The Turinese communists were in a singular case (deriving from their cultural familiarity with the syndicalism of Sorel) because they had understood this process of historical contradiction perfectly, though they were not themselves able to launch an examination of the relations that ought to have linked the myth to practical action. Their declamations against the state were originally understood by the writers of the *Ordine Nuovo* as declamations against the bureaucratic state; the very ideal of a new order derived from the wish to inherit the unfulfilled demands of the Risorgimento, and their profession of internationalist faith was a foreign policy adopted in opposition to French imperialism. As for their struggle against capitalism, it was tinged with a polemical lament for the economic inadequacy of capitalism in Italy.

So the main lines of their critique were quite unconnected with the ideology of state socialism. Gramsci descends directly not only from the revolutionary theorists but also from liberal thinkers with a problem-based approach [*problemisti liberali*], like Salvemini, Einaudi, Mosca, and Fortunato.[36] Tasca, Togliatti, and Sanna[37] had the same ideological roots.

36. On Mosca see the essay in Chapter 1. Giustino Fortunato (1848–1932) directed and published the first socioeconomic research in south Italy and in spite of his conservative ideas played an important role in inspiring a critical awareness of the limits of the Italian liberal state.

37. Giovanni Sanna (1877–1950) was among the founders of the Italian

This means that the inadequacy of their experiment cannot be attributed to the immaturity of their ideas, which in fact derive from the traditional currents of liberal and autonomist thought that were always the typical instrument for the critique of Italian history. The explanation must lie instead in questions of character and internal administration.

The Communist Party, with its ideals of liberating revolution against bourgeois bureaucracy, was a practical example of an artificial organism that grew up under a protectionist regime. It is organized in bureaucratic departments; its personnel are functionaries dependent on a salary just as much as, or even more than, trade union mandarins are. Its administrative systems correspond to a parasitical method of life.

Because of its unpopular and aristocratic nature it seemed to place itself above the real conditions of Italian life. Its initiatives were abstract, neither adapted to nor controlled by the effective participation of the masses. Nationalists and *patriots* have repeated the banal accusation about "Russian gold," but we can ignore them: the real danger and the real immorality lie in the fact that, since they are not financed by donations and thus exposed to the sanctions and the sacrifices of individuals, the party lacks any incentive to make changes and also one of the fundamental criteria for gauging validity and success. It chose to branch out by adapting itself, in the most bourgeois and reactionary way, to the administrative partition of the kingdom (to have a section in every commune was its fondest dream!), and didn't stop to think that a revolutionary party needs to build itself around forces rather than offices and that the geographic distribution of the sections has to correspond to the effort and will of the party members, to follow a rule of autonomy, not a bureaucratic plan. Naturally, when the going got rough, an *employee* would fold rather than hold firm against the advancing enemy.

Communist Party and among those who inspired the council factories. An expert on the agrarian problem, he had been close to Gaetano Salvemini.

The heroic spirit was lacking, so there could not be any desperate resistance. When the central payroll department shut down, the functionaries scattered.

The same effects of this protectionism were observable in the journalistic activity of the party. There was a paper, *Ordine Nuovo*, born of the sacrifices of a mature and conflict-hardened working class. In the first months of its life it was the most intellectual periodical in Italy: everything in it was organically conceived, done with a spirit of sacrifice and an ideal of liberty, the headlines, the theater reviews, the letters from workers, the articles by Lenin, the fiction supplement. An even rarer miracle followed: the workers themselves read it and discussed it like culture fanatics.

Then an unexpected order from the executive (not unconnected to petty personal motives) founded two new dailies, *Il Lavoratore* at Trieste and *Il Comunista* at Rome. Italy was divided into three strictly delimited zones each of which was meant to have its own periodical and no other in order to avoid competition, and since there was not the staff for three papers, they broke up the Turinese editorial team, sending Togliatti to Rome and Pastore to Trieste. The end result was three unreadable papers. Only the proletariat of Turin had the specific attributes needed to support a political paper of its own by making that paper an expression of its own life. Clearly it is impossible to bring to life aristocracies and mature individuals out of decisions taken by boards of trustees and executive committees. Instead of representing local mentalities and reflecting original tendencies, the communist papers turned into the most boring collections of writings by Bukharin and Zinoviev, in ill-conceived homage to the Third International.

Such conditions of political protectionism produced artificial constructs of moral life. Closed in small groups, unable to act, the communists consumed themselves in a sterile critique of the maximalists, while the rank and file, notwithstanding the notional veto on splitting up into factions, were rocked by re-

ciprocal mistrust and fierce personal hatreds of the kind unique
to conspirators. The prevailing atmosphere was romantic, intolerant, and intolerable, an arid sectarian spirit of disintegration. The finest members had to occupy themselves with matters
insidiously particular and therewith wasted their liveliest abilities. In less than two years they were worn out. Fascist persecution, instead of making them into martyrs and symbols of rebellion, simply made everything they did ineffectual, condemning
them to start again every time by scrutinizing their own consciences and their own maturity. Organizations cannot be improvised: they are worth as much as the traditions that have
nourished them and the effort they cost. Rather than finding the
vigor of rebirth in the struggle for liberty, the communist organizations collapsed as soon as the leaders suffered a moment of
fatigue.

COMMUNIST FEMINISM

> We have to persuade the female proletariat at home that the in-
> dustrialization of domestic work, which the communists pro-
> pose, can emancipate them from household slavery and make
> their capacities and energies more utilizable.[38] And while that
> will be good for the collectivity, it will really help to meliorate the
> condition of women, guaranteeing them the chance to elevate
> themselves spiritually and to safeguard their health and their
> beauty. (Camilla Ravera in *Ordine Nuovo*)

I s elevating women an independent moral problem, distinct
from the moral problem of elevating all human beings? Femi-
nists say it is, but when pressed for details, they rarely go beyond
a generic invocation of juridical equality, entirely contained in

38. Original title: "Femminismo comunista"; a section of an article entitled "Esperienza liberale [IV]"; from *La rivoluzione Liberale* 1, no. 10 (23
April 1922), p. 40, signed "Antiguelfo." Translated from *Scritti politici*, pp.
339–41.

the demand for voting rights. In a democratic regime, in the representative regime, the *vote* is only one of the ways through which individuals bring their will to the state. That women are entitled to it no one denies. But to say that their exclusion from this entitlement up till now has been an enormous injustice is blatant demagogic exaggeration, since there were infinite other modes of self-affirmation open to female initiative. But it is clear nonetheless that these infinite ways attain consecration and permanence through the vote. There were some who pointed to the risk that if they did voice their will, it seemed likely to be reactionary, since they had formed their political notions within the restricted domain of the family and would be inclined by historical tradition to see social problems from a quasi-physical viewpoint of conservatism and economic individualism. In reality, however, the dialectic of wills, once they actually become effective, overrides all exclusivism: the family problems that preoccupy women, once they become the object of political debate, force those who are posing them to adopt an attitude that is no longer limited and sentimental. The training of individual women in that is part of the training of everyone to see things with a *political*, not fragmentary, consciousness. The emergence of a moral will, of a serenity above egoism, in a woman who contemplates her problems is a universal impulse that men feel in the same way. Recriminations and subtle distinctions are the tricks of suffragists.

Once the problem is put in these terms, the communist critique of bourgeois society and the bourgeois family becomes a necessary phase of female participation in political life. The concept of the industrialization of domestic work signifies an aspiration to free the political mentality of women from every sort of sentimentalism and from limited emotional horizons. Getting rid of all the ways of *poeticizing the household* will further the task assumed by historical liberalism of forcing all human beings to think and act realistically. In that respect too, communism is realistic. It combats an idea with an idea, a tradition with a purely formal will.

So their polemic takes on the force of a spiritual liberation and renounces all of history with a heroic myth, because that appears to be the only way to make progress and overcome the crisis. While various committees for "the vote for women" talk about moral superiority and inferiority, about rights, and so on, drafting eighteenth-century declarations of abstract Jacobin liberty, the program of communist feminism is measuring up to the only unavoidable current need, which is political and not moral, which is for action and not intentions, for will and not juridical justification.

But instead of wishfully imagining empirical programs, this effort has to focus on a myth: the *industrialization of domestic work* is an expedient of the grossest simplicity, a piece of economic infantilism, as long as it is invoked as a measure to be taken by the state, as the triumph of order and uniformity. We need to accept the revolutionary and creative part of the program and reject the reformist illusion. In this sense, the struggle against familial sentimentalism may be the most lucid and rigorous way for women to acquire their familial function integrally (meaning in political reality). That the communists should confront this task before anyone else is naturally logical, because it is in their interest more than in anyone else's to block any ingenuous and instinctively reactionary translation of feminist prejudices into politics.

PARADOX OF THE RUSSIAN SPIRIT

Tartar Byzantium

SITUATED between Europe and Asia, longing to rise above Asiatic primitivism, unable to attain European culture, Russia did not win a position for itself in the spiritual life of humanity before the nineteenth century.[39] This lament for the inadequacy of the nation's accomplishment was a commonplace among Russian thinkers of the previous century. But the intellectual class did not succeed in passing from this sentimental attitude of abstract recrimination to something more constructively concrete.

The people were absent from political life, beyond the pale of the state and culture, did not know their own strength, and were incapable of creating for themselves a clear consciousness (in praxis) of their own will and their own destiny. The state, offshoot of a theocracy, was the heir of Byzantium and the negation of modernity. The intellectual class did not derive its vitality from the needs of the country (because the latter were suffocated) and therefore—necessarily—lost itself in cultural caprice while aspiring to freedom: from that flowed arbitrary theories, a culture unacquainted with the most intimate social torment, an intemperate need for disputation reduced to criticism. These elements defined the Russian national conscience before the revolution, and to understand them we must not be content to consider them in the abstract, as static results; rather, we must make the effort to see how they came about and how they grew up around the problems that history posed.

Our investigation of the process of development presupposes a point of arrival that sheds light on all the rest: the revolution. In that extreme act the period of preparation gained its final validity, which is also a criterion of dialectical evaluation.

Theocracy

The age-old malady of Russian life, its prehistoric spiritual immaturity, took the form of mysticism and theocracy. Russian mysticism was the first moment of thought. To use the language of the philosophy of knowledge, we could say that it affirmed un-

---

39. Original title: *Paradosso dello spirito russo*, part 1, "La lotta delle idee." Translated from *Scritti storici*, pp. 293–309.

differentiated unity, a unity of aspiration without any principle of real determination. An elementary historical consciousness begins to appear when, faced with the tumultuous flux of social data, the spirit affirms itself as distinct from every other fact and locates the abstraction of itself (in its inconsistent purity) in an ideal world delivered from all the physical laws that trammel it. Theocracy was the primal form of social life into which this effort of thought organized itself. The abstract ideal became the law of practice. Having discovered a world of mystical purity, the spirit wants immediately to conform to it. Theocracy is the system without the dialectic, the motionless ideal of transcendence.

The first ruling class in this country of sparse commerce and uncertain communications saw their most heartfelt interests embodied in this doctrine of social conservatism and devotion to the established aristocracy. They introduced into the sermons the Church addressed to the people the idea that the riches of others have to be respected as though divine. The transcendence of the doctrine thus revealed functioned as a guarantee of obedient popular submission.

In describing the process, we have assigned limited theoretical value to this transcendence and the theocracy to which it gives rise; but precisely because we are dealing with a static value (reduced to the simplicity of a formula of identity), the interest of the historian must be directed—more than to defining it (or pondering the definition)—to investigating its pragmatic validity, its capacity to create new effects and new practical relations.

Catholic theocracy, born with the great legacy of the Greco-Roman world and imposed on persons whose sense of individual and political values was extremely strong owing to tradition, expressed itself, during the period of mystical preparation, in the enthusiasm of religious life, in the spontaneity of sentiment, in the vitality of individual pulsations, and practically generated the organization of the Church, an ideal organization that is also practical, a Church that is also a state, a transcendental unity that creates (to be created out of it in turn) popular unity and democracy. (The Church in Italy is also the communes.) For Western man the Middle Ages represents a discipline out of which has come the unshakable conviction that free life and social life are inseparable; for modern man the Catholic heritage excludes anarchic aberrations (without needing to deny or limit the value of the individual).

Extraneous to Greco-Roman culture, Russia was unable to have a Middle Ages (a discipline); its early history was a prehistory of fantasy, concealing slavery. The soil and the climate, the squalid immensity of the unvarying steppe (exposed to the violence of the Tartars) constituted, for a primitive people, insurmountable obstacles to the formation of industrial and commercial life. Unacquainted with earthly goods, incapable of seeing in life on earth anything besides nature and physical pleasure, the Russian turned to the heavens, or rather split himself between heaven and earthly brutality, between ascetic solitude and vodka. The impulse to unity was absent because the idealization of practical activity and economic individualism was absent.

With the world of reality deconsecrated, the Russian could accept slavery, could support every external constraint without his ideal becoming operational and combative (nonresistance to evil). This mysticism reinforced with indifference precluded any autonomous practical organization—hence the state had to arise in Russia not out of the spontaneous consent of individuals and their culture but from external imposition.

The people did not know how to construct their Church. The clergy was born as an emanation of the government, as a tyrannical bureaucracy, indifferent to any religious and theoretical interest, extraneous to the national life. It is worth pondering Trotsky's idea that a clergy was unable to emerge spontaneously because of the lack of abundant sources of food. The clergy emerged artificially and subsisted by robbing the people of their bread every day, without fulfilling any function that would—for the people—have validity.

Whereas the first modern European civilization was religious, the Russian clergy was not capable of elaborating a dogma, did not promote any philosophy, did not initiate a literature. No reforms or heresies arose out of concrete debates about ideas—only sects, out of otiose Byzantine questions about rites or even about orthography.

The Russian people, whom all intellectuals consider the most religious of peoples, did not have a religion. The twin poles of their faith were a mechanism of rites and formulas, socially unproductive, and a morbid religiosity that cloaked a disturbed and violent individualism with mysticism.

To this situation of cultural dearth there corresponded analogous economic circumstances that reacted upon the condition of the spirit and reinforced static mysticism. Scattered across the steppe, the people did not feel the need for centers of movement and progress, did not succeed in building cities based on commerce and industry, remained strangers to any state unity. The history of Kiev and Novgorod was swiftly cut off by foreign interventions. Before the *muzhik* [peasant] there stood the Moscow government, tyranny imposing itself without respecting the wills of individuals, in fact ignoring them, and placing over them a bureaucratic organization that, while it could annul and repress them, could not comprehend and distinguish them.

Moscow also signified the clergy: another bureaucracy that governed because it ignored. In the context of civilization, Moscow counted as a bureaucratic capital. The Russian people remained an aggregate, without system, cut off from life, incapable of opening up to the originality of others. A notable effort to tear Russia out of this isolation was made by Peter the Great, the cruelest of the absolute monarchs.

The Intelligentsia

Peter the Great responded with the audacity of a warrior to the ineluctable dilemma that Russia faced: to stand either outside

Europe in oriental barbarity or with Europe in the guise of pupil and conqueror of empires. Unburdened by a cultural tradition, Russia ran the course of its history in a few decades. The Russians, more than all other peoples, have this candid and rash audacity to start afresh. The work of Peter the Great was not a fine gesture made suddenly by a superior and capricious will; it corresponded rather to the requirements of foreign policy and the economy and gave direction to an obscure drive for renewal, the hidden efforts of individuals. The result was the intelligentsia: not an artificial product, not the aberration of individuals, but the legitimate moment of a malady, the irrepressible element of a crisis. The generic psychology of the movement was imparted to it by the effort of imitation to which the learned devoted themselves, their gaze fixed on the West.

The first phases of the growth of the intelligentsia were encyclopedism and aestheticism. During the reign of Catherine we observe the tumultuous and vulgarizing spread of the ideas of Montesquieu, Beccaria, and the other encyclopedists. The need to know took the form of the most naive quest for many new notions, and when it encountered an analogous movement in France, born in a very different spirit, it assimilated its ideas in the most summary fashion. The polemics between Novikov and the empress are the record of this dilettantish, superficial, and imprecise divulgation. It was not for the obvious intellectual reasons that Catherine opposed Novikov—the first to instigate a movement of bourgeois culture, which was later revived, in a minor key, by Schwarz and Fedor Krechetov,[40] an

40. Gobetti gives the names of many Russians of the nineteenth century in a phonetic transliteration into Italian. For well-known individuals, the form of the name used here is the one familiar to an English-language readership—for example, Dostoevsky. For less well-known names, the form given is the one used in the corresponding entry in Joseph L. Wieczynski, ed., *The Modern Encyclopedia of Russian and Soviet History* (Gulf Breeze, Fla.: Academic International, 1976–). Several individuals named by Gobetti proved impossible for a reader without competence in Slavic studies to trace in this

implacable, but literary, adversary of despotism. She did so out of a concrete political conception, a new personal element that she added to the inert cultural material gathered in the West. Catherine's political position, which was profoundly ambiguous, was inspired by the corrupting and taming reason of state that was once falsely attributed to Lorenzo the Magnificent: autocracy made itself revolutionary in order to crush the opposition to the dominant power. The intelligentsia attached itself the government and, like a new clergy, was suffocated by it. Catherine reached her goal only in part: she weakened and held back the movement but did not suppress it.

The opponents of reaction suffered persecution and became more popular, precursors and symbols of retaliation. Aleksandr Radishchev (1749–1802), exiled to Siberia, obtained resonant, perennial glory. As superficial as his regal persecutor; a compiler of works derived almost verbatim from Locke, Voltaire, Rousseau, Raynal, Diderot, etc.; a rotten writer (with flashes of imitation, in the manner of Sterne), he also became the symbol of revolution for Russia on account of the heroic sufferings he endured in opposing the central power.

Radishchev is a typical representative of the first intelligentsia: he combated serfdom exclusively out of homage to the humanitarianism of his Western sources; he made himself the champion of Western forms of popular sovereignty without understanding that they would not abolish the submissiveness of the people to tyranny; on the agrarian question he expounded ideas that were sensible in Germany but became abstractions in Russia, even when discussed in technical terms (liberation from serfdom, the surrender of the propriety right of usufruct, etc.).

The French Revolution and the Napoleonic wars did not bring new elements to the battle of ideas, but they sharpened the drive for renewal. The people took part in the wars with the

---

or other repertories, and thanks go to Professor Robert Johnson for identifying them and providing a transliteration of their names. [Translator's note.]

heroic spirit of the old legends, and while others were discoursing about autonomous activity and democracy, they were content to sing new *byliny* or to adapt the old ones to the new events. The Napoleonic campaigns roused very different impulses in the aristocratic officers who had fought in them with military ardor and had learned in them the necessity for action. It was they who planned the Decembrist revolution, filled as they were with the spirit of French ideologies and prepared to face the scaffold, as Radishchev had faced exile. With the abstractness of Jacobins, in a country that knew nothing of political ideologies, the Decembrists thought to bring about the "liberation of the peasants" by summoning the Duma, as though it were possible to abolish age-old enslavement through a legislative act.

They were reduced to elaborating abstract programs of renewal and constructing schemes and divisions on this utterly elementary and naively inchoate basis. The Society of Salvation, which arose after the Napoleonic collapse, was divided into a Northern Society and a Southern Society. The leaders of the two parties, Murav'ev and Pestel', were both incapable of thinking through a concrete revolutionary program. The dissension between them was highly academic but heralded the ardent conviction, the political aspirations, and the formidable polemics between westernizers and Slavophiles.

Murav'ev, a westernizer in his own way, was the one who aspired to the regeneration of Russia through the formation of an aristocracy; his ideal program was composed of all the commonplaces of European liberalism: freedom of conscience, freedom of religious faith, freedom of association. Amid these generic affirmations his agrarian program was alluded to in a wretchedly simplistic utterance: "Let serfdom and slavery be suppressed." Mimicking the Western myths of liberation, he believed that he was challenging an aristocracy; but the Russian ruling class was condemned to remain a mechanical bureaucracy as long as the principle of choice did not depend on popular struggle. Nor was he able to reach the people with his declarations of liberation,

since they cared not about legal recognition of an abstract capacity to possess but about effective possession. In France the
problem of the revolution was legislative because it was a question of recognizing a new, de facto condition of democracy; in
Russia it was not so much a question of recognition as it was a
question of creating the new state, the new democracy. When the
people deserted Murav'ev's standard, they gave him a fine lesson
in political concreteness: those who stood by him were a handful of intellectuals divorced from practical reality and without
any political influence. The program of Murav'ev was redolent
of the legalitarian, moderate aspirations of the northern Russian
mercantilist bourgeoisie.

The thought of Pestel' was also premature in the political environment of Russia. It contains intuitions that are more realistic, but they are not followed up—for example, this statement:
"You may proclaim a republic, but that will only be a change
of name. The main question is that of land: it is necessary to
give land to the peasants. Only then will the goal of the revolution be reached." In fact, the necessity was not that the peasants
be given land but that they should seize control of the land and
that their maturity, as virtual proprietors, should be expressed
in this act of occupation (not improvised but historically determined). Pestel', however, hostile to any integral revolutionary movement, a worshiper of the state in his reformism, incapable of understanding the importance of the associationist
movement in the spiritual evolution of Russia, was at bottom
promoting ideas of renewal in a perfectly theocratic and tsarist
spirit. Against Murav'ev's individualism he opposed a form of socialism (in the etymological sense). Against liberal and communist agrarian ideas he opposed an ingenuous statism, showing
himself incapable of rising above the subtly abstract antitheses
in which his action became enmeshed.

The reformism of Pestel' is easily explainable in the context
of the struggle of the social classes in Russia at that time. He
belonged to the southern landed aristocracy, ruined by the war,

that was discovering the insufficiency of agriculture based on the slave system the hard way, through economic crisis. None of his practical proposals has survived; his historical importance lies in the heroism that led him to sacrifice himself and that, more than all his projects, served to inspire others. The fate of the Decembrists did not nullify but consecrated the principle of the political contest and social redemption and made the people face the problem of direct revolutionary action that had remained until then the domain of an insulated minority.

In the decades that followed the Decembrist uprising the protagonist of Russian spiritual life was the tsar. To him fell the unsought honor of being able to disperse certain kinds of intellectual fogginess by persecuting the intelligentsia, forcing them to adopt a greater concreteness of thought and action. The agrarian reforms themselves, initiated by the tsar to undermine the revolutionary initiative, had the virtue of making the peasants focus on the important economic questions and of liberating them from the fantasies and dreams of the cultivators of literature.

Herzen, concerned mainly with the history of the intelligentsia, saw this period as the most painful in Russian life. But in fact, from 1825 to 1835 liberalism had no power to create new developments, and poetry had to take the place of politics. Lacking a moral center, the first phase of Russian culture (encyclopedism) had been grossly content-based, without strong formal expression or unitary psychological interest. Now disorganized empiricism was replaced by the most superficial, immediate, and sentimentally egoistical form of organized arrangement: aestheticism, the external consideration of things. In Russia, romanticism, which in Europe had been a philosophy of liberty, shrank to the literary disputes of Polevoi against Kachenovskii. Accustomed to Muscovite autocracy, Pushkin, Griboedov and Lermontov nevertheless remained bound by their individual aesthetic problems, estranged from the interests of the Slavic soul. It is true, as Dostoevsky observes, that Pushkin shed light on the morbid phenomenology of Russian intellectual society, which was "historically ripped out of its native soil and set over the people. He threw into relief, before our eyes, the negative type of agitated, untamable individual who does not believe in the soil of the homeland, or its forces, who in the end denies Russia and himself (that is, his society, his intellectual stratum born of his own earth), who has no wish to have dealings with others and is content with his own sincere suffering. Aleco and Onegin gave rise in due course to a quantity of similar types in the history of Slavic literature." But of this malady Pushkin was not only the observer, he was also the representative, and so unable to speak the word of consolation that Dostoevsky erroneously looked for, nor point to the secret of true Russian life in the soul of the people. Not to Pushkin, entirely given to Western romanticism, but to the exegete himself belongs the thought that Dostoevsky attributes to him: "have faith in the soul of the people, from it alone expect salvation, and you will be saved." Pushkin's messianism, his ability to incarnate the genius of other nations, points merely to his versatility as an imitator: Dostoevsky confused a literary problem, a question of style, with a political and social problem.

Driven by demands he was unable to perceive clearly, wandering in a purely literary culture, Pushkin was the culmination of a crisis for which no solution was then in sight. The only word of consolation that he was able to speak (not proclaim) was not a political proposal or concept: it emerged from his own torment, revealed itself to him with limpid expressivity in his most serene works of poetry. Faced with indistinct, aestheticizing romanticism, the healthier Russian spirit turned solitary and lost itself mystically within the bounds of the individual.

Slavophiles and Westernizers

In the fifteenth issue of *Telescope*, the Moscow journal that continued the political traditions of the suppressed *Telegraph*, there appeared the "Philosophical Letter" of Petr Yakovlevich Chaadaev, one of the most weighty examples of thought to appear in Russia in the last century. Chaadaev's "Letter" came after ten years of silence; it analyzed with ferocious precision the vices of the spiritual formation of Russia and ended with a sweeping condemnation. Many of Chaadaev's ideas may seem valid even today for the critic of Russia. His thought has a systematic character that casts a spell and makes it seem irrefutable.

But in our exegesis we have to go beyond this initial striking fascination, which tends to elevate the "Letter" to a position far above the development of Russian history and thus fails to account for its genesis. We have as well to distinguish the significance the "Letter" had in its historical context, in the eyes of those who first read it, from the significance that we, through an error of history and system, might attribute to it. The fact that Chaadaev renounced his own ideas a few years later should make us extremely cautious in evaluating them.

Even when Chaadaev expresses concepts that others might with good reason judge to be modern, the enduring point of departure is still a dogmatic element, the spirit is still that of theocracy. Chaadaev proposes, and indeed imposes, the direction and the center of Catholic thought on disorganized Slavic mysticism, and for that reason he appears to us solid and systematic. In reality, his critique lacks positive capacities. His weighty affirmations are destined to lead to nothing because they have not been attained for a creative purpose or value. His truth cannot become revolutionary. There is a more ample revolutionary capacity in the mystical immediacy of Christianity than there is in the finished and mechanical truth made by Catholicism. Chaadaev's conception is not activist, because it culminates in a revealed faith that, once known, is mechanically handed down.

From a standpoint of Catholic realism, Chaadaev affirms the superiority of practice over theory and exalts the value of discipline over the Western ideology of freedom: he sees clearly the importance that Catholicism and the Middle Ages have had in the spiritual formation of Europe, and he understands the consequences for Russia of its popular apathy and isolation. But his theoretical perceptions do not complement a program of action. His stance might have permitted him to overcome permanently the bitter conflict that was about to spring up between westernizers and Slavophiles, but he showed himself unequal to this task and let himself be swept along by the malady of his contemporaries. In an early phase he accepted the simplistic dogma of Catholic revelation, but later, forgetting the interpretation that he himself had given of the policies of Peter the Great, he abandoned himself to Slavophile rhetoric.

In the midst of these excesses we find the characteristic affirmation of the necessarily autonomous character that the spiritual development of peoples must assume, the firm faith in the formative value of history and in what almost amounts to the inversion of praxis, and a fierce battle against all the rationalistic prejudices imported from eighteenth-century France. But this living nucleus of thought remained undeveloped in Russia down to the Bolshevik revolution (the voluntarism of Bakunin was not sufficiently realistic, nor did it contain an awareness of the logic through which action makes history). On the other hand, the Slavophile themes in Chaadaev have weighed on the spiritual life of modern Russia.

The dissension between westernizers and Slavophiles was a direct consequence of the policies of Peter the Great and did not bring a single new idea into the Slavic intellectual movement. In a nation struggling to emerge from prehistory through elementary effort, amid the multiple suggestions and motifs of thought, few ideas can be maintained undeviatingly, and they flow and return following the simplest of laws. Themes dominant for a century in Slavic culture were reborn with greater intensity and clarity in the Slavophiles and westernizers.

The clash between westernism and traditionalism had something ingenuous and unreal about it when it was first manifested. A civilization exists inasmuch as it is capable of understanding and assimilating the traditions of others from the point of view of its own tradition. Any claim for solitary originality or purely passive imitation is naive.

But the abstract point of this antithesis became concrete in Russia because of the specific need to bring a backward country up to the level of a civilization with which it had to communicate in order to survive and which was already highly developed. Clearly this goal could be achieved through an equilibrium between the tendency to rapidly assimilate foreign ideas and the tendency to defend the need for autonomy against this excess. Slavophile and westernizing were the names of the two currents, and since, after the early examples of intemperate polemic, they had to reach a point of equilibrium, the union of the two forces was achieved in the second half of the nineteenth century by Dostoevsky, in an abstract intellectual systemization. The real synthesis, however, would have to come from a theory that saw the value of economic autonomy in the efforts of the people.

Rather than examine separately the thought of Stankevich, Belinskii, and their followers and, conversely, that of the brothers Aksakov, Samarin, and Khomiakov, it will be opportune to note the identical process of culture from which their declarations sprang. A sentimental love for freedom, theorized in light of Hegelian and Schellingian concepts, prevailed on both sides.

But the idealistic declarations of the German philosophers were understood according to a curious antirealistic deformation characteristic of naive persons, to whom history appears not as experience but as revelation. Belinskii, who passed from Schelling to Hegel in a sentimental evolution that Miliukov has clearly portrayed, was full of literary prejudices. Having affirmed the unity of the spirit and the nonexistence of distinct, independent categories (aesthetics, ethics, logic), he did not think to develop the concept theoretically and instead deduced, through a process of merely empirical validity, a naturalistic doctrine limited to the literary domain. His culture was the culture of Catherine taken to the most vigorous quantitative intensity; the result in his case was the state of mind of a man of intelligence who is bored with finding so much ignorance around him and incapable of understanding why it is inevitable, who thinks that in order to get rid of it, it will be enough to supply everyone with copies of the books that he himself has read. His positive qualities of refined taste, dialectical agility, the powerful imagination of a rebuilder (which will all continue, albeit with a stronger dose of sociology, in the critics of the succeeding generation—Chernyshevskii, Dobroliubov, Pisarev—down to the emergence of nihilism) indicate a character rich in fascination who remained the educator of Russia and the idol of its youth for many years. Yet he lacked realistic preparation and the sense of economic forces that could have brought him closer to the people.

The aestheticism of Belinskii—although it is rooted in a solid intelligence—is intellectualistic abstraction, culture applied to the surface, just as the mysticism of Khomiakov is the expression of obscurantism and Hegelian dogmatism as understood by a Catholic subversive.

Slavophilism formed a grossly simplistic myth out of the traditional prejudices of the Russian soul, sentimental contradictions that remained historically undeveloped in a perpetually unsatisfied aspiration for transcendent activity (mystical palingenesis); accepting the Hegelian prejudices concerning the historical predestination of peoples, it posited its myth as a term of universal progress. It made divine individual catharsis the palingenesis of history. Slavophile intellectualism did not go beyond these general and generic principles. Its aim of going to the people remained, as it had to, unfulfilled, and when it was fulfilled, it had no formative value: underneath, there was too much dilettantism and superficiality.

The logical continuator of Slavophilism was Aleksandr Herzen, who after a long attachment to westernism and the ideology of freedom embraced messianic popular drives and also cultivated his Russian dream. The novel element in Herzen, which

will become a commonplace in the second phase of Slavic intellectualism, consists in an economic vision of the social problem,
which takes the place of the old mysticism. The conclusion is a
primitive socialism based on the *mir* that excludes violent individual initiative and practically reduces the state to statism. We
will find the beginnings of a critique of these ideas in the Bolshevik revolution.

Mysticism and Marxism

Although Dostoevsky sought to elaborate a doctrine reconciling Slavophiles and westernizers, his own ideas grow out of the
internal development of the Slavophile myth, and an analysis
of his thought will reveal the leading ideas of the movement in
their most complete logical expression. The following declaration grows directly out of the mystical exaltation of Kireevskii
and Khomiakov:

> The intellectual class in Russia is the most elevated and the most
> seductive of all the elites that exist. In the whole world there is
> nothing that resembles it. It is a magnificence of splendid beauty
> that is not yet sufficiently appreciated. Try preaching, in France
> or England or wherever, that personal ownership is illegitimate,
> that egoism is criminal. All will back away from you. How could
> individual ownership be illegitimate? Is there anything, then,
> that would be legitimate? But a Russian intellectual will be able
> to understand. He began to philosophize as soon as his con-
> science was awakened. Thus, if he touches a piece of white bread,
> a dismal picture immediately presents itself to him: "This bread
> was made by slaves." And the white bread tastes very bitter to
> him.
>
> He feels love, but he sees his inferior brother who lives in
> squalor and sells his dignity as a man for a few coins, and then
> love loses all its fascination for the intellectual. The people have
> become his idée fixe; he searches for a way to bring himself in
> contact with this taciturn crowd, to mingle with them. Without

the people, who for thousands of years carry all of Russian history with them, without love for the people, a naive and mystical love, the Russian intellectual would be unable to conceive of himself. For this reason he sets himself to searching, anxiously, scrupulously, and continuously, for the true, for what the people and the peasants know to be true! He renounces everything that constitutes the pride, the ordinary happiness, of mortal man: it is from the villages, from the fields, from the black earth, that intellectuals receive their moral ideas. They would be ashamed to live while forgetting the little peasant, and from the peasant they have borrowed their celebrated formula "Life according to truth, and not according to law and science." It is true that in the West science dominates, along with the consciousness of juridical and historical necessity. But in Russia love dominates. We believe in it as in a mysterious force that in a moment obviates all obstacles and instantly brings into being a new life. This image of a new life, an interior life, is always to be found in the heart and in the head of every Russian intellectual, and we are always impassioned by this true life based on love for one's neighbor, which cannot be comprised in any formula except the formula dictated by the heart.

This populist verbosity explains better than any comment from us how any effort to make philosophical thought systematic must of necessity waste itself in naive philosophical poverty, in sentimentalism swollen by a forlorn vision of universal suffering. The interpretive efforts of Russian writers and critics to find a philosophy in Dostoevsky have in the end produced formulations that run counter to any sort of philosophical seriousness: revelation of the eternally youthful, messianism, etc.

The *autochthonous* Russianism, for example, that a Slavophile exegete attributes to him is only a sign of his audacity as fantasist. The fact is that, with no Middle Ages as background, his spontaneity, far from constituting an original aspect of his thought, gives it an essentially antihistorical character; and his feeling of fear at the prospect of death leads him to affirm the eternity of life, but in a poetic form.

In these factors, even though the Russians insist on seeing in him the ardor of a prophetic soul, we see only the limits of a tormented individualism. When Dostoevsky wishes to escape from this dead end and enter history, he succeeds only in positing an abstract dualism between divinity and humanity in which humanity is atheism, blind nature, immorality that never succeeds in overcoming itself and that is sanctified by piety, by the messianic expectation of a revelation historically assigned to Holy Russia, who will bring infinity and eternity to pass. But even the infinite and the eternal are not theorized philosophically; rather, they are thought of by Dostoevsky as something absolutely immense before which one feels a shivering sensation. His love is for humanity in general: faced with an individual, he sometimes has a feeling of disdain and sometimes one of exclusively aesthetic contemplation; and universal love itself is still dictated to him by an individualistic sentiment: the fear of solitude. His attempts at philosophy all dissolve into empirical psychology.

The political action that flowed from this attitude was vague and messianic. The mystical aspiration for the infinite, the eternal, became a school of bad influence in which any kind of realism was negated out of reverence for the mists of spiritualism; and the people were encouraged in their wish for an anarchic social organization in which any consciousness of individual values and any strong spirit of coexistence in a state were lost.

Nationalist preaching fell on ground favorable to distortions; it fed exasperated prejudices and maladies that already harshly burdened the history of the people with a constricting immobility. The most complete lack of preparation to feel the importance and the limits of the economic problem hindered the adequate development of impulses of thought that might have proved healthy and productive.

The spiritual position of populist intellectualism, which remained static for almost forty years and out of which were indirectly born, in social life, the two revolutionary failures of 1905 and 1917, was the culminating point of the mystical Slavic crisis. The intelligentsia revealed its impotence to accomplish its task as the germs of modernity gradually filtered into the people, from whom it was increasingly split off. Its purely intellectual experiences were suffocated in a vicious circle.

While this process of dissolution was concluding, we find the first signs of a realistic social critique in the Marxists. But in Russia even Marxism followed its own course and had to undergo severe crises of development and misunderstanding. In the wake of Herzen, it was the Slavophiles who first rushed to adopt Marxism when it was imported from Germany, and they completely falsified its spirit, just as they had falsified Hegelianism. The nihilists were the fruit of this aberration: men of enthusiasm who took part in action with an aestheticizing mentality, out of abstract heroism, out of abstract purity.

The adhesion of the intelligentsia to Marxism goes back to the years 1880–90 and was the most immediate consequence of the collapse of the hopes of *Narodnya volya:* drained of strength in the face of the progressive rise of the proletarian movement, which had resolved by now to choose its own road, they saved themselves with equivocation while in reality corrupting and weakening the system, to which they brought their own nebulousness. Russian socialism after 1890 was still messianic and based its concept of socialization on the prehistoric *mir.*

The vital seeds of orthodox Marxism remained hidden, almost suffocated, but still ready to shoot up promptly amid this disorganization. By rigidly accepting historical materialism, the Bolsheviks destroyed the cloudy ideals that kept the people outside the world and reality. They made the equation between reality and force, life and individuality, thought and economic activity, and posited the need to make an autonomous movement emerge from below, one not limited to the declarations of principle of the intelligentsia, and ready to range its forces against tsarism. They knew that ideas cannot grow out of isolated brains, that philosophy arises out of history, that the great political struggles presuppose an awareness of interests, a sense of responsibility, and economic individualism. It was not their intention to educate the people by revealing the truth to them: they were working to make the people understand the conditions of their own freedom, to make them feel themselves a proletariat and feel responsible for their own fate. In the battle against tsarism and capitalism they gave a necessity and a direction to the revolution.

SOVIET RUSSIA

I

THE commentary on the Russian revolution published in Italy bears witness to the pitiable shortcomings of our political vision and the complete inability of our culture to provide us with the sketchiest historical interpretation—in sum, our incapacity to attain scientific objectivity on questions like this.[41] Italian writers discussing Russia stubbornly refuse to give up didactic history in the slightest degree: they are unable to see the facts of the revolution as historical facts that have to be examined for what they are, and are determined at any cost to interpret and exploit them to promote political revolt or political reaction in Italy. Any notion of a global interpretation is completely foreign to such writing; in Italy we are still ignorant of the whole movement of thought and propaganda that led to the revolutions of 1905 and then 1917 in Russia. But no one can understand the content of the political parties in Russia without relating them to this mystical and practical background.

A second extremely serious defect in our historians arises from their inability to distinguish among their sources. Those in Italy who call themselves liberals derive their criteria of evalua-

41. Original title: "La Russia dei Soviet"; from *Rivista di Milano*, 20 February 1921. Translated from *Scritti politici*, pp. 197–206.

tion from, and base their judgment on, writers of the Russian intelligentsia (populists, socialists, revolutionaries) who are quite incapable of perceiving concrete social reality clearly: dreamers, not doers; deluded sentimental agitators, *progettisti* (if I can use that barbarous term),[42] not politicians. The mentality of the Russian intelligentsia is just as abstract as that of the eighteenth-century Enlightenment, and if you follow mystical intellectuals like that, you wind up opposing Bolshevism because it is not socialist enough (meaning the kind of infallible socialism represented in Italy by Treves, Turati, and the rest of that third-rate crew).[43]

Our bourgeoisie will make use of every available tactic in the propaganda campaign it has launched against Bolshevism. The renewal of our historiographical culture had freed us from a number of old methodological biases, but now they are welcomed back: once again doctrines and ideas are scorned, and *facts* are exalted. Our journalists enumerate a series of facts against the Bolshevists, such as the difficult conditions of life in the new regime, hunger, cold, and so on, and draw negative conclusions, without recognizing that if these facts are accepted and tolerated by the people in Russia, that signifies that there is a driving spirit superior to the facts, and if you want to understand the facts, you will have to pay attention to the spirit. Events are diminished and misunderstood in light of this false realism and dogmatism about the empirical fact (which is in reality inter-

42. The word *progettista* normally means "designer" or "planner," but here and, I believe, in all the other the texts translated for this volume, Gobetti uses the plural form in the more unusual sense of "propounders of extravagant ill-thought-out schemes." Usually I translate it with a paraphrase. This, however, is the only instance in the texts selected for translation in which he italicizes the word and draws attention to it by calling it "barbarous," so I have let it stand in the original Italian. In the seventeenth and eighteenth centuries the English word "projector" meant exactly the same thing; it is familiar to readers of Swift, for instance, in that acceptation. [Translator's note.]

43. Gobetti is referring to the main leaders of the Italian Socialist Party.

preted implicitly and in the most narrow and superficial manner, so that the force of the interpretation is kept hidden and doesn't appear). Certain bourgeois papers have sent their correspondents to Russia so that they could report at first hand that truly not everyone is happy under the Bolshevik regime and that every worker does not have a chicken in his pot every day. Now, that kind of reporting might be enough to deter many of our proletarians, invincibly *bourgeois* in spirit, from revolution, but it does not help us to understand the historical phenomenon, precisely because it denies the spiritual factor that is its essence. Our socialists have reason to compare this pseudo-historical approach to that of the good Father Bresciani: although they too, as party men, are neither able nor obliged to emulate De Sanctis and are condemned, just as much as Father Bresciani,[44] to see no further than newspaper articles and to hold to their particularistic point of view.

II

Campodonico does not escape these aberrations in his recent volume.[45] His perspective on Soviet Russia is also distorted by his concern to score points against Bolshevism in Italy; his denial of the revolution's work is limited to an attitude of false real-

44. Francesco De Sanctis (1817–83) was the most important literary critic of the nineteenth century and the author of a seminal history of Italian literature. In his youth he went into exile in Switzerland, where he taught at the University of Zurich. He was influenced by German Idealism, and after the unification of Italy, he became professor of Italian literature in Naples. He linked his interpretation of Italian literature to the formation of political beliefs, and his ideas inspired more than one generation of scholars and intellectuals, from Croce to Gramsci. De Sanctis's criticism of the Catholic writer Antonio Bresciani (1798–1862), a Jesuit and a harsh critic of liberalism, was used by Gramsci to exemplify a noneducative form of national-popular culture.

45. Aldemiro Campodonico, *La Russia dei Soviets (saggio di legislazione comunista)* (Florence: Vallecchi, 1920; "Uomini e idee," no. 2), a volume of 370 pages. [Author's note.]

ism (the Christian realism, in the manner of the later Schelling, of the reactionaries of our own Risorgimento as critiqued by De Sanctis and Bertrando Spaventa).[46] He registers facts that appear detrimental to the Bolsheviks, attesting to the deficiencies of their regime and the harm caused. But Campodonico is not dogmatic only about facts; he is dogmatic about law too, claiming to examine and dismiss all of Bolshevism through a review of its legislation. This claim had already been put forward by Labry,[47] but with shrewd disclaimers that are missing here, replaced by presumptuous abstract tendency to simplify. Campodonico wants to demonstrate that "the great reformers of the East" have not made "substantial innovations" in legislation. But that demonstration gets us nowhere. It is not juridical innovation that matters; it is political reality. The law is an empty form if it is not brought to life by the social action of individuals (which is the true law), since the study of a body of legislation cannot be insulated from consideration of the historical traditions that generated it and in which—uniquely—form acquires content, and reality development.

This truth escapes Campodonico; he insists (p. 240) on believing that there exist "odious systems" that discredit those who have created them wherever they appear; but any system is good or bad, hated or approved, according to the environment in which it exists. Law as a pure schema is a nullity, the wording gains its force from the reality to which it is adapted. You will explain the revolution to us if you explain its spirit: that would be a real innovation. We are told that "this book advances no claims," but in fact it advances the most grotesque of intellectualistic claims, presenting us with a cadaver ("the essential lines of Soviet legislation," which are as such *abstract limits*) in the belief that it is bringing us face to face with a living body (the new

46. See Chapter 2, note 28.
47. Raoul Labry, *Une législation communiste (Recueil des lois, décrets, arrêts principaux du gouvernement bolchéviste)* (Paris: Payot, 1920). [Editor's note by P. Spriano.]

regime in Russia). I, too, have little sympathy for the mentality of those like Serrati or Bombacci.[48] I have the same repugnance as Campodonico for the ideology of the Russian maximalists. But these are states of mind: they have to be put aside in order to do history. Labry is certainly right (p. x) to see Russian legislation as the expression of the consciousness of that people, but it is that principally to the extent that the effort to legislate is adequate to reality and individuals are adequate to the effort to legislate. On the basis of the *complete* corpus of Bolshevik law you might construct a kind of history of the revolution. But that corpus itself has to become history; the progressive development of the legislation has to be comprehended for what it is in reality: a ceaseless attempt to solve the problems that ineluctably arise as life is lived. Then law, as a schema that comes into force and in time decays, is really history, the living symbol (created, destroyed, replaced) of a living reality. If Campodonico had thought through the eleven lines that serve as a preface to his book and the appalling ingenuousness of his assertions, he would not have offered us this absurd compilation.

III

Now that I have pointed out the fundamental mistake in his overall approach, let us see whether there may not be something noteworthy and valid in his specific observations. In explaining "how Bolshevism came about" Campodonico alludes glibly (pp. 11–12) to the influence of Germany on the Russian extremist parties and reaches this entertaining conclusion: "It is a question of a general revolt by the soldiers of the Petersburg garrison, who did not want to leave for the front and made up their minds to avoid the risks and dangers of the war once and for all, etc." There you have the whole mystery solved: it was nothing but

48. On Serrati see Chapter 2, note 35; and on Bombacci, Chapter 1, note 23.

a little cowardice. Campodonico, for all that he has read Trotsky's marvelous book on the revolution, loves to keep things very
simple. In any case, his book completely ignores the Russia that
existed before the revolution: the whole mystical movement, the
revolutionary culture of the intelligentsia and the peasants,
which was a potent stimulus to action just because it was fantastic—all of it passes him by. But without that, nobody can understand Russia in war or Russia in revolution, or the work of Trotsky and Lenin.

Trotsky, a Marxist with an extraordinary knowledge of how
the popular mind had been formed, wanted an anarchic revolution, the only kind with a chance of not turning reactionary
(Kerensky's constitutional democrats were reactionaries), the
only kind capable of breaking the bonds of age-old servitude
and promoting social activity. Trotsky, because he understood
the need for an anarchic movement as the first phase of reconstruction, is the true founder of the new Russian life. Nothing
could be given voice except the will to autonomy for its own sake,
the responsibility: a people shaking off its chains falls back into
slavery if it lets itself be organized. The manifestation of its will
must have no other object than itself: in denying tsarist egoism
individuals affirm their own egoism, but that is the only way for
them to reach true liberty. Arbitrariness will become liberty, necessity, social organization, but before that it has to be arbitrariness, will, and action for its own sake, without purpose. Anarchy
is the first moment, anarchy so that all men can assert their will.
Tsarism is negated, and the experience of the people begins.

Trotsky's second problem was to promote the formation of a
new ruling class ready to assume the role of true heir to the previous state, of a *new order,* while this revolution was spreading,
while the anarchic phase was running its course. The first problem belonged to the past; it was the unfolding of things that had
previously been implicit and obscure. The second was a contingent problem of force, which he solved by relying on the sailors

of Petersburg for a coup d'état and on the workers rather than the managers for organization. Then came Lenin: his problem was the problem of relations between the minority that imposed itself during the phase of anarchy and the other citizens clamoring for power. And so after the anarchy—after the dictatorship—the way is paved for democracy (agrarian): a form of government in which the new energies that have been awakened may settle down and begin to develop themselves. Thus the cycle is completed and Russia renewed. But naturally, the concreteness of this history eludes the abstract reasoners of juridical empiricism—just as it eludes the theorizers of Bolshevism as universal revolution and a category of the spirit.

IV

In his second chapter Campodonico sets about examining the legislation of the Bolsheviks, or rather he lets the law speak for itself, and I have already sufficiently shown the absurdity of that claim. In fact what Campodonico does is discuss a small number of laws compared to those compiled by Labry, so that far from giving us the full picture, he doesn't even give us the chance to fairly evaluate a part of the legislative activity of the Bolsheviks. Not only does he not give us the results of original research of his own, he does not even take the trouble to translate from Labry's French, contenting himself with clipping the texts of the different laws from "Documenti della rivoluzione" in *Avanti!* This collection, carelessly done and full of mistakes, meets the crude standards of propaganda. Campodonico, who is not a socialist, ought to have been able to do better than the socialists, at least on the level of scholarship.

At page 42, citing the first volume of the documents of the Soviet constitution, Campodonico says that in the new socialist regime that is taking shape there are not supposed to be any more distinctions of caste nor *state power*. Now, it is hard to be-

lieve that the Bolsheviks would have written down a huge blun-
der like that, since it contradicts everything we know about
the thought of Lenin and Trotsky. It appears that the word in
the original Russian was *upravlenie,* i.e., "government," as the
French translation would seem to suggest. That is, the Bolsheviks desire that the people themselves become the state, reducing
governmental mediation to a minimum and making state and
government coincide as much as possible. We might have a debate about the value and the viability of this proposal, but we
can't simply misunderstand and misrepresent it for the sake of
raillery. Likewise, on page 46 he refers to "incomes," whereas the
word in the original is "taxes." In reporting article 25 of the constitution Campodonico says that the peasants elect a deputy for
every 250,000 inhabitants, whereas Buisson,[49] Labry, and Vichniak [50] say one for every 125,000 inhabitants. And in fact the latter
has to be the right figure. Campodonico has wantonly accepted
the incorrect figure given by Lazzeri.[51]

I will not continue to point out these factual errors, which
document the inexperience and the shallowness of the author,
and will concentrate instead on a few grave errors of interpretation. Campodonico evidently has no idea of what a soviet is.
On page 26, after comparing it to the *mir,* he ends by maintaining that it is similar to our workers' leagues and unions [*sindacati*]. But the resemblance is superficial. The importance of the
soviet lies in its organizational character, which proceeds from
below as an expression of the working class gathered in the factories with the capacity to offer a form of coexistence and collaboration of all the elements of production: in fact, if one thinks

49. Etienne Buisson, *Les bolschéviki (1917–1919): Faits-documents-
commentaires* (Paris: Fischbacher, 1919). [Editor's note by P. Spriano.]

50. Vichniak, *Le régime constitutionnel et administratif de la Russie bol-
schéviste* (Paris: Imprimerie Union, 1919). [Editor's note by P. Spriano; he
gives only the surname of the author.]

51. Gerolamo Lazzeri, *Il bolscevismo, com'è nato, che cos'è. Resultanze*
(Milan: Sonzogno, 1919). [Editor's note by P. Spriano.]

about it, a soviet of this sort might be the only remedy against the industrial trusts and the rapacious workers' unions with their bureaucratic apparatus.

About local organization in the new Russia Campodonico has nothing to say. And yet he ought to have noted the immense effort made by Lenin to bring about decentralization: in an immature country corrupted by a tsarist bureaucracy, even the provisions for local autonomy degenerated at first, by a curious twist, into bureaucratic bloat, so that Lenin had to centralize the right of command in order to dominate the bureaucracy and really decentralize. This apparent paradox accounts for the uncertainty of Russian administrative law (which Campodonico is satisfied to point out without trying to explain). With great satisfaction, he throws the spotlight at every turn on the cruelty of the Bolsheviks, who arrested their enemies (p. 69), and introduced compulsory labor (p. 161) and military discipline (pp. 283–84). As well, he describes at length the state of hunger and cold in which people are living (p. 260). He fails to see that all these facts, in substance, only give rise to a new question: How is it that the Bolsheviks obtain compliance? Why does their government continue in place? It will not do to say that the answer lies in their use of violence. Violence only works when there is someone capable of exercising it, and others are prepared to tolerate it. And this exercise and this toleration are the external expression of an inner fact that is rooted in the spirit of the people. In Russia the explanatory factor is precisely that people support the Soviet government: Lenin's government is "moral" because it is the only one the citizens recognize. For that matter, the report of the members of the General Confederation of Labor (amply summarized in the newspaper *Il Resto del Carlino* for 6 October 1920) leads to the same conclusion. Those who drafted it, though their intent was openly hostile, end by asserting that the peasants in Russia "have definitely obtained more advantages than disadvantages from the revolution" and "are ready to de-

fend the new regime against any reactionary attempts." That is
the secret of Soviet success, and it can't be understood within the
framework of standard anti-Bolshevism. No wonder that Campodonico doesn't understand it, since as usual, his analysis is
completely unhistorical. Albeit a liberal himself, he doesn't even
think to undertake a serious critique of Lenin's economic legislation, something we would have been glad to read because it is
our view as well that the real deficiency of the new regime lies
here (though it is perhaps inevitable during the phase of transition). But all Campodonico does is report the laws and let it go at
that, with the hint of a grin, when he ought to have been studying
how they came to be, what the errors are that vitiate them, what
remedies have been applied in practice and in succeeding legislation. A challenging problem, you may say, given the limited ac-
cessibility of the sources at the moment. But not insuperable.
You would need to be a little less deficient in historical culture
and bibliographical erudition and perhaps a little more diligent
in searching for documents. But Campodonico must believe that
things like that are just trifles, since he is not even acquainted
with *Ordine Nuovo*,[52] though it has made available numerous
documents and published interesting analyses and revisions, or
with the study published by Caffi in *Voce dei popoli* (numbers
5, 6, 7, and 12),[53] the most interesting writing on the subject in
Italian. This accounts for many of the gaps in his research. One
might note, for example, that the Bolshevik tax system, though
technically very backward, is nonetheless a notable attempt to
apply exactly the kind of taxes on luxury spending that students
of finance consider the most perfect and the best adapted to the
times. As for the laws about insurance, they too ought to be taken
for what they are, a first experiment. It is ridiculous to compare

52. *Ordine Nuovo* was the journal founded by Antonio Gramsci in 1919.
Gobetti spoke extensively of it in his essay "The Communists," included in
this chapter.
53. Andrea Caffi, "La Russia bolscevica e l'Europa," in *La voce dei popoli*,
1918–1919. [Editor's note by P. Spriano.]

them to the perfect English system. In sum, to do this kind of work you need a historian's eye, not a journalist's breeziness.

V

Let me take the liberty of quoting myself to conclude these observations on method, which I hope may prove to be of some use to anyone who cares to revisit the subject along the lines I have indicated. I wrote the following a little over a year ago (*Energie Nuove* for 25 July 1919, pp. 132–39) and was accused of being paradoxical. If I now repeat, in light of the points I have just clarified, the interpretation I gave then, I think it must be conceded that a year of further developments have justified my position.

It is our view that we have to see two factors and two results in the events now occurring in Russia. But here in Italy opinion has focused on only one.

The Marxist experiment in Russia has undoubtedly failed; the old objections of liberal economics against the supporters of state ownership are stronger than ever, and Bolshevism reinforces them. Every writer on the subject has observed this. But there is another fact that nobody in Italy has observed, least of all the socialists.

The Russian revolution is not just a socialist experiment. They are laying the groundwork for a new state there. Lenin and Trotsky are not just Bolsheviks; they are the men of action who have awakened a people and are busy re-creating its soul.

Our mentality and our systems cannot interfere when judging the Russian revolution, and above all we cannot import the memory and the weight of our own interests. The experiment in socialization has failed for now (and, we believe, forever) because it runs directly counter to the interests and the mentality of human beings. But even as evidence of this failure, the revolution has been useful and necessary. Confusion and disaster have mounted: the struggle between peasants and the workers has ravaged the whole country. Yet Lenin and Trotsky have remained.

When history smashed their initial intentions and programs, they and the whole people renewed themselves. They passed from anarchy to statolatry, trying every tactic. But the Russian people have for certain begun to form a political consciousness in these years, and for that reason the soviets were necessary, even if they were not welcomed by the people at first, even if they will necessarily have to make way for other institutions better adapted to the manifestation of the popular will. Only in the throes of a crisis like the present one could the chance of liquidating both tsarism and the utopia of the abstract reasoners as active elements of history present itself.

That is what the work of Lenin and Trotsky represents. At bottom, it is the negation of socialism and an affirmation and exaltation of liberalism. History will have to recognize this. Tsarism is dead, and with it the tsarist mentality. Russia is rising to the level of civilization of the Western peoples, who are naturally failing to grasp what is happening.

4 FASCISM AND THE
MISSED LIBERAL REVOLUTION

THE REASONS FOR OUR OPPOSITION

THE spirit of our inquiry might have absolved us of the duty to say anything about fascism, which was identified in the preceding pages as a historical parenthesis, an example of unemployment in the economy and the unemployment of ideas connected with all the errors of our coalescence into a nation.[1]

This book makes the assumption that Italy will succeed in finding the strength within itself to overcome its crisis and resume the drive to be part of Europe that appeared to manifest itself, in certain episodes at least, of the Risorgimento.

It therefore happens that our objections to fascism are all prejudicial, and what we see as error the apologists of fascism claim as merit, that is, the capacity this movement showed, in an hour of suspension and uncertainty, to end the tension among the Italians and make them complicit in a banal revival of patriarchalism—when the solemnity of the crisis imposed on the citizens the categorical imperative of coherence, free political contest, and self-government. Historians will regard the Facta[2]

---

1. Original title: "Le ragioni dell'opposizione"; from Gobetti, *La rivoluzione liberale* (ed. Perona), p. 163.
2. Luigi Facta (1861–1930), a moderate liberal, was the head of the Italian government who had to face Mussolini's challenge to the state. To stop

cabinet as the most curious of ironies, almost the caricature of a providential will that gave the Italians a weak government, a government that washed its hands of responsibility, so that the citizens would learn to shoulder the inevitable responsibility of the political contest and state initiative themselves. As long as the contest among the parties of the postwar era remained undecided, none of the roads to the future was precluded. Fascism rescued us from that nightmare: the Italians failed their test of modern seriousness, and the genius of the race plucked from the debris of Renaissance adventure the legendary figure of the condottiere leading his band, imposing paternal discipline on the restless serfs.

IN PRAISE OF THE GUILLOTINE

FASCISM wants to cure the Italians of the political contest and reach the point at which the roll is called and all the citizens declare that they believe in their country, as if the whole of social praxis could be fulfilled simply by restating convictions.[3] It would take too long to teach them the superiority of anarchy over democratic doctrines, and, anyway, certain kinds of praise are delivered most convincingly by practice. *Actualism*, Garibaldianism, and fascism are expedients by which infancy, with its incurable trusting optimism, loves to contemplate a world simplified to its own dimensions.

Our polemic against the Italians is not based on any preference for supposedly more mature foreign cultures, nor does it

---

the march of the Blackshirts who converged on Rome in October 1922, Facta proposed to declare a state of emergency, which however the king rejected.

3. Original title: "Elogio della ghigliottina"; from Gobetti, *La rivoluzione liberale* (ed. Perona), pp. 164–66. In an introductory sentence, here omitted, Gobetti states that he is citing one of his previous articles in *La Rivoluzione Liberale*, dated 23 November 1922, but Perona adds in a note that he has considerably revised the text.

arise out of reliance on Protestant or laissez-faire doctrines. Our antifascism is an instinct before it is an ideology.

If there is any point to a comparison between new situations and roughly similar ones of old, then we would wish our pessimism to be the serious kind, Old Testament pessimism without palingenesis, not the literary pessimism of the Christians (the delusion of optimists). The conflict between seriousness and D'Annunzianism[4] is ancient and incurable. We need to distrust conversions, believe in history more than in progress, and think of our work as a spiritual exercise performed from internal necessity, not for the sake of becoming known. There is one abiding value in the world: intransigence. And we are, in a certain sense, its desperate priesthood at this time.

We fear that there are few so courageously radical as to suspect that with a *metaphysics* like this we could possibly be engaged with the political problem. But ingenuousness like ours is more competent than certain ideological theories and has already detected the objective presence of an insolent political realism in certain autobiographical theories.

We feel concern at the spread of a fear of the unforeseen, which we will continue to label provincial in order to avoid more alarming definitions. But certain underlying defects, even in a people who are "grandchildren" of Machiavelli, we would not be able fully to grasp even at the hour of final reckoning. Fascism in Italy is a sign of infancy because it signals the triumph of the facile, of trust, of enthusiasm. We could analyze Mussolini's cabinet as though it were just another governing ministry. But fascism has been something more: it has been the autobiography of the nation. A nation that believes in collaboration between the social classes and that steers clear of the political contest because of laziness has to be regarded, and guided, with some circumspection. We confess it was our hope that the battle between fascists and social-communists would continue with-

4. See Chapter 1, note 54.

out a break. We planned *La Rivoluzione Liberale* from September 1920 and began publishing it in February 1922, with faith in the political contest that through so many corruptions, itself corrupted, still surged up. In Italy there were people getting themselves killed for an idea, for an interest, for a rhetorical contagion! But already we could see the signs of exhaustion, the longing for peace. It is hard to grasp that life is tragic, that suicide is more of a day to day practice than an exceptional measure. In Italy there is no proletariat and no bourgeoisie, only middle classes. We knew that; and if we hadn't known it, Giolitti would have taught us. So Mussolini is nothing new; but Mussolini offers us experimental proof of that unanimity; he attests to the nonexistence of heroic minorities, the provisional end of heresies. Certain spells of drunkenness are as good as confessions, and the fascist palingenesis has inexorably confirmed the impudence of our impotence. You can't ask for the spirit of sacrifice from a people of D'Annunzians. Our thoughts also turn to that which can't be seen; but going by what you can see, you would have to admit that the war was in vain.

In the absence of real, distinct, necessary interests the Italians desire discipline and a strong state. But it is hard to imagine Caesar without Pompey, or a strong Rome without a civil war. You may believe that guardians are useful, and justify Giolitti and Nitti.[5] But masters only remind us of the Pazzi Conspiracy [*La congiura dei pazzi*]: in other words, they carry us back to the political customs of a bygone age. Neither Mussolini nor Vittorio Emanuele of Savoy has the virtues of a master, but the Italians certainly have the souls of slaves. It is painful to have to think back with nostalgia to Enlightenment ideas of freedom and to the age of conspiracies. And yet, let's be totally frank, there are some who have anxiously awaited the coming of persecution against individuals so that a spirit would be reborn out of suffering, so that this people would recognize itself in the sacrifice

5. See Chapter 1, notes 10 and 15.

of its priests. In us, in our firm opposition, there has been something quixotic. But we felt that there was a desperate religiosity too. We can't delude ourselves that we have rescued the political contest: we have guarded its symbol, and we have to hope (alas, with what skepticism) that tyrants are tyrants, that reaction is reaction, that there are some who will have the courage to hoist the guillotine, that positions will be defended to the end. We can benefit from the fascist regime, try to make it yield all its fruits: we want blows so as to wake a few people up, we want the hangman so as to make it clear how things stand. Mussolini may make an excellent Ignazio di Loyola. Where is there a De Maistre[6] who can supply a doctrine, an intransigence, for his sword?

THE *CAPITIS DEMINUTIO* OF THEORIES

THERE is no De Maistre, no doctrine in the apologetic literature of fascism.[7]

For fascism, theories are agreeable ideologies that have to be improvised and adapted to fit circumstances. Adventures they find more attractive than ideas, and the latter, deprived of their dignity and autonomy, are reduced to servile functions.

The similarity of fascism to the Counter Reformation serves as a resource for the neo-Guelph program; the liberalism of De Stefani[8] can satisfy the most popular expectations surrounding

6. Joseph De Maistre (1753–1821), a diplomatic and political theorist, was one of the most prominent philosophers who inspired the Restoration. A critic of modernity and individualism, De Maistre interpreted the advent of the liberal state as the debacle of political authority and the entrance of social interests in the political sphere. Among his works are *Considérations sur la France* (1797) and *Les Soirées de Saint-Pétersbourg* (1821).

7. Original title: "La capitis deminutio delle teorie"; from Gobetti, *La rivoluzione liberale* (ed. Perona), pp. 166–73. *Capitis deminutio* is a term from Roman law signifying the loss of citizen rights; the most extreme form of *capitis deminutio* was enslavement. [Translator's note.]

8. Alberto De Stefani was a representative fascist economist and a minister in several fascist cabinets.

the myth of the balanced budget; national syndicalism offers the *masses* bread in exchange for dignity; nationalism and patriotism satisfy the most philistine instincts of the enthusiastic classes.

In an all too successful book, which Mussolini was content to have recognized, even abroad, as a statement of his program, an honest fascist ended by drawing all the most obvious consequences from the warning of Missiroli:[9] "Fascism will be the mature conscience of the new democracy; and as such it will have to make peace with socialism, or it will be worse than nothing, a tardy and impossible reactionary attempt." But the fascism of Pietro Gorgolini is simply the Giolittism of Fera, a political anthology of all the programs of the *Left* after Depretis.[10] Wilsonism and state socialism, laissez-faire confused with the economics of the *just* price, demagogic finance, defense of small landholders and an attack on the large ones—this was the poetic demagogy precociously heralded by the messenger and not abjured later by the work of the fascists in government.

Anyone who failed to adopt these simple recipes immediately drifted close to heresy and was barred from popularity. The mediocre attempt at theory by Grandi[11] remained an isolated piece of naïveté. Anyhow, the proposal to *make the masses loyal to the state* cannot be realized by inventing new proposals for national syndicalism. While Grandi hopes that popular support will endow the movement with a kind of religiosity, he fails to see that he is repeating the aberrations (born of Enlightenment ele-

9. See Chapter 1, note 35.
10. Gobetti is comparing fascist ideology with previous forms of statism and is trying to convey the sense that it is a low-grade synthesis of the Italian liberal tradition. Pietro Gorgolini (b. 1891) was a journalist and a fascist leader. Luigi Fera (18769–1936) was a liberal and a supporter of Giolitti. On Depretis see Chapter 1, note 11.
11. Dino Grandi was among the early fascists and was one of the leading politicians during the twenty-year-long fascist dictatorship. On 25 July 1943 he contributed to the collapse of Mussolini's government.

gance) of nationalism, modernism, and syndicalism, the critical notes of intellectuals.

As for the thought of Agostino Lanzillo,[12] one might actually recommend it to anyone who finds themselves short of arguments in the debate with fascism. It is easy to see why he follows Mussolini: because of the fervor of interventionism and fitful anti-intellectual inspiration. Even so, Lanzillo's philosophy of intuition remains considerably more accomplished and informed than some of the crudely relativistic declarations made by fascist leaders and followers and even opens up a few possibilities of criticism and intelligence. He prophesied the nature of fascist government in these terms, at the beginning of 1922:

> In society at present we note that the state is increasing its power every day. The military force that it has at its disposal is much more overpowering now than it was before the war, because confidence in the use of arms has greatly increased, and the citizens are much less shocked by incidents of armed repression—in fact, hardly shocked at all. The means of transmitting orders, of repression, and of defensive organization are formidable, virtually invincible. If we suppose, following the hypothesis advanced earlier, that some categories of workers may join with elements of the governing class for the purpose of political control, the result will be a political combination so strong that the force it will have and will be able to deploy against the rest of society will be practically limitless.

We are led to wonder, faced with a prospect like that, what passes through the mind of a supporter of laissez-faire, an enemy of state intervention, nationalism, and militarism like Agostino Lanzillo, given that fascism is about to become the heir, in the worst sense, of socialism.

12. Agostino Lanzillo (1886–1952) was an economist who passed from socialism to fascist corporatism. He dissociated himself from fascism in 1931. After World War II he became a journalist on the newspaper *Il Corriere della Sera*.

Of the three criteria most cherished by Lanzillo, *laissez-faire, anti-intellectualism, experience in dealing with the economy,* I do not know which, if any, will survive under a government of paternal Catholicism in a state that intends to control not only the private economy but also consciences and the ballot box. It is true that by now he can take pleasure in his old prophecy that *the war will have the effect of making men totally uninhibited in the use of force,* but among the new disciples of the *conception of warrior life* he will search in vain for the aptitudes he hoped for in a ruling class capable of limiting the *persistence of aggregates* and the *instinct for combinations,* a ruling class of individualists and libertarians against organized mediocrity. Certainly the members of the new warrior class that Lanzillo counted on to be instinctive individualists have shown themselves to be barbarously bureaucratic instead, and their instincts for monotony do not offer much hope for a unitary solution to regionalism with religious respect for the personalities of the regions!

His invitation to fascism to make itself the voice of the middle classes was the only one heeded, but on seeing the results, we would like to hear Lanzillo explain how exactly he perceives a *heroic soul* in fascism and whether his quotation from Sorel concerning their *violence* isn't badly misapplied.

For our part we will offer him a libertarian antithesis to the problems that he puts. Laissez-faire in fact locates the natural boundary of the economy in political mediation, which similarly has its own necessities and autonomous requirements; so it would seem to follow that quite proper criticism of rash strikes and of facile maximalism by third-rate political hacks should not automatically justify the exaltation of juridical syndicalism in the hope of one day having a government of *producers!* To invoke a government of *producers* when in fact proportional representation alone would be marvelously effective in promoting the political contest and the free formation of parties means taking fright at the prospect of liberty and seeking refuge in the medieval consolations of corporatism. The fascists' hatred of politics because of a preference for literary idyll and practical economic adaptation is the worst symptom of the decadence of our customs and the softness of the characters who want a return to the repose of the Middle Ages. The constitution of Carnaro was the first warning;[13] then collaborationism and fascism, the royal guard and the youth squads, were the assiduous expedients of the tremulous fantasy.

Mussolini's government exiles criticism to the convents, offers weak people a religion of the state, a praetorian guard, a Hegelian philosopher in charge of the schools; initiatives are annulled within the ethical state. It offers immature Italy a cradle that may be the tomb of *civil consciences* turned private, after eliminating provisionally, through yet another alliance with the rich, the two problems that might have been the *Bastille* of the Italian people: relations between the state and the working classes, and the encounter and antithesis between industry and agriculture.

Who today is discussing laissez-faire and the Southern Question? The monarchy has buried the democrats and the political contest. Speeches about government by experts and technicians have the same nature as sermons on divine grace and the holy spirit: they served to rob us of a constitution that they were supposed to improve, and to erect a new monument to paternal theocracy.

But a discourse on theories is not called for when the overriding question is one of absolutely thoughtless instincts. Symbols turn out to be more significant than ideas. Hence you would not need to add very much to the portrait of the author that adorns another extremely odd apologetic book[14] to have the

13. The constitution of Carnaro was the outcome of Gabriele D'Annunzio's occupation of Fiume (Rijeka, then in Yugoslavia; now in Croatia) in 1920 in an attempt to return it to Italy, against the resolutions of the Conference of Versailles.

14. Umberto F. Banchelli, *Le memorie di un fascista, 1919–1922* (Florence: La Sassaiola Fiorentina, 1922).

complete biography of the fascist, for evidently the brazen display of military medals defines the contours of the individual much better than a list of his books or a description of his style. The comparison to a primitive tribal leader armed with rugged physical exultancy and alluring talismans automatically springs to mind because of the crude similarities, and it is not contradicted by the vivaciously bureaucratic narrative, amateurish and open. The document acquires a singular interest the moment one looks at things from a distance, so that they take on a certain relief—as if Umberto Banchelli were the new vassal of a new king as illiterate and bellicose as Theodoric, as ferocious as Alboinus. But he himself seems to have more of the roughness of Paulus Diaconus than the smooth erudition of Cassiodorus, deriving his respect for intellectuals like Prezzolini and for Soffici,[15] from the way the two friends are unfailingly indulgent toward adventurous thoughtlessness and sometimes even toward the new barbarians. Who knows, perhaps Soffici will willingly add his own jovial approbation to Banchelli's invectives against the doctrines "of the German-Jew Karl Marx, or rather Mordecai, since that was his real name, which he changed in order to be acclaimed and believed by the ignorant crowd of his time." Truthfully, only a perversion of the sense of values in the darkest depths of night can explain the sailor's metaphors that occur in this humble chronicle, in which, during the election battle at Florence, the fascist action group is assigned the task of "preventing eight cen-

15. Giuseppe Prezzolini (1882–1982) was the founder of the Florentine avant-garde journals *Il Leonardo* (1903), *La Voce* (along with Papini), and *Il Regno* (along with the nationalist Enrico Corradini [1865–1931]). He used to sign his articles with the pseudonym Julian the Sophist. He aimed at renewing Italian national culture by purifying it of its academic positivism and injecting new streams of thought, such as irrationalism, futurism, and neo-Idealism. In 1930 he left Italy for New York, where he taught at Columbia University for many years. Ardegno Soffici (1879–1964) was a leading futurist and, with Giovanni Papini (1881–1956) founded the journal *Lacerba*. See also Chapter 4, note 25.

turies of Italian art and citizen sacrifice from being dirtied by the effigy of the Hebraized Russian Asiatic, Lenin." On the other hand, the literary ambition of the uncouth chronicler candidly evokes a comparison with the Florentine age of the Guelphs and Ghibellines in connection with the revival of *street fighting* .

But there is no point in wasting overripe metaphors on such banal everyday facts. Only rarely in the fascist do we come across the respect of the barbarian for the knowledge that is denied him; and certain kinds of religious veneration flourish with difficulty in the dull heart of the clumsy professional warrior. The daily newspapers speak with more exactness of the fake assertiveness of "underage" generals and deputies. In Banchelli's *Memorie* too, the veneration and prophecy of Catholic Italy, the applause for absolutist monarchy, the fear of the Jews and plutocracy, the protests against Mussolini for not wanting state industries, conclusively portray the candor of certain spiritual epiphanies. One is tempted to gather examples of the style:

> By now, all this overflow of parties has made it known how needful it is to put an end to parties altogether and reduce them numerically to perhaps one alone.
>
> And crush dialect speech as far as possible and not permit any printing in dialect, which nourishes the spirit of local particularism. . . .
>
> There can be but one Catholic power, there can be but Rome, which may decide one day to rid Europe of the Turk and give back to the temple of Santa Sophia the Christian significance that gave rise to it.
>
> Woe to anyone who dares to lay hands on the sacrosanct economic gains of the proletariat! If a real and true monarchy comes to pass, it will have to be, through the agency of a responsible king, the stern father of the proletariat.

The analysis might become more severe if we were to demand an accounting, from Banchelli's legitimate and responsible guardians, for these artless remarks. In that case, Banchelli's moralizing criticism of democracy would have to be seen as the suitably insolent rebellion of the ill-taught pupil against his inadequate teacher. Really, oughtn't we to regard these lads as misfits deserving our deep pity? They learned little from their democratic elders and the tumult of events except degenerate behavior! Fascism is like any other kind of childishness for us; it has its own painful justifications and would be better served by a confessor or a preacher than by an instructor in politics. They grew up like wayward foundlings, and nobody taught them what a hard apprenticeship lies in store for the artisan of social contingencies. The war was a game in which they recognized their own depraved precocity. Today the truculence of the barbarian disguises only fear, nor does an open spirit lead to generosity; rather, bravado alternating with obedience reveals nervous exhaustion, the poverty of inhibition, the decadence of the race. Futurism, then, must have been the drunken, dejected proclamation of this fundamental inner barrenness. It comes down to substituting the fascist dagger for the German stick and entrusting the exercise of one's own freedom to someone else. In politics, opposition to democracy signifies a nostalgic return to the paternal state; in criticism, the procedures are metaphors, as with the alchemists. Instead of the philosopher's stone, the explanation for everything varies from the hidden plutocracy to Jewishness (the shape in the clouds puffed up by a thousand winds), or the way some have elbowed their way into the top positions, or even commerce and industry as a whole. Banchelli's book is full of complaints about the lack of fascists who are old-fashioned gentlemen and malicious questions about how the fiery leaders of some fascist action group have been handling the group's money. In these crude internal quarrels, the rule seems to be to call one's political adversary a thief.

Our memory is a little blurry, so we won't revive certain items of gossip, but when such decadent behavior is judged, its historical significance will be readily apparent. Let no one hide their

natural concern about the denial of the most elementary digni-
ties; for the immature spirit of fascism lies precisely in their not
even knowing how to make themselves respected for doing their
job. The recourse to myth instead of experience, the anthropo-
morphic view of the complex realities of contingency, reveal that
they are not ashamed to be simpletons and do not try to hide it.

The remedy for our deficiencies is supposed to be a stereo-
typed discipline, but they lack the nerve to let order arise out of
free disorder. The spirit of adventure is unsuccessful in locating
tradition, and their laments about moral degeneration show a
failure to comprehend that outside the political contest there is
no criterion of ethical renewal.

WE AND THE OPPOSITIONS

I T is important at this point to give a precise historical outline
of the nature and origin of the movements opposing fascism.[16]

When the fascists marched on Rome, at least two sorts of
antifascism immediately sprang up. The first was the resistance
to the coup d'état on the part of the losers: the antifascism, not
to mince words, of the old democrats and liberals who had been
ministers or supported the government after the war, as well as
of disappointed supporters of fascism.

The approach these opponents took was consummately parliamentary. They felt no natural repugnance toward the winners, had not the slightest intention of working for a new generation, felt anger and resentment above all because their own
plans had been upset and they saw power slipping out of their
grasp. This was a widespread feeling that even Salandra and Giolitti shared.

16. Original title: "Noi e le opposizioni"; from *La Rivoluzione Liberale* 3,
no. 17 (22 April 1924), p. 65, signed "La Rivoluzione Liberale." Translated
from *Scritti politici*, pp. 641–44.

These were not opponents; they were simply disoriented. None of them comprehended the historical situation of which fascism was the outcome; they persuaded themselves that what they had here was a passing phenomenon, one they could defeat if they were shrewd, and that was best handled by dealing, collaborating, setting out preconditions as bargaining chips.

One of the leaders of the opposition, who was being courted by Mussolini to get him to come to terms, sent back the following reply: Dissolve the national militia, restore legality, and then we will treat with you, collaborate, perhaps even make some sacrifices. An absolutely Mussolinian response. And in fact the criticism of the papers and the individuals whom our friend Ferrara[17] defends was all technical criticism, de facto collaboration, the purpose of which was to set out a program Mussolini would have to accept and, along with it, the men who were momentarily excluded.

None of the so-called democrats and liberals had realized that Mussolini could not be shackled with programs, that he would betray any agreement and beat all comers at the game of shrewdness, that he had to be unmasked by an example of fierce intransigence leading to a historical situation in which the effective political contest would nullify the habits of paternalism and the dictatorship of wealth masked as personal dictatorship.

That would have been real antifascism, real politics on the part of the opposition. But no one will contradict us when we say that only *La Rivoluzione Liberale* took this position right from the start. In the early months there was no other opposition to Mussolini's regime so desperate and inexorable. More than a tyrant, in Mussolini we were fighting a corruptor; and in fascism, more than dictatorship, paternal guardianship. Rather than complain insistently about the loss of liberty and the violence, we aimed our polemic against the Italians who were not fighting

17. Mario Ferrara (1892–1956) was a liberal journalist and then a fascist one . After World War II he wrote for *Il Corriere della Sera*.

back, who were letting themselves be tamed. We offered a diagnosis of the economic immaturity of Italy that both coincides with and determines the immaturity of the political contest and the diminishment of personal dignity.

If these notions, which the majority saw as paradoxical, have now become commonplace, if *La Rivoluzione Liberale*, which was meant to be a small clandestine intellectual review, is now read and discussed by the liberal and democratic oppositions, our only role has been to elaborate them and repeat them to the point of tedium. Hence it is that many old-style liberals and democrats have been introducing a few of the new ideas about liberal revolution to which Ferrara refers into their outmoded habits and ideas. Hence it is that if before they defended *liberty* in order to treat with Mussolini and cleverly outplay him, they have ended up by seeing liberty as an absolute value, as a matter of human dignity, and as a principle of the political contest and the formation of parties, over and above *liberty as method*.

Caramella[18] noted that we ought to remain diffident of these new converts. That is perfectly legitimate, and above all it coheres with our own premises in light of the fact that our own antifascism has always eschewed small tactical considerations and little personal games. If fascism is the product of a historical crisis, then there is an inescapable imperative to review the antifascists critically and prefer some to others. We refuse to make common cause with all the enemies of the regime, and we do not think we can beat it with coalitions and ministerial crises, but rather by extirpating the roots from which it springs.

At the risk of having our words misunderstood, we continue to point out that in Mussolini we are fighting against the same historical vice—magnified—that made possible the Depretis era and the Giolitti era in Italy.[19]

18. Santino Caramella (1902–72) was a mediocre professor of philosophy and a neo-Idealist.
19. See Chapter 1, notes 11 and 10, respectively.

Of course the old liberals and democrats cannot fully accept language like that. As for the ones who youthfully and admirably refused any pact or complicity with fascism, it has to be made clear that the resistance they are offering now is a liquidation and a condemnation of their own past as supporters of the government and parliamentary dealmakers. Only when they have probed their own consciences can we accept them as companions in our revolutionary struggle. There can be no more question of defending their past record or bewailing their lost position, no more question of singing the same old songs.

Fascism has accomplished this at least: to offer a synthesis of Italy's historic ills taken to their extreme consequences—rhetoric, courtiership, demagogy, *trasformismo*.[20] To combat fascism has to mean remaking our own spiritual formation, working for new elites and a new revolution. Fascism is the legitimate heir of Italian democracy: eternally pro-government and conciliatory, fearful of free popular initiatives, oligarchic, parasitical, and paternalistic. Orlando and De Nicola were both on the *listone* with full entitlement and in exactly the same spirit.[21]

When the opposition talks about democracy and liberalism, it has to know that it is working for the future, against the current; it has to know that fascism is the government that an Italy of persons without an occupation, an Italy of parasites—an Italy still far from the modern democratic and liberal forms of social life—deserves. And it has to know that to combat fascism we have to work for a complete revolution in the economy and in consciences.

20. On *trasformismo* see Chapter 1, note 11.
21. On Orlando see Chapter 1, note 15. Enrico De Nicola (1877–1961) was a moderate liberal in the pre-fascist parliament and a professor of constitutional law. He was nominated president of the state in the months that preceded the proclamation of the republic. The *listone* was the electoral list that the Fascist Party made in 1924 along with democrats, liberals, and Catholics in order to secure (as it did) an absolute majority in the parliament.

A PROBLEM OF FREEDOM

ONCE again we are faced with the problem of how to interpret our Risorgimento, for current events in Italian life are stripping away our illusions and laying bare the fundamental ambiguity of our history: a desperate attempt to become modern while remaining lovers of literature with a (non-Machiavellian) vanity about our cleverness, or Garibaldians with the emphatic style of tribunes of the plebs.[22]

The freedom we are discussing here as a challenge to the dreams of absolutism of the new Masters should not therefore be compared to the verbose passions of the radicals, who showed the true measure of their impotence in Mazzinianism.

Political Italy has to seek freedom as a virtue of the state, a virtue less vulgar than the servile discipline imposed by a militia. And while "a people of artists could imagine nothing more beautiful than a second Rienzi mounting the Capitol with theatrical pomp," a question of autonomy may very well present itself as a question of style and passion for the spirit of those who are founders of the state.

The true contrast of the new times, and of our older history too, is not between dictatorship and freedom; it is between freedom and unanimity: the historic fault in our political formation would, on this view, consist of an inability to weigh degrees of difference and to maintain, when engaged in opposition, an honest intransigence arising from the sense that antitheses are necessary and that the contest is meant to coordinate them, not suppress them.

The dignity of these liberal methods is repugnant to the philosophy of dictators—theorists of contentious government, ignorant of the secret duplicities of the demiurgic art. Cavour's warning that "the government cannot fill the role of the jour-

22. Original title: "Problema di libertà"; from Gobetti, *La rivoluzione liberale* (ed. Perona), pp. 9–10.

nalist" goes unheeded amid the facile and dogmatic usages of tyranny.

We would never seek to apply the English experience, however it will be judged in the long run, as a timeless model. Nevertheless, a movement for liberation that stands for economic responsibility and popular initiatives, renouncing the sterile ideologies of *discipline, order,* and *hierarchy,* will emerge only from the molding of habits and forms that are not provincial. The Italian problem is not one of authority but one of autonomy: the absence of a free way of life was the fundamental obstacle over the centuries to the creation of a ruling class, the growth of modern economic activity, and the emergence of an advanced technical class (highly skilled labor, entrepreneurs, investors). And those were the inescapable conditions and premises for a courageous political contest, the infallible instrument for selecting and renewing a governing class.

IN DEFENSE OF PROPORTIONAL REPRESENTATION

I N Italy constitutional questions continue to be regarded as questions of form, as though all peoples had not given proof of their aptitude for self-government and their diplomatic abilities in the creation of electoral mechanisms best adapted to their specific historical circumstances and in the harmonization of state institutions and free initiatives.[23]

The single-member constituency was the ideal system in a country (England) that had rejected feudalism in order to fortify itself against a state-worshiping sovereign. Economically and politically it is still a feudal form; it presupposes a limited number of electors and the existence of an aristocratic class, and it is suited to a traditional, sedentary way of life untouched by the

23. Original title: "Difesa storica della proporzionale"; from *La Rivoluzione Liberale* 4, no. 5 (1 February 1925), p. 22. Translated from *Scritti politici,* pp. 809–12.

spirit of adventure. It is a system the peasantry takes to readily, uninterested as they are in participating in the life of the state, content to elect a deputy but unable to control him.

When the deputy is unable to speak in defense of his interests as a feudatory, the tendency of the single-member constituency is toward the formation of a class of politicians who all too easily slide into the practice of grubby parasitical politics. This process occurred, in extremely demagogic forms, in Italy, where the agrarian interest did not attain stability, and the rhetorical instinct transformed the representative into a tribune of the plebs.

Against this background, proportional representation appeared rightly to signal the period in which a unitary form of life was going to take hold in Italy at last—following the torment of the war and the socialist ascendancy—with a profile of ethical and political seriousness. This idea was promoted by the Popular Party, which was the one to launch in Italy, to the extent possible among the Italians, a revolution with a Protestant character, both on account of its liberal-Christian ethics and on account of the laic, Cavourian spirit with which it viewed clericalism (Sturzo and Donati).[24]

The advantage of proportional representation was not that it was a tool of the conservative forces, as some think. Rather, it was revealed in creating the preconditions for the political contest and the normal development of the work of the parties.

On this topic we have a few things to add that depart quite a lot from the consensus. The postwar period was characterized by the breakdown of old habits and by ideological controversy: the general conditions were not unlike those of Europe in Luther's time, strongly favorable to a movement of a religious kind, in the sense of a Christian reform of Catholicism. The most important evidence of these exigencies is not the various mysti-

24. On Sturzo see the essay "Luigi Sturzo" (Chapter 1). Donato Donati (1880–1946), a professor of constitutional law, was forced to resign from his job because of the laws that forbade Jews to hold public office.

cal and confessional episodes (Papini, Manacorda, Zanfrognini, *Conscientia*)[25] but rather the endeavor of Sturzo, which has the credibility of a broad social movement. Proportional representation gave these voices the means to act on a national scale and present a platform and a discipline. Democracy found its liberal atmosphere: proportional representation obliged individuals to fight for an idea; it encouraged interest groups to form and tended to make economics subordinate to politics.

One of the worst signs of postwar fragmentation was not the class struggle but the danger that the classes might break up into narrowly focused groups, that interests would prove stronger than ideas and that corporatism would replace the habit of revolutionary syndical struggle taught by Marx and Sorel. The danger, though no one perceived it, lay in the organizations representing the professions—a concept dear to all the unoccupied intellectuals from Murri to Rossoni.[26] Only proportional representation had the power for a few years to turn these divisive forces to account, constraining them to bring their interests to the political table; there they are naturally drawn into alliances, renouncing exclusivism at just the moment each is affirming and declaring it most strongly.

In order to win, fascism had to upset the liberal-conservative results of two experiments in proportional representation, setting those who knew nothing of political rights against the army of voters.

25. *Conscientia* was a scholarly journal of prestige among the antipositivists of the beginning of the century; it published interesting articles on existentialism, pragmatism, and Idealism. Giovanni Papini founded *La Voce* along with Prezzolini. He embraced an irrationalist philosophy and gave a vitalist and Nietzschean interpretation of William James, who acknowledged him as the representative of pragmatism in Italy. Guido Manacorda (1879–1965) was a poet and an Idealist professor of philosophy in Naples. Pietro Zanfrognini (b. 1885) was a writer and a philosopher.

26. On Murri see Chapter 1, note 6. Edmondo Rossoni was the founder of the Socialist Union in 1918. He became the general secretary of the fascist labor organizations.

The fascists are accurately guided in their fight against proportional representation by their bosses' instinct—though they are a curious lot, these bosses, since they want to present us with their stratagems for achieving a vulgar restoration as though they were futurist discoveries. The critique of proportional representation on the ground that it makes majority government impossible is as futurist as Marinetti's discovery of Alexandrian forms in art.

In the Italian experiments, the importance of the moralizing effect of proportional representation was seen in its tendency to dissolve majority governments. Where a majority holds power with complete security, you have a veiled oligarchy and nothing else. The formation of a government majority through the electoral process is always the result of negotiations and ambiguities (the Gentiloni pact);[27] blackmail is the tool systematically employed by the tyrant to make the ranks of the democratically enfranchised the slaves of his instincts.

Modern life thrives on antitheses and contrasts that are not reducible to schematic form; blocs and concentrations are only a simplistic way to try to find unity. The logic of political life lies in variety and dissent; government emerges out of it through a dialectical process that varies in concrete detail according to the varying input of the different parties. Proportional representation has succeeded in creating an environment in which a coalition government can work (exploiting the influence of the parties who join it even when they are in conflict), eliminating any possibility of things like the *Gentiloni pact*. The Nitti[28] period

27. The *Patto Gentiloni* was the secret agreement that the Catholics made with the liberals in 1909, according to which they would vote for the liberals in exchange for the promise that the liberals would launch a friendly policy toward the Church. In making that agreement the Catholics promised in fact to participate in the national election, in spite of the Vatican's *non expedit*, which forbade Italian Catholics to take part in the political life of the country. The pact was the best example of Giolittism.

28. See Chapter 1, note 15.

will—in this respect and apart from any criticism that might be made of the figure of the minister—remain an ideal of political education vainly longed for and hoped for.

In that muddled and difficult period, when proportional representation brought clarity that helped the government to save the country, we were given the first example of the capacity of the Italians to live in a modern democratic system: outside of that experiment, the only alternative left was the Middle Ages we are living in now.

A MISSED REVOLUTION

To a detached observer, the postwar history of Italy would appear to herald the onset of the political contest and preparation for the effective exercise of freedom.[29] The civil war, which put all the parties and all the forces to the test, constituted the most intense expression of this new will.

But this ferment, these hopes, were not backed by the directing energies, the aristocracies, capable of interpreting and reinforcing them. The old elites survived, and the new ones reproduced their lack of preparation, because they were formed by the coarsening experience of the war and messianic restlessness. The influence of the two groups around *L'Unità* and *Volontà*, who had no natural bent for political militancy, was not enough to redeem the politics of the combatants.

Nor were the old parties able to understand and express the new needs; instead, they were enervated by an insurmountable attrition between their work of interpretation of the real and their praxis. For four years the political contest did not succeed in giving the measure of the social struggle.

29. Original title: "Una rivoluzione mancata"; from Gobetti, *La rivoluzione liberale* (ed. Perona), pp. 31–32. From the third paragraph to the end, the text is adapted from "A Manifesto," pp. 121–123 above.

Liberalism lost its efficacy because it showed that it was incapable of understanding the problem of unity. Clericalism, having sung a requiem for the liberal idea, died out in a party that was aiming at a conservative result through a democratic praxis. Socialism, which somewhere inside had the raw material to make the idea of the future succeed, revealed the poverty of its attitudes when the moment for action came, and expressed, in Turati, its impotence as a governing party. It accepted the legacy of a corrupt democracy instead of remaining faithful to revolutionary logic.

The only revolutionaries in Italy were those communists who, spellbound by Lenin, saw the revolution as the test of the political capacity of the working classes, of their readiness to form the state. But not even Marxism could bring leaders into being, though it could inspire the masses.

The postwar workers' movement has nevertheless been the first laic movement in Italy, able to take the modern revolutionary significance of the state to its ultimate logical consequence and to decide the battle against dead faiths with a new ethics and a new religiosity. There was a failure to comprehend the national value represented by this revolutionary workers' movement. The leaders failed in their duty because they were afraid, but flattered at the same time, to be part of government. The unitary politics of Serrati, on whom the fate of the revolution depended at one point, revealed itself to be a pernicious Giolittism without the competence of Giolitti and ill equipped to dominate situations with serene confidence.[30] Only struggle can lead to cohesion and discipline. The unitary function is carried out by the government in any case; for it to keep out of the fray is the essence of morality.

In the thought of Serrati the conflicting aspirations of peasants and workers became embroiled before they were even fully

30. On Serrati and Giolitti see Chapter 2, note 35, and Chapter 1, note 10, respectively.

articulated. For the political contest to have its own rhythm of responsibility, it is necessary instead that interests be affirmed autonomously from below, as if obeying some principle of separation. Reconciliation is always the result of the contest and always new: to affirm it a priori means nullifying the free forces just as they are surging up. And the revolutionaries were in fact initiating a reactionary practice.

INDEX

Alfieri, Vittorio, xxxv, xliii, 112*n*23
Antifascism, 213; Croce and, 55–57;
  movements, 223–224, 226
Antiliberal movements, xxiii
Apathy, political, 77
Apoliticism, xix, lii, 133
Autonomy, individual, xvii, xxi, xl;
  as Italian problem, 228; and liberalism, 128; and politics, 98; and
  religion, 138; and rights, xx; and
  self-reliance, xxii, lv–lvi
Autonomy, moral, xxviii
Autonomy, political, xvi, xxi,
  xxvii–xxviii, xxxvii–xxxviii, xlii,
  xliv–xlvii; and democracy, xl; as
  Italian problem, 228; and liberalism, 128; local, xlii, 85; and
  order, 137; and political action,
  204; and reformism, 163; and
  republicanism, xlv

Bagnoli, Paolo, xxiii*n*7
Bakunin, Mikhail, 164
Balbo, Cesare, 114
Banchelli, Umberto, 219–221
Baretti, Il, xxv, xxxiv
Beccaria, Cesare, 185
Berlin, Isaiah, liii
Bobbio, Norberto, xvi*n*2, xlv*n*28,
  xlvii*n*31
Bolshevik Revolution, as a liberal
  revolution, xli
Bolsheviks, 202, 207, 209
Bolshevism, 200, 202–205, 207;
  Italian reaction to, 200–201
Bourgeoisie, 86–92; and the mod-
  ern world, 89; spirit of, 88

British Empire, 96–98
Bureaucracy, Russian, 184

Calvin, John: as founder of liberalism, xliii; and Martin Luther, 138,
  229
Campodonico, Aldemiro, 201–208
Catholicism: and absolutism, 74–
  75; antiliberal role of, xvi, xlii,
  121; and failure of Italian romanticism, 113; and fascism, xxxix,
  138, 218–219; liberal, xxix*n*13,
  115; and liberalism, xxxi, 6;
  Machiavelli and, xxxi; moral
  legacy of, xxviii, 117–118; and
  Popular Party, 6; and Protestantism, 137; and Slavic mysticism,
  191; and theocracy, 182; tradition
  of, 113. *See also* Protestantism
Cattaneo, Carlo, xxviii, xxxv, 22,
  144, 147
Cavour, Camillo Benso, conte di, 9,
  104*n*20
Chaadaev, Petr Yakovlevich, 190–
  192
Citizen(s), 90, 119; and fascism,
  129, 212; and French Revolution,
  xxxii; versus "man," xliv; participation of, 83; peasants as, 86;
  psychology of, 157; responsibility
  of, 84; and the state, 65
Citizenship, xviii, xxviii, xliv; individualist core of, li; Trotsky on, 4
Class: and classes, 71; concept of,
  88; myth of, 91; ruling, 90; social,
  213; socialist concept of, 70–71;
  "working-class aristocracy," 158,

On Liberal Revolution

PIERO GOBETTI

Edited and with an introduction by Nadia Urbinati
Translated by William McCuaig
Foreword by Norberto Bobbio

This book is the first English-language edition of a collection of writings by one of Italy's most important radical liberals, Piero Gobetti (1901–1926). In thirty-five thought-provoking essays, Gobetti proposes an original and challenging notion of liberalism as a revolutionary theory of both the individual and social and political movements. His theory is of particular relevance in the wake of the collapse of Marxist socialism, as non-Western countries with nonliberal or antiliberal cultural and moral traditions confront the problems of transition toward democracy and liberalism. Gobetti's ideas continue to influence in important ways today's heated debates over the nature of liberalism.

Gobetti was the first Italian scholar to identify "two Italys": one enlightened and modern though small and weak, the other premodern, traditional, and dominant. A witness to the seizure of power by the fascists, Gobetti became convinced that Italy's hostility to liberalism could be overcome only with a cultural revolution. Endorsing a radical liberalism, he nevertheless believed that the communists, led by Antonio Gramsci, could play a crucial role in democratizing Italy by helping to develop a secular culture. For a liberal state to subsist and grow, Gobetti argued, there must first be a transformation of both the economic structure and the legal and moral culture of the society.

Nadia Urbinati is assistant professor in the department of political science at Columbia University. **William McCuaig** lives in Toronto. His previous translations include *Liberal Socialism* by Carlo Rosselli and *Italian Foreign Policy* by Federico Chabod.

Italian Literature and Thought Series
Paolo Valesio, *General Editor*